The Clinical Erich Fromm

Contemporary Psychoanalytic Studies
9

Contemporary Psychoanalytic Studies (*CPS*) is an international scholarly book series devoted to all aspects of psychoanalytic inquiry in theoretical, philosophical, applied, and clinical psychoanalysis. Its aims are broadly academic, interdisciplinary, and pluralistic, emphasizing secularism and tolerance across the psychoanalytic domain. CPS aims to promote open and inclusive dialogue among the humanities and the social-behavioral sciences including such disciplines as philosophy, anthropology, history, literature, religion, cultural studies, sociology, feminism, gender studies, political thought, moral psychology, art, drama, and film, biography, law, economics, biology, and cognitive-neuroscience.

The Clinical Erich Fromm
Personal Accounts and
Papers on Therapeutic Technique

Edited by
Rainer Funk

Amsterdam - New York, NY 2009

Cover photo: © DVA

Cover Design: Studio Pollmann

The paper on which this book is printed meets the requirements of "ISO
9706:1994, Information and documentation - Paper for documents -
Requirements for permanence".

ISBN: 978-90-420-2573-8
© Editions Rodopi B.V., Amsterdam - New York, NY 2009
Printed in the Netherlands

Printed by Printforce, the Netherlands

Contents

Roger Frie: Foreword   vii

Rainer Funk: Introduction   1

PART I: ERICH FROMM ON THERAPEUTIC PRACTICE

    Erich Fromm: Being *Centrally* Related to the Patient   7
    Erich Fromm: Factors Leading to Patient's Change
            in Analytic Treatment   39

PART II: RELATIONSHIP AS DIRECT MEETING

    Rainer Funk: Direct Meeting   59
    Marianne Horney Eckardt: From Couch to Chair   71
    David E. Schecter: Awakening the Patient   73
    Dale H. Ortmeyer: Conveying Hope to the Patient   79
    Harold B. Davis: Directness in Therapy   85

PART III: ERICH FROMM'S THERAPEUTIC PRACTICE
IN THE MIRROR OF SUPERVISION

    Ruth M. Lesser: "There Is Nothing Polite in Anybody's
            Unconscious"   91
    Robert U. Akeret: "What Have You Learned about
            Yourself from Your Patient?"   101
    George D. Goldman: "What Is this Patient Really After?"   105
    Arthur H. Feiner: "Now, Look here..."   117

PART IV: REMINISCENCES OF ERICH FROMM—
PSYCHOANALYST AND PERSON

    Anna Gourevitch: Elation and Fortification   125
    Ralph M. Crowley: Psychoanalysis: An Adventure
            in Learning to Think Critically   127
    Edward S. Tauber: Words are Ways   131
    Jay S. Kwawer: His Main Interest: The Human Passions   135
    Bernard Landis: When You Hear the Word,
            the Reality Is Lost   137

Michael Maccoby: Fromm Didn't Want to Be a Frommian   141
Jorge Silva García: His Way to Clarity and Humaneness   145
Salvador Millán and Sonia Gojman de Millán: His Deeply
       Inspirational Presence and Thoughtfulness   153
Gérard D. Khoury: A Crucial Encounter   161
Leonard C. Feldstein: Fromm's Genius Was
       in His Actual Presence   169

References   171

About the Contributors   177

Acknowledgements   181

Erich Fromm's Writings on Psychoanalytic "Technique"   183

Foreword

Roger Frie

As a result of the growing technocratic culture of contemporary psychotherapy, it is becoming increasingly difficult to preserve a space for critical
reflection and the uniqueness of the therapeutic encounter. A number of
powerful factors—pressures from insurance companies, the pervasive
drive towards medication, and a general indifference to the complexity of
psychological change and development—are transforming how psychotherapy is practiced. Whereas psychoanalysis once provided a lens through
which social and political forces in human experience could be critically
examined, contemporary psychotherapy is often conceptualized a purely
technical undertaking. But psychotherapy and psychoanalysis are more
than learned techniques; they are always grounded specific ideas and theories about the nature of human experience.

Erich Fromm's writings remind us that the practice of psychotherapy and psychoanalysis always takes place within sociopolitical and cultural contexts, and that these contexts inevitably determine the objectives
and the manner in which any analysis is undertaken. As Fromm states in
Man for Himself (1947a), "Psychology cannot be divorced from philosophy and ethics nor from sociology and economics" (p. ix). At the heart of
Fromm's work is a unique interdisciplinary outlook that bridges sociology,
philosophy, economics, psychology and psychoanalysis. While Fromm is
identified with each discipline, he is not defined by any one of them indi-
vidually. Indeed, as a theorist, writer and public intellectual, Fromm rejects
doctrinaire outlooks and rigid definitions. And as a practicing psychoanalyst, Fromm similarly eschews the codification of clinical technique and
rejects prescriptive ideas about how to practice.

Fromm developed his clinical approach in response to the restrictions imposed by classical psychoanalytic technique, the reigning therapeutic paradigm of the time. In contrast to Freud and classical psychoanalysis, for whom technique is grounded in a positivist and deterministic
theory of drives, Fromm celebrates the uniqueness of the "direct encounter" with the patient. Fromm seeks to remain true to the patient's lived experience, without imposing a restrictive technique or universalized theory
on the vitality of interpersonal interaction. Yet much less is known about
Fromm as a clinician and psychoanalyst, than as a writer. Fromm's psychoanalytic practice was immensely important to the formulation of the
ideas for which he is so widely recognized. Indeed, what is often over-

looked is the fact that Fromm was first and foremost a clinician, and maintained an active practice for forty-five years.

Fromm's psychoanalytic education and clinical trajectory speaks for itself. Fromm completed his doctorate in sociology from Heidelberg in 1922 and began his psychoanalytic training several years later. Fromm was introduced to psychoanalysis by Frieda Reichmann, his colleague and future wife, and subsequently trained with Wilhelm Wittenberg in Munich, and Karl Landauer in Frankfurt. Fromm completed his psychoanalytic training with Hanns Sachs and Theodor Reik, graduating from the Berlin Institute. In 1929, Fromm became one of the founders of the Frankfurt Psychoanalytic Institute. That same year, Max Horkheimer's invited Fromm to join the Frankfurt Institute for Social Research—later known as the "Frankfurt School"—where he was appointed the director of social psychology. Following the rise of National Socialism in 1933, Fromm left Germany, finding his way to New York, where he eventually joined the other émigré members of the Frankfurt School.

Although Fromm was trained in classical psychoanalytic theory and technique, his studies in social psychology led him to conclude that the individual psyche is inherently social in nature. In the Appendix of his first major publication, *Escape from Freedom*, Fromm (1941a) describes the intrinsic relation of the individual and society:

> The fundamental approach to human personality is the understanding of man's [sic] relation to the world, to others, to nature, and to himself. We believe that man [sic] is primarily a social being, and not, as Freud assumes, primarily self-sufficient and only secondarily in need of others in order to satisfy his instinctual needs. In this sense, we believe that individual psychology is fundamentally social psychology, or in Sullivan's terms, the psychology of interpersonal relationships. (p. 290).

Fromm's rejection of psychoanalytic drive theory spelled the end of his association with Freudian psychoanalysis and the work of the Frankfurt School. This led first to a professional association with Karen Horney, and subsequently with the interpersonal psychoanalysts, Harry Stack Sullivan and Clara Thompson. Together with his ex-wife, Frieda Fromm-Reichmann, Fromm, Sullivan and Thompson founded the William Alanson White Institute of Psychiatry, Psychoanalysis, and Psychology in 1946. With its focus on understanding the social contexts of human experience, the White Institute became the home of interpersonal theory and practice. For the next years, Fromm oversaw the new institute's faculty and training committee. In 1950, as a result of his wife's health, Fromm moved to Mexico, where he founded the Mexican Institute of Psychoanalysis. Over the next two decades Fromm continued to teach and supervise at the White Institute and at a variety of American universities, dividing his time between Mexico and the United States.

As a member of "loyal opposition" within the growing field of psychoanalysis, the White Institute initially had relatively little impact on the psychoanalytic mainstream. Indeed, outside of the White Institute, Fromm's main influence was not on psychoanalytic clinicians in the first instance, but on the educated public and on academics interested in applying his analytic perspective to the study of social, cultural, and political trends and processes. However, within the White Institute, there were many psychoanalytic candidates and colleagues who had the opportunity to work with Fromm and experience first-hand his unique and important interpersonal approach to therapeutic work.

Rainer Funk's edited book provides an immensely valuable service because it presents Fromm's clinical ideas and clinical style through the voice of his supervisees, students, colleagues, and friends. Funk is ideally situated to undertake this study: he has published extensively on Fromm, is the executor of Fromm's literary estate, and an executive member of the International Erich Fromm Society. His book provides a timely and important addition to our understanding of Fromm. It fills a gap in the secondary literature on Fromm by demonstrating the way in which Fromm was an especially skillful and talented clinician, in addition to being a writer of great renown.

By offering first-hand accounts of their work with Fromm, the contributors help readers to grasp how the "clinical Erich Fromm" worked in his psychoanalytic practice and how he conceptualized clinical case material. In the process, this book deepens our appreciation of Fromm as a thinker, clinician and a human being. Most importantly, perhaps, it reveals how Fromm's therapeutic approach, which emphasizes direct encounter with the patient and values the contextualization of experience, remains directly relevant for the changing culture of contemporary psychotherapy.

Although I am of a younger generation than the contributors to this book, Fromm's writings had a strong influence on me (Frie 2003). I chose to undertake my analytic training at the White Institute in large part because of Fromm and the tradition he represents. As a faculty member of the White Institute, Fromm's work continues to be important to my clinical work and my teaching. However, analytic training in North America today is more practice-focused and less intellectually oriented than it was when Fromm taught at the White Institute. In general, students and analysts tend to learn from direct clinical reading. Unfortunately this also means that Fromm's writings are not as widely read as they once were. For therapists and analysts who wish to know Fromm not only as a writer, but also as a practicing clinician, this book provides an important step towards reaching that goal.

Funk's book should also help to dispel certain stereotypes of Fromm that have arisen over the years, foremost of which is the erroneous belief that Fromm's therapeutic approach was that of a stern European analyst who valued confrontation. Quite to the contrary, these personal accounts paint a picture of Fromm as someone who was related and sensitive to the needs of others. Indeed, it is precisely Fromm's ability to be engaged with others and their contexts that remains most salient.

For contemporary clinicians who value political engagement, Fromm demonstrates that the political and psychological realms of experience are always inherently connected. Engagement with the other person thus necessarily implies engagement with sociopolitical forces and contexts. Fromm teaches us to pay attention to the reality of all forms of social and political conformity and oppression, both in the lives of patients and in our own lives. Fromm helps us to appreciate the therapist plays an important role in analyzing not just the patient's mind, but the way in which all psychological life is inherently social and political in scope.

As such, Fromm's ideas come out of a rich tradition of "philosophical anthropology," largely in the German language (Taylor 1988). Fromm's work delves into the implicit presuppositions of the theories we use to understand and explain human experience, and points out their inconsistencies or blindness to other assumptions that are also operative. In the process, Fromm seeks to develop a clearer conception of the human being. The critical reflection on what it means to be human is precisely what is of significance here, whether within and beyond the therapeutic setting. This book illustrates the wealth of Fromm's approach, and picks it up at the moment when psychoanalytic psychotherapy is confronting a challenge to its whole way of thinking and practicing.

Ultimately, Erich Fromm, the practicing psychoanalyst who is portrayed in Funk's edited book, does not fit any restrictive definition of who the clinician is or should be. Both as a thinker and as a psychoanalyst, Fromm defies disciplinary distinctions. I can think of no better reason to recommend reading this book, or to reread Fromm's rich body of work.

Associate Editor, *Contemporary Psychoanalytic Studies*
Associate Professor, Simon Fraser University, Vancouver
Faculty, William Alanson White Institute, New York

Introduction

Rainer Funk

Erich Fromm is remembered for many things: as the author of *The Art of Loving* and *To Have Or to Be?*; as a social psychologist and explorer of the authoritarian character; as a humanist, psychologist of religion, and student of the nature of aggression; and as a member of the Frankfurt School, a lively interpreter of Karl Marx, and a socialist with humanist leanings. Far less is known about another Fromm—the practicing psychoanalyst, the therapeutic teacher, and the clinical supervisor.

The objective of this book is to introduce Fromm as a practicing psychoanalyst and to familiarize readers with his therapeutic "technique." As such, this book seeks to explore answers to a series of important questions: What were the therapeutic goals that Fromm set himself? How did he shape the therapeutic relationship? What pathways to the unconscious did he favor? How did Fromm choose to work with transference and counter-transference, defense and resistance? What role did he see the psychoanalyst's own personality as playing in therapy, and where did he stand on the issues of analytic neutrality and abstinence? When and in what ways did Fromm use interpretation? How much truth, and how much directness, did he think his patients could tolerate? Which kind of therapeutic setting did he prefer? What did Fromm consider of primary importance in the therapeutic process? And how did he conceive of the connection between social reality, mental images and irrational forces?

In deciding to proceed with this book, two considerations were uppermost in my mind. One is the almost complete lack of awareness of Fromm's therapeutic approach. This is hardly surprising, given that Fromm himself hardly published anything on the subject of technique and—correctly in my opinion—refrained from creating a school of his own.

A number of attempts by Fromm to formulate his psychoanalytic "technique" were broken off. To be sure, he did clarify his theory of psychoanalysis in terms of numerous case histories; but not one of these derives from his own work with patients. In 1965, Fromm applied for a grant so that he could embark on a four-volume "systematic work," as he called it, on humanist psychoanalysis, which was to contain a chapter entitled "Psychoanalytic Technique." By 1973 his labors had reached a point where he could publish *The Anatomy of Human Destructiveness*, the first volume of the projected work. In a letter to Professor Kalinkowitz dated

July 20, 1973, Fromm announced that the second volume would deal with psychoanalytic technique, but instead he began to write *To Have Or to Be?* And when finally, in 1978, Fromm wanted to edit the transcripts of one of his clinical seminars, he was forced to stop because of his declining health. To this end, the handful of Fromm's mostly posthumous writings on psychoanalytic "technique" at the end of the book.

But there is another consideration that led me to publish this volume. Almost thirty years after Fromm's death, the ranks of those who knew him personally or through their psychoanalytic training are sadly thinning. So it seemed timely to ask for their impressions, insights, and memories. I was grateful to receive the contributions now gathered in this book. They are of value in every way. I have elected to supplement them with several earlier reports, obituaries, and memoirs, mostly taken from the pages of *Contemporary Psychoanalysis*—the mouthpiece of the New York-based William Alanson White Institute, of which Fromm was a co-founder. The journal has rendered outstanding service in keeping Fromm's therapeutic legacy alive and well in our time. I wish to thank that Institute for letting me reproduce the aforementioned texts.

The book is divided into four parts. As indicated above Fromm published very little about his particular therapeutic "technique" and how he related to his patients therapeutically. Part One of this book consists of two clinical papers from his literary estate: "Being *Centrally* Related to the Patient" and "Factors Leading to Patient's Change in Analytic Treatment," both of which were published posthumously. Part Two through Four present the views of Fromm's pupils. Indeed, all of the contributors to this book have personally experienced Erich Fromm in a variety of contexts and in a host of ways. Some underwent therapy with Fromm, or were trained by him; some asked Fromm to supervise their clinical work; some knew him through his academic lectures and clinical seminars; still others knew him not only as students and trainees, but as a colleague and personal friend. The encounters with Fromm described by the contributors are surprisingly varied: some contributors recall their meeting with Fromm in idealized ways; others still feel like students of a Zen master who disciplined them. All the contributors, however, recognized Fromm as an outstanding human being and psychoanalyst—as a therapist who has an uncanny gift for engaging the other directly and immediately, and with enormous presence.

In Part Two, the contributors explore the encounter with Fromm from the perspective of the relationship process. The direct, face-to-face mode of encounter sought and favored by Fromm in every kind of relationship prompted the contributors to consider two questions: first, what was unique to Fromm's approach; and second, to relate Fromm's understanding of the face-to-face encounter with how he actually practiced therapy. It quickly becomes evident that Fromm's therapeutic approach diverged from the general run of traditional psychoanalytic technique.

In Part Three, contributors introduce readers to Fromm's supervisory style and objectives, drawing on actual experiences of supervision with Fromm. These accounts, some of them highly detailed, give a vivid sense of how direct Fromm could be in sizing up the patients before him, including their unconscious aspirations, and how quickly Fromm saw through the deceptive maneuvers patients used to stave off their core feeling of isolation and impotence. At the same time, Fromm could be equally unsparing—though not without empathy—in his dealings with therapists. He quickly sensed in them a dread of their patients. Fromm confronts therapists when he feels they are reduced to the role of an accomplice, either because they have not yet managed to tap into the healing powers of those they seek to help, or are not yet sufficiently aware of their own role and needs in the therapeutic process.

Part Four considers Fromm from a more personal perspective. Contributors recall not just the training analyst, the supervisor and the therapist, but also what Fromm was actually like in the flesh. Idiosyncrasies and biographic details have the power to illuminate what was exceptional in Fromm's way of doing therapy. At the same time, these personal accounts of Fromm strengthen the impression that such exceptionality is not to be sought in a "technique," at least to the extent that a technique can be copied and applied as a routine. Rather, for Fromm the issue is to ensure that practicing psychoanalysts have personalities that have been given an exceptional shaping: that is to say, the ability to directly encounter whatever is destructive, sick, or productive in one's patients depends on whether therapists are willing, and able, to directly encounter these selfsame dimensions in themselves. Success here presupposes daily self-analysis, which Fromm always sought to practice.

The texts that follow were edited at various points for publication. Omissions and additions are indicated by square parentheses, e.g. [...]; the standard American form of address (given names, family name, academic title, etc.) was sometimes abbreviated. In those contributions that were previously published, the use of the masculine pronoun has been retained, even if this is now outdated.

PART I

ERICH FROMM
ON THERAPEUTIC PRACTICE

Being *Centrally* Related to the Patient

Erich Fromm

MY UNDERSTANDING OF WHAT IS BEING UNCONSCIOUS

If one uses the term, "repression", as it is usually used by Freud and as it is used in analytic literature, one thinks primarily of something which *was* conscious and then was repressed. While in my concept here I refer to that which is *not* conscious, i.e. both to that which has been conscious, and to that which we have never been aware of. Therefore, perhaps it would be better to word the concept *"dissociation",* rather than "repression", because in the concept "dissociation" one can more easily comprise both: that which has emerged and that which has not emerged in awareness. It does not have quite the active "pushing back" quality. To give another example of the kind of dissociations I have in mind, representing that which we are not aware of: You have seen the face of a person, let us say, who is well known to you; you have known him for many years, and one day you suddenly see the face entirely afresh. Suddenly, you see this face with what you would describe simply as a greater degree of reality. You know the face; you could describe it, you see a quality, you see an essence, which is much more real than anything you have seen before, and actually for a moment you have the feeling, "I have never seen this face before, it is completely new". What happened? You are aware of something in the reality of this face, which you have not been aware of before. The face was always the same, that is to say the man or the woman was always the same; you are always the same, but you had a veil and you did not see. You were, what one might say, half blind, and suddenly your eyes open and you see.

The whole process really of making the unconscious conscious is a process which could be described as seeing, and actually you have in the mythological literature the symbol of blindness, utter blindness, and then you become a seer. Tiresias is blind and he is a seer. Oedipus becomes blind and eventually he becomes a seer. Faust, in Goethe's *Faust,* becomes blind at the very moment when he sees and he says then that an inner radiance emanated from him.

This concept of repression in which we talk about not being aware of that which exists within ourselves, is based on the premise that *all is really inside us*. Or, if we put it differently, that we know everything, except that we do not know what we know. If I assume I have never before seen you as I see you now, then I must, in my way of putting it, assume I really knew you before, but I was not aware of what I knew. If I had not known you before, if I had been really blind, then I would only be able to speak of a new insight, rather than of a hidden suppressed, unconscious insight, which has emerged.

I believe, indeed, that we have everything inside us, not only in the sense that we are all human and that there is nothing human which is alien to us, because there is nothing human which is not in us, from the child, to the criminal, to the insane person, to the saint, to the average person. I would say, we are also aware of all that, but at the same time we are not aware; we sense it. This one of the reasons why pointing to reality— which, in my way of thinking means the same—has such a peculiar effect on people. Because the truth touches only upon something one knows, and once this chord is touched one almost cannot help responding.

The lie does not touch upon reality, the lie touches on nothing, and therefore you can say a thousand lies, because you touch on nothing: you touch fiction, you touch unreality, but once you touch reality, which means you say the truth, then something in the person tends to respond, because what you say hits upon that which he knows and yet does not know. Of course I do not mean that the process is this simple, that the person will necessarily respond; because there might be defenses against his responding—that is what we call resistance, then he will not respond. But, nevertheless, I would say this is the hope for the human race, that in fact truth makes us free, as the New Testament says [John 8:32].

In us is a sense of reality—of our inner reality and of the reality outside—to which one can appeal with a true word. If one could not do that, then I think the analytic method would really be essentially impossible, except as a method of persuasion. There is a very interesting Jewish Talmudic myth about this, which says that before the child is born, it knows everything, but to be born with this knowledge would be so painful that out of mercy an angel touches the child and does away with all his knowledge. What I say here corresponds pretty much to this myth. Unconsciously we know everything and yet we do not, because it is indeed very painful to know and at the same time there is nothing more exhilarating, which do not even exclude pain, than to know, than to be in touch with reality.

Another point I should like to stress is the *connection between individual repression and social repression.* It is true that we mostly have to do with social repression and that there are only individual variants, individual deviations, which work above the social repressions, and they make for more or less repression in this or that area.

How does social and individual repression work together? If you take for instance a mother who gets anxious every time the child does something "bad" and then reacts, the child senses this anxiety, and the child becomes highly sensitive to the notion "bad". Take for instance a mother who is obsessionally compulsive, and whose fear of badness is a good deal more intense than that of the average person—take the nineteenth century cultures—then indeed this mother may be some thirty percent above the average in her obsession with good and bad. But, nevertheless, this child will have great difficulties getting over the anxiety produced by mother's anxiety about good and bad, because of the culture in which it finds itself; this is supported by the whole culture, the culture never denies the basic principle of the mother's influence. And, of course, in general, we must not forget that the mother, the father, the family are not accidental individuals which happen to be in a culture, they are formed by the society, that is to say, in the first few years the child is rarely in touch with society as such. But it is in touch with its agents, namely the parents whose characters are formed by society and whose sociological function it is to prepare the child characterologically to become that which the society wants.

If the parents are really crazy—and by really crazy I do not mean it in a psychiatric sense, but I mean completely outside the culture in which they live—then the child has actually a much better chance to get away, not to be impressed by the influences. In fact, really crazy for better or worse, that does not matter. Once a child grows up a little bit more these parents will then stand out as being outside the majority, outside of what is considered to be reasonable, normal, and so on.

Let me say a few more words about the concept of unawareness of experience. What actually happens when we have an *experience?* Let me give an example: We have a ball and we throw the ball and the ball rolls, and we say: "The ball rolls". What do we actually experience when we say "The ball rolls?" I think we experience only the following: Our mind confirms our knowledge that a round object on a relatively smooth surface, when pushed, rolls. In other words, when we say: "The ball rolls", we make an intellectual statement that really amounts to saying that we are able to speak. We know this is a ball and we know the law of nature that a ball rolls. But what happens to a little boy of four when the ball rolls? What happens is that he really sees the ball rolling. That is an entirely different experience; it is a beautiful experience; it is an experience—you could call it an ecstatic experience—in which the whole body participates in this beautiful thing of seeing a ball rolling. Some of us for instance, have this experience more clearly when we see people playing tennis. Let us assume that we are not interested in who wins, but we just follow the beautiful movement of the ball going back and forth. The simple act of a rolling ball usually appears boring to us after the second time. Why are we bored? Because we feel we already know that the ball rolls. But for the little boy, it is not a matter of knowing it. For the little boy it is a matter of seeing this movement, which is a full experience.

Like some other people, I believe that any thought, which is not already dissociated, is not only a thought of our brain, but a thought of our *body*. We think with our muscles; we think with everything in our body. If we do not think with our body, if our body is not participating in a thought, then it is already a dissociated thought. This I know is true in thoughts about things, about people. If, for instance, you see a little teddy bear with a very smooth, nice surface, and you say: "Isn't that beautiful", but you do not feel anything in your fingers, an impulse to stroke it, I would say that your statement: "Isn't that beautiful" is not true. It is one of these statements we make every day a thousand times: "Isn't it nice", "I feel fine"— but really you have not had the experience, which allegedly is contained in the sentence: "Isn't that beautiful".

Somebody sees a mountain. What is the first question? "What's the name, what's the altitude?" Once he knows these data cerebrally, he files them away. You see a person and ask: "Who are you?"—and you expect first the name, then the age, then the marriage status—in other words, the passport. Actually, this is beautifully expressed in Ibsen's *Peer* Gynt, where Peer Gynt, when he begins to doubt his identity, eventually asks himself: "Who am I?" and, he answers: "My passport". These are the data which are experienced as "I"—and this is where it ends.

In our way of speaking, in our way of saying, "this is me", or "this is I", "a ball rolls", "this is a rose", "this is a mountain", we are already dissociating from the total experience, the affective part, and are already making a statement. It sounds like a full statement, but is actually a dissociated statement because we are not aware of the affective experience, which exists and yet does not come into awareness. This is the point where the unconscious really begins in daily life.

You do not understand a person unless you know that *life is paradoxical*, and therefore that you have to think paradoxically in order to understand it. A few examples: I can make the statement: "I am unique. I am as unique as my fingerprints are unique. There is no other human being, nor has there ever been or will be anyone like me". I can make the statement: "I am you, I am everything, there is no individuality, no uniqueness in me at all". If you would make these statements by saying: in some respects I am unique and in others I am not, then of course you have no truly paradoxical statement. This statement fits very well, with Aristotelian logic, because you do not really contradict yourself. You say: "Here I am unique, here I am not". The statement which I am making here is meant in a paradoxical sense. It is not so much a matter of statement, but of experience. Do I experience myself, at the same time, (and the same subject, I,) as completely unique, and as completely not unique—as completely as "I" and as completely as that which I share with every human being and to some extent with any living being: with a fly, or with a flower; namely, the quality of life in me? Do I experience both aspects of my life, or don't I?

Our consciousness, our awareness, is greatly influenced by Aristotelian logic. It is very difficult to experience a reality which can be experienced only in paradoxical terms. What we tend to do is to separate the two poles of the paradox, and then to feel either one. We are either completely unique; or we feel like the Christian mystics often felt, I am nobody, I have no individuality, I do not exist and I am completely dissolved in God or in mankind; or as a profoundly masochistic or submissive person may feel, who has no sense of individuality. As soon as in any polarity we separate the two poles, the same thing happens—if I may use a simple analogy—as when you have a positive and negative pole of electricity. If they are at a certain distance, you will have a spark. If you separate them completely, there is no spark, and if there is no distance at all there is no spark either, the current will just flow through.

I do believe that with regard to the basic facts of life, we have to live in the paradox, and *we have to think in the paradox, if we want to understand life.*

Another example where we deal with a paradox is the factor of time in analysis. Actually, you or I can wake up, can break through the defenses, any minute, right now, and it may take years. Experientially, there is a paradoxical attitude, i.e. I expect that it may happen right now, and I expect it will take years. But if you separate the two poles, if you assume logically that it will take many years, then you will not expect it to happen right now. If on the other hand, you are convinced it will happen right now, you will be terribly disappointed tomorrow if it has not happened. In the literature, and I am sure there are other examples. I can give an example of this paradox from the Talmudic literature, about the expectation of the Messiah. In the Jewish tradition the Messiah was expected to come at any moment, to come right now. At the same time, the Talmud had a very strict and rather urgent message: One should not push the Messiah, one should not be impatient. There is a concept of patience—impatience, namely of a paradoxical patience, in which you are prepared every moment, and yet you also expect it may happen after many years or sometime in the life of mankind; it may happen now or in thousands of years.

The question is of inner experience: of being able to feel both attitudes at the same time in spite of the fact that they are contradictory. Also the next example has to do with the attitude toward the patient: For any person whom one really understands or tries to understand, one has a feeling of responsibility. I am responsible for you, because once I get close enough to you, you might say: "You are my brother", and I am indeed my brother's keeper. But, at the same time, with equal truth I have to say: "I am not responsible for you at all. You are responsible for yourself; God may be responsible for you, your genes may be responsible for you, the whole universe may be responsible for you, but not me". But, again, this is a paradox, which one has to experience, because if you tear the two sides apart, then you either feel guilty and you feel an unrealistic responsibility, or you feel irresponsible. In fact you can hardly help anybody; you will only harm him if you only feel responsibility. If you feel only irresponsibility, then you are indifferent and cannot help either. The attitude I am talking about is again to live in the paradox that both statements—I am responsible, I am not responsible—are equally true, and I live in this, and with this contradiction.

I could give many more examples of such paradoxes, but I will not do that. All I want to do really is to make this point clear, which in our Western thinking is very difficult to grasp fully. This is so strange to us: the true experience of two contradictory facts, two contradictory statements, and the capacity or the willingness to live with these contradictions, and not to think that *because* they are contradictions, they cannot be true, or cannot be real.

ALIENATION AS A PARTICULAR FORM OF UNCONSCIOUSNESS

The problem of alienation is really a continuation of the topic of repression, or of unconsciousness, or of dissociation, because alienation is perhaps the most frequent and the most characteristic form in which we, in this culture and at this time, dissociate experience. Alienation is, you might say, a particular form of dissociation, or you might even go further and say, all dissociation is a form of alienation. Nevertheless, I think this must not prevent us from talking about it very seriously.

To describe the mechanism of *alienation* in psychological terms: By alienation I project an experience, which is potentially in me, to an object outside of me. I alienate myself from my own human experience and project this experience onto something or somebody outside, and then try to get in touch with my own human being, by being in touch with the object to which I have projected my humanity. That holds for alienation and idolatry. The two terms refer exactly to the same phenomenon. One term is used by Hegel and Marx and the other is used by the prophets of the Old Testament.

Both terms, alienation as well as idolatry, mean that I deprive myself, I empty myself, I freeze, I get rid of a living experience. My own thinking, my own loving, my own feeling is projected onto a person or thing outside. I can get it back by the relationship to this thing, which has become the representative of that which I have deprived myself of. I abdicate so to speak certain human powers, put them onto the emperor, onto the pope, or whatever it may be, and from now on, this figure *out there* represents me, but I am bound to him, because if I am not close to him, I am lost, because, he has my soul. In Goethe's *Faust*, Mephisto, as long as he is important to Faust, really has his soul. He has part of him, but Faust gets away from him and comes on his own.

The prophets of the Old Testament have expressed in many ways, what they call *idolatry*. In the concept of idolatry, we do, of course, not deal with the question whether there is one God or many Gods. For the prophets of the Old Testament, idolatry means that man worships the work of his own hand and bows in front of *things*. In this process man becomes a thing himself. In this process, he limits himself, reifies himself, kills himself, because he becomes dependent on things into which he has projected his human powers, but which are now in the hands of the saints.

These "things" can be idols, as you read in the prophets. A man can take a piece of wood; with one half he makes a fire and bakes his cake, from the other half he makes a sculpture and worships it as his God. Or, it may be the state, or a powerful institution. It may be anything. What is common for all is the fact that man always abdicates his own creative powers and is in touch with them only indirectly by submitting to the idol, by worshipping the idol.

Marx more than anyone else has clarified the concept of alienation. Actually alienation is at the center of his system and particularly in his main works this becomes clear. In the *Economic-philosophical Manuscripts (1844)* he says: "The object produced by labor, its product, now stands opposed to it as an *alien being,* as a *power independent* of the producer" (MEGA I, 3, p. 83). If you read the prophetic description of the idol, you will see that it is an almost literally identical description. And in order to deepen Marx's concept of alienation I quote from the *German Ideology:* "This consolidation of what we ourselves produce, which turns into an objective power above us, growing out of our control, thwarting our expectations, bringing to naught our calculations, is one of the chief factors in historical development up to now".

If you really listen to Marx's words then you are forced to think of the atomic bomb, because that indeed is the "consolidation of what we ourselves produce, which turns into an objective power above us, growing out of our control, thwarting our expectations, bringing to naught our calculations", and indeed it threatens to do so.

Today the *bureaucracy is* an idol to which we project our own will, tomorrow it may be an electronic computer, because bureaucracy is only, you might say, an imperfect step compared to what an electronic computer can do much better and much more correctly. You feed it with data, the data are collected, processed and given a certain principle and you come out with what sounds like a decision. It is a logical consequence of certain data, processed under certain premises.

If you speak today with the average person, let us say, about the danger of war, he will say: "This is all too difficult for me, I do not know". Not only the average person, many persons who ought to know, will say: "I do not know, let them make the decisions". The average person has stopped to think, has projected his power of thinking and wanting on a bureaucracy outside himself and is in touch with his own human quality of wanting and thinking only inasmuch as he worships this bureaucracy. The bureaucracy is an idol of decision-making.

God today is an idol of love and wisdom. People are not loving, and they are not wise, but since it is difficult for man to live completely without love and wisdom, they go to churches and worship God. Since they have projected love and wisdom onto God, they are once a week in touch with their own love and wisdom, by going to church, or by using the name of God. At least they feel they have not completely lost their love and wisdom, but they are alienated from it; it is not theirs anymore, it is what they get back from God. It is not an experience, but an indirect being-in-touch-with what they have already lost, but not given up.

The *hero* is an idol of courage. I have no courage, but if I identify with the hero and worship the hero, I am in touch with whatever courage I might have.

Words in general and *thoughts,* become generalized idols. They substitute for experience. Needless to say, what we have here is a most ambiguous phenomenon. Actually if you utter a word, by uttering the word, you alienate yourself already from the experience. The experience is really there, only just the moment before you say the word. Once the word is said, it is already over there. At the same time, of course, this holds true also for an abstraction, it holds true for a concept. But it is obvious that this is also a process of increasing differentiation, of increasing thought. Here again we deal with a paradoxical problem; you utter the word to express something and the moment you have spoken it, you have already killed what you were expressing. The ambiguity of "words", the ambiguity of "concepts", and yet all that matters is really where the word comes from. If you utter a word which comes from your experience, then the word will remain in the living context in which it is spoken as an expression of the experience. If you utter a word which comes from your brain and which according to its contents should came from experience, then your word is empty and is nothing but an idol, a little idol.

Let me mention a few instances in which this problem of alienation is particularly significant from the standpoint of what we go through in *psychoanalysis.* By "we go through", I mean both: being analyzed or analyzing somebody.

Take, for instance, *transference.* Of course, one can look at transference from the standpoint of Freud, as a repetition of the infantile image of the parents. That is in a sense perfectly true. But I would say there is a difference between the child's love for the mother, and the transference feeling for the analyst in the figure of the mother, because the child still loves the mother in a non—alienated way. It *really* loves the mother. The mother means her milk, her nipple, her skin, her smile, her arm, but this is not an alienated experience. But what happens in the transference situation? Especially in the very violent transferences, I impoverish myself, even more than before I went to the analyst, because now I have found an idol. I project, being desperate about my own powers, being desperate about my own strength. I project all I have got, or all I have left, onto the person of the analyst and then try to get in touch with all my human richness by being in touch with the analyst.

You may call it submission, love, or whatever it is, but actually it is the same process as idolatry: emptying oneself is a condition of complete submission-dependency because now I have even ceased to exist authentically. I have now become completely dependent on the idol. This becomes a matter of being or not being, because I lose myself completely if the idol leaves me. This can happen in more extreme forms and it can happen in milder forms. I do not mean that what I am saying here about transference is in contrast to Freud's theory, or that of many other people. The two concepts do not exclude each other at all, or do not even contradict each other. This is just one aspect, as I see it, of the transference situation.

Another example of alienation in many patients, or in many of us, one might call the *idolatry of the self-image.* There is the self-image of grandiosity: the hero, the genius. Or there is the self-image of the terribly modest, kind and good person. There is any number of self-images. Actually, what happens is that the self-image becomes the idol, whom one serves. That is to say, to put in front of oneself this little statue, call it modesty, goodness, wisdom, intelligence, brilliance, anything; or surliness, or even cruelty, because that is also a self-image. In some patients it is simply the phallic worship.

I am referring to the subtle process in which one's own self-image is an idol. You transfer whatever is alive in you to the idol and now live reflectively in terms of the idol. You do not act genuinely anymore, but as your own idol makes you to act. You see a person who is quite consistent in his actions and yet he is frightened because his actions lack authenticity. He has emptied himself, erected the idol of the self-image, lives according to this idol but he is never himself, and that is why he is frightened.

Obviously in analysis, it is terribly important to understand not only the self-image but to understand the mechanism of alienation or idolatry with regard to the self-image. Actually you find quite frequently that this self-image is built up as an escape from a negative self-image. Take the boy, let us say, who by his father and mother, or God knows by what circumstances, has been impressed by his own worthlessness, badness. He has a self-image which is worthless, but not only that; "I am dead, I am unbearable, I am objectionable, I am not accepted". This self-image, if he would hold on to it, would practically lead to destruction, because he would really worship Moloch, to whom one sacrificed one's children. Thus he escapes from this negative self-image, to a self-image which he may steal from somebody. He chooses the analyst, he chooses god knows whom, as his little idol in the flight from the unbearable self-image which he developed originally. He is forced to worship the idol of the self-image, because otherwise he feels always in danger of being driven out and of being confronted with the original negative self-image, the original feeling of utter worthlessness.

Another problem is the *idolatry of thought.* A person talks and believes that his experience is in the word, and is not aware anymore that the experience is not in him, that the word or the thought has become the little idol. Using the words gives an impression of being in touch with what the word means, when I have in fact emptied myself from the experience, and am in touch with it only indirectly by being in touch with the word which is supposed to represent the experience.

Another example of alienation is the *fanatic.* Maybe I could take Arthur Koestler's *Darkness at Noon* (1941) as an example. There you have a higher functionary of the Communist Party, who has been in the Party for many years, who has been a quite a decent human being. (By decent I do not mean saintly, or something of the kind, but with some normal human feelings towards other people). In the process of being a high functionary of the Party, he must actually kill more and more of all that is human in him. Eventually, all humanity in this man has been killed. He feels nothing anymore, he cannot.

What happens is that the Party becomes to him the idol of all that is human. The Party represents human kindness, solidarity, brotherliness, hope, love—everything. He must become the slave of the Party, because having emptied himself of all human quality he would became insane, he would lose his human identity, were it not for the fact that by submission to the Party he remains in touch with qualities which were originally his. Then comes the particular quality of the fanatic, and that holds only for the fanatic. By making these qualities into an idol and forming them into something absolute, by the complete submission to this idol, he experiences a kind of strange, fiery passion. Or maybe I shouldn't say "fiery" passion, I should say "cold" passion.

If you love, if you see, if you hear, if you enjoy, there is excitement, there is intensity connected with a real experience. The fanatic has an intensity which is not connected with what the experience pretends to be, namely, the love for mankind, freedom or whatever. His excitement is the excitement of the complete submission to the absolute. Here you have a paradox, which Koestler expressed very well in the paradoxical title *Darkness at Noon*. If I were to choose a symbol, I would choose `burning ice'. That is to say, the fanatic is burning, but at the same time everything is completely frozen, the ice burns; he is frozen, he has emptied himself completely, he has projected completely all that is human to the idol that he has chosen, this hate, or this nationalism, or anti-semitism, or God knows what. It does not make any difference. But, he experiences the intensity of the complete submission and thereby of being in touch with what to him is absolute humanity. Of course, one can do the same with God too, provided God is an idol. It is important to understand the psychology of the fanatic from the standpoint of the alienation and the subsequent idolatry.

Another example is *mourning*. There is a type of depressive mourning in which the dead person, or even my own dead Self becomes an idol, and all that is good is transferred to that idol, and I remain alive only in relation to my connection with the dead, either with the other person who is dead, or my own dead Self.

One of the most important clinical concepts, which has also to do with alienation, is the *alienation of the Self*. In regard to the concept of the Self—the image that the Self has about himself—I should differentiate between two concepts: between the *Self* and the *Ego*. What do I mean by the experience of one's Self as an Ego? I mean exactly the alienated experience which I have been talking about, and which you find in so many, if not in most, people today. The alienated person looks at himself as he would look at an outsider: I have an image of myself. I do not want to stress here whether the image is right or wrong, but that we see ourselves as a package and from the outside.

When we think "I", we really experience ourselves as we experience another person, although we shouldn't experience another person that way either. We experience ourselves as a thing which has many qualities. Then you have the kind of ruminating which you find in a person: "After all, I am intelligent", or "I am pretty", or "I am kind", or "I am courageous" and so on. Actually, this is only the description of that thing over there. This Ego concept is an alienated concept of the image I have of myself as a thing, which I carry through in life and with which I want to do something in life.

The concept of Self, as I see it, is the experience of myself as "I" in the process of being the subject of my action. By "action" I do not mean primarily that I do this or that, but that I am in the process of being the subject of my human experience. *I* feel, *I* think, *I* taste, *I* hear, *I* love. And there are many more things, which are the whole range, all the expressions of human faculties. If I am not synthetic, but the authentic subject of my activities, then indeed, I experience myself in the moment of being active as the one who acts. But I do not experience myself as the Ego.

The one who experiences his Self as an Ego experiences only his package. He looks from the outside and asks: "How have you done it?" or: "How will you do it?" By asking himself: "How will you do it?" he asks himself: "What will be the impression this little package makes on the world, what will be the price tag, if you please?" To that same extent, of course, I am inhibited in being, in experiencing myself as a subject of my *powers.* And on the other hand, to the same extent to which I experience myself as the subject of my powers, I do not contemplate my Ego. That is actually what the New Testament means as far as I understand by "slay yourself'," or what the Zen Buddhists mean when they say "empty your-self'. It do not mean "slay yourself'. This slaying yourself means simply forget about your Ego, because this attempt to hold onto your Ego, to look at yourself from what some people call the objective standpoint, actually stands in your way of being. The experience of "I" or of "self" exists only in the process of being, in the process of relating, in the process of using any kind of human power.

I can explain the other person as another Ego, as another thing, and then look at him as I look at my car, my house, my neurosis, whatever it may be. Or I can relate to this other person in the sense of being him, in the sense of experiencing, feeling this other person. Then I do not think about myself, then my Ego does not stand in my way. But something entirely different happens. There is what I call a *central relatedness* between me and him. He is not a thing over there which I look at, but he confronts me fully and I confront him fully, and there in fact is no way of escape.

I wanted to mention this here as one of the most important psychological or clinical instances of alienation because you can see why this is alienation: As soon as I experience myself as that nice, intelligent doctor, whatever he may be, married with two kids, and so on, I do not experience anything. I put my experience in that image I assume. Because the image is that of the kind, nice, intelligent doctor, I am kind, nice and intelligent.

I have talked about the problem of alienation as a particular form of unconsciousness, namely the unawareness of inner experience and the pseudo-awareness of experience in the alienated person who deceives himself about experiencing when he is actually in touch with thought, in touch with the idol, and so on.

There is what you might call an original anxiety, which exists in the experience of separation. We have to overcome this primary anxiety which usually does not exist manifestly but potentially, by compensating for this isolation in various ways, to overcome it. If I say, "compensating" I really mean only the regressive ways, because if we take the progressive way, as I see it, namely the full development of human powers in over-coming alienation, there is no more compensation. If a person has really woken up—if a person has really seen the reality of his Self, has thrown away most of his Ego, then indeed there is no need to compensate for anxiety anymore, because there isn't any.

If I say, there is no anxiety, I do not speak about my personal experience because I have not been enlightened and I have suffered a lot of anxiety, less now than I used to, so I do not mean to say that this is all very simple. I am talking about something I know. But I do know, and I have known, a few people who did not feel any anxiety, not because they had repressed their anxiety, but because they had solved the problems of their lives. These people have been very important for me as models, to help me see what is possible. I doubt whether I ever will achieve it, and I do not speak in this sense, but nevertheless what matters is how far one goes.

Doctor Suzuki once made a remark, which I think is quite pertinent also to analytic work. He said:

> Take a room which is completely dark, that is to say, absolute darkness, no light. As soon as you bring one candle into this room, the situation is totally changed. Before that candle came, there was absolute darkness, and when this candle comes, there is light. Now then, you bring ten candles, and a hundred candles, and a thousand candles, and a hundred thousand candles, and the room gets lighter and lighter and lighter ... That makes a great deal of difference. And yet the decisive event happened when the darkness was broken by the first candle.

I personally think of human development in terms of an increasing light. I think it is important to bring the first candle into one's own life, or into the life of the patient, if this can be done.

I differentiate between what I call here the basic or primary anxiety and the secondary anxiety, by which I mean simply the anxiety which is aroused when one of the compensatory mechanisms is affected. To give an example: A person has compensated for his anxiety by the image of himself as a successful man, who is always successful. But one time he's a failure—bang. Then the compensation do not work anymore and then the original anxiety comes out, but not in reference to the original problem—that of separateness, but in reference to the problem of the compensatory mechanism.

As long as you share your defects, i.e. your pathology, your inability to be fully developed, to be productive—as long as you share it with the group, usually you do not have a manifest neurosis. Because you have the very reassuring and very important feeling: "I am like the rest, I am not isolated, I am not sticking out ... I am not alone, I am not separate". While, if you happen to have a kind of problem which does separate you, which is not the usual manifestation, very often because you are the more sensitive person, because your individuality has not been rubbed out so drastically, because you have not been so smudged—then, indeed, you feel isolated, and then out of anxiety you produce certain symptoms which we call neurotic symptoms. This is the problem of all neurotic symptoms, the non— adaptation to society by the person who suffers from being crippled to a certain extent. I am aware that there are many complex factors in it. But what I do mean is, that we must differentiate between the fact of being crippled, of the narrowing down, impoverishment of human faculties, of aliveness, and manifest symptoms, and that this makes a great deal of difference.

IMPLICATIONS FOR BEING RELATED TO THE PATIENT

The aim of the analytic process is to help a patient grasp his hidden total experience. I emphasize the "hidden" experience, but also the "total" experience, because I do not think the understanding of partial, small, isolated aspects of that which is hidden is enough for more than a symptomatic cure. I think to cure symptoms, the understanding of the isolated hidden or repressed experience, which leads to that symptom formation, will indeed very often be enough. For a change of character, I think the aim of the analysis must be to grasp the hidden "total" experience. That is to say, I cease to be a thing, I cease to be a stranger to myself, and I begin to experience what I am—experience what I really feel, what I really experience. From this, of course, follows a few statements of what analysis is not.

How we should not be related to the patient.

1. Psychoanalysis is *not a historical research into the past* of a person. Historical research into the past is important only inasmuch as it makes it easier for the patient to have certain memories and to renew or to relive certain feelings of his childhood, to be able to experience what is now repressed, which is now apart from him, namely something he feels now. So we must always protect ourselves from letting the analysis deteriorate. Historical research has value only when it is part of uncovering what the hidden experience is that the patient has now.
2. Psychoanalysis is not either a study of childhood patterns and learning from them in order to manage the world better now. To give a well—

known example: You were afraid of your father, that is why you are afraid of authorities, and when you meet your boss, then remember that, after all, you are afraid of him because you were afraid of your father, and this will help you. This would be similar to saying to a hypochondriacal patient, who is in a panic when he has a cold or this or that little symptom, when he comes to the doctor for the first time: "Look, you are a hypochondriacal person, every little thing causes you this anxiety, so next time you have a cold and you think you have tuberculosis, remember that this is a mechanism of a hypochondriacal person". That is very relieving and it is very good. I am not criticizing, only saying that one should not spend years to drill these things into the patient. He can learn it quicker elsewhere, it is important, it is useful, it is helpful, but it is not analysis.

3. I also do not consider as analysis what sometimes happens explicitly or implicitly, as if psychoanalysis were a kind of teaching a patient the skill of living. It takes a wise man to do that, and I am sure one can sometimes find such a wise man, who can teach the skill of living. This is very important and very helpful, but it is not what our profession is about. We are not counselors of wisdom. We promise something very specific: We are specialists in the understanding of the unconscious, that is to say in helping the patient to experience dissociated material. And we promise, furthermore, that there is a reasonable chance, that if we do that, the patient may feel better.

I think we have to live up to this promise, because otherwise I do not think we have any right or claim to call ourselves psychoanalysts. Sometimes we may give the patients a piece of our wisdom if it is there—that can never do any harm. Sometimes we may explain to him or her some simple facts of life. But if we do so, we should say: "Now, look here, I want to give you a piece of my wisdom", or: "I want to explain to you a fact of life". But we should not do it in a disguised analytic form as if we were making an interpretation. But while all this is very useful sometimes, I think the essential thing is that we must make a decision about what psychoanalysis is: Is the essential thing to help the patient in uncovering his dissociated material or is it not?

Premises for understanding the patient

Analysis is—to use a traditional formula—the understanding of the unconscious of the patient. That is the formula since Freud's day, and I would still say that is a correct, good formula. That is what we are there for—to understand. I would rather not use the word "unconscious" of the patient. I would rather say: to understand the patient better than he understands himself; to understand that experience which exists in him, which is there and yet has not come to his own awareness, is obscured from him, is separated from him.

This leads us to the question: How do we understand another person? If you have a person, in this case a person called patient, who is like me, I understand him, provided I understand myself. If I do not understand myself I will not even understand a person who is very much like me. But let us assume for a moment that I understand myself, I know myself, I am aware of the reality inside of me. Thus I would understand another person who is very much like me. But we do not select patients in that way, and we cannot. So how do we understand a person who is entirely different? How do we understand a person whose temperament is different, who is this, that and the other way? I do not have to describe to you how different people are. I think there is one answer: it is all there within us.

I am using again the same broad and rather unscientific formulation. What I mean is, *everything is inside* us—there is no experience of another human being, which is not also an experience we are capable of having. There is no string—if the other person were a violin, not with four but with a hundred strings—which, when vibrating, does not touch the same string in ourselves. The only difference is—and there my example of the strings becomes pointless—that in one person one thing is stronger, in another person the other thing is stronger. But if I try to understand a criminal, a man who has murdered and stolen, I can only understand him if I become aware of the criminal impulses within me, under the influence of which I could murder or steal. It is true, I am not a criminal, so I assume in him these impulses are much stronger, they are uncontrolled, and so on. But they are there in me as well.

This is saying essentially what Freud has already said. But I want to point out that this is true not only with regard to bad things. If I want to understand a saintly man, a good person, I can only understand him if this good person is also in me. If a person has nothing human within him, if there is no impulse of goodness, of kindness, of love, of health, then I would indeed say he has ceased to be a human being. There is nothing in the other person, which is not also in me. That is the only basis on which I can understand any other human being, especially the being who is very different, or the being who is very sick, provided we are not so sick. If we are also sick, we sometimes understand certain things better.

This is one premise, as I see it, for understanding someone. But secondly, the question is: What do we mean by "understanding"? For instance, Edward Glover wrote, in his *The Technique of Psychoanalysis* (1955) that actually a psychoanalyst does not know anybody any better than a layman, before that person has been on the couch and has given himself up to free association. He claims that intuitively, immediately, directly, we have no knowledge, and that the only knowledge we acquire is through the laboratory experiment of having a person on the couch and then receiving the associations. Of course, that is a way of understanding and of academic psychology, the way of the natural sciences. But I believe in that way we do not really understand. We talk about a person; we remain outside in the same way I was describing before, we remain outside of ourselves. We can talk endlessly about ourselves: "I am this and I am that, I am hostile, I am not hostile, I am masochistic, and what not", and yet we remain on the level of talking *about* ourselves. I believe, and this is a belief to which I have come more and more over the years, that indeed we understand a person fully, only inasmuch as we are *centrally related* to him.

If we really understand the patient, then we experience in ourselves everything the patient tells us, his fantasies, whether psychotic, or criminal, or childish. We understand only if they strike that chord within ourselves. That is why we can talk with authority to the patient, because we are not talking about him anymore, we are talking about our own experience which has been made manifest through his telling us what he experiences. This is indeed where the patient analyzes us. I do not mean that he analyzes us by saying anything, although that sometimes happens too— and I must say that I have learned some of the most important things from what some patients have said about me in analysis. However, I am not talking about that part.

If you relate to the patient, not as a thing over there, whom you study, but if you try to experience in yourself what the patient feels, then indeed you will experience the whole realm, the whole world which is not in the conscious mind, and by being in touch with it, you analyze yourself, because you become more and more aware. I would say this is the unique thing about the psychoanalytic profession, which I do not quite see in any other profession—that in curing the patient, we cure ourselves.

Provided we start out with this kind of relatedness and we start out after our own analysis is finished successfully, we start out with a readiness to see. I would define a successfully finished analysis as one in which we can begin to analyze ourselves. Increasingly we become aware of ourselves, in other words, the resistance is broken down to a point where we can go on by ourselves. But I think the patients are a tremendous help, because they just hit you over the head, again and again and again, with things which are in yourself.

Some analysts react to that with a feeling of guilt. They feel: "For heaven's sake, we are treating people, and I am much sicker than they are", which is a kind of Self—discouraging reaction. But there's also a different reaction: "For heaven's sake—I have seen something new again this is me". If we really permit ourselves to feel that, instead of running away from it and feeling guilty, I think we have made considerable progress.

Being centrally *related to the patient*

I want now to speak more specifically about one thing which is the most difficult to put into words—what I call *central relatedness.* In the first place, I have to say I do not think I can explain it. It cannot be put into words, because either you experience it or you do not. Just as hard as it is to actually put into words the difference between experiencing my "I" as an Ego, as an object, and the experience of "I" as an active subject of my powers, in which I forget about myself, although I am most fully myself in the process of expressing myself.

The most convincing and natural symbol of what I am talking about is actually sexual love, because in the act of sexual love, whether you are a man or a woman, you forget yourself. If you do not stop thinking about yourself, you are even impotent or—in the case of a woman—frigid. As soon as you are not *in* the experience and the full subject of your experience, but you become an object who thinks: "How am I doing?" you will be incapacitated, even on the physiological level. Actually sexual love in this sense is one of the most significant natural symbols of being related. I am not saying that two people who sleep with each other are necessarily related for that reason. This is wisdom almost only of our body, and I am sure there are many people whose body is quite wise and whose mind is utterly stupid. I think there are other people whose body may not be wise and who may yet be tremendously related to other people. In other words, I do not mean that there is any one-to-one relationship between sexual behavior and the general characterological pattern. I use it only in the sense of a symbol. So I would say there is no description, which is adequate, there is only a description of certain aspects.

When I use the concept "central relatedness" I mean the relatedness from center to center instead of the relatedness from periphery to periphery. Although these are only words, I think we have some sense of what we consider central and what we consider periphery. Relatedness from center to center means to be interested: We are interested in another person, we listen attentively, we listen with interest, we think about the person, and yet the other person remains outside. In other words, we relate ourselves, think ourselves, think about the person as psychologists in the laboratory will, quite legitimately, think about the rabbit, or the chemist will think about the fluid: it is a matter of utmost interest, he is concentrated on it, and yet it is over there, I am here.

We should try to be aware of the difference between lack of interest, interest and what I call the direct meeting with the other person, not only with regard to our patients, but with regard to everybody. We will find a great deal of the kind of interest which corresponds to our own contact with ourselves as an Ego: He's there, he's nice, he's intelligent, he's a little weak, he's a little strong, he's this, that and the other. But we still think *around* him. We think about him, but we do not see him fully.

The Indians and many other philosophers have a word, "This is you"—"This is you—I do not have to describe you, I do not have to write a treatise about you—this is you". I see you as I can see myself, this is me. "If I really see another person, or if I truly see myself, I stop judging. I am not saying judgment is wrong, on the contrary. I think we have to judge others and ourselves, it is a rational function. If we do not see that we are going to hell, where the hell are we going? We have to judge where we are going. What corresponds to either principle and what corresponds to the laws of human nature? But actually this judgment is a judgment of reason. If you really see a person, and he may be the vilest villain, you will stop judging provided you see that person fully. If you see yourself, whatever you are, you will stop feeling guilty, because you feel: "This is me".

If you have the full experience of seeing the other person you really stop judging. This is what every great artist and dramatist conveys to you. The Shakespearean villain ceases to be the villain. Take, for example, the *Merchant of Venice:* He is an ugly figure, but nevertheless, the way Shakespeare has painted this merchant of Venice, he is not a villain. He is he. God knows why he is that way. God may have created the circumstances. He is he and he is me, too. In the process of seeing him fully, I can say: "So this is you". I am neither tolerant nor judging.

It is not a matter of tolerance, that is different. I want to emphasize this, because it is so frequent among psychologists today to say: "Well, if I understand why he is that way, I won't judge him so hard". This is all part of liberalism, to say: "The fact that the criminal is a criminal was caused by the circumstances, so I will put him into a nicer prison". I am not speaking of tolerance here, I am speaking about an entirely different phenomenon, which does not exclude tolerance. At the moment when you see yourself or another person fully, you do not judge because you are overwhelmed with the feeling, with the experience: "So this is you", and also with the experience: "And who am I to judge"? In fact, you do not even ask that question. Because in experiencing him, you experience yourself. You say: "So that is you" and you feel in some way very plainly: "And that is me too".

To be centrally related to others is something which we ought to practice, and in which we can get quite far. For me personally, Zen Buddhism has been a very effective way to overcome an attitude of judging, which stems from my own biblical background. One day I woke up and it was completely gone. Not that I was more tolerant, it was just gone, because there was a new experience. So I am not saying: "Look here, that is simple". I speak from the experience of someone who has spent many, many years in trying to learn more and more. If I see the other person—what happens is not only that I stop judging but also that I have a sense of union, of sharing, of oneness, which is something much stronger than being kind or being nice. There is a feeling of human solidarity when two people—or even one person—can say to the other: "So that is you, and I share this with you".

This is a tremendously important experience. I would say, short of complete love, it is the most gratifying, the most wonderful, the most exhilarating experience, which occurs between two people. This is also one of the most important therapeutic experiences which we can give to the patient, because at that moment the patient does not feel isolated any more. In all his neurosis or whatever his troubles are, the feeling of isolation, whether he is aware of it or not, is the very crux of his suffering. There are many other cruxes, but this is the main one. At the moment when he senses that I share this with him, so that I can say, "This is you", and I can say it not kindly and not unkindly, this is a tremendous relief from isolation. Another person who says, "This is you", and stays with me, and shares this with me.

I have had the experience increasingly through the years that once you speak from your own experience and in this kind of relatedness to the patient you can say anything and the patient will not feel hurt. On the contrary, he will feel greatly relieved that there is one man who sees him, because he knows the story all the time. We are often so naive, to think that the patient must not know this and the patient must not know that, because he would be so shocked. The fact is the patient knows it all the time, except he does not permit himself to have this knowledge consciously. When we say it, he is relieved because he can say: "For heaven's sake, I knew this always".

Freud used the symbol of the mirror in the sense of symbolizing the detachedness of the analyst—the so-called scientific laboratory attitude. The symbol of the mirror has often been used in a different sense, namely the mirror which receives everything and does not keep anything. It is not a matter of whether it is right or wrong, it is just a symbolic use. I think indeed an essential factor of the kind of relatedness I am talking about is that I receive everything and do not want to keep anything, to retain anything. I am completely open to the patient. At this moment, when I speak with the patient or the patient speaks with me, there is no more important event in the world for me or for him. I am completely open to him, and all I promise him is just that: "When you come to me, I will be completely open to you, and I shall respond with all the chords in myself which are touched by the chords in yourself". That is all we can promise, and that is a promise we can keep. We cannot keep the promise that we'll cure him. We cannot keep the promise even that we will understand everything, but we can keep the promise of being completely open, and to respond.

I have to be related to the patient, not interested in him as a scientific object, but I have to be *related* to him. This is so very ambiguous, it is so shallow and yet, one can only understand it if one has had an experience of the difference between liking somebody, being interested in somebody and feeling fully the central relatedness to a person: "This is you".

In this process I must forget that I am the doctor, that I am the analyst. I must forget that I am supposed to be well, and the patient is supposed to be sick. And I must not forget that this is also paradoxical. If I forget this, it is too bad, because my activity will then be lacking in centeredness, which is necessary. But at the same time, I must forget it. Because as long as I am the doctor and there is a patient, as long as I am not relating to him as one human being to the other, I am treating him like an object. As soon as I think: "I am normal and he is nuts", I cannot experience the fact that we are the same, in spite of the fact that we are not, at the same time. And also, as long as I think I am curing him, I do not experience the full situation of relatedness.

Seeing the patient means to see a person as the hero of a drama, of a Shakespearean drama, or a Greek drama, or of a Balzac novel. That is to say, you see here a unique piece of life in human form, born with certain qualities, who has struggled, and—this is remarkable—has survived in this struggle, with difficulty, but this has given him specific and peculiar and individual answers to life.

To be born raises a question because of the inner dichotomy of human existence. We have to answer this question at every moment of our life, not with a thought but with our whole existence. There are only a few answers to these questions, namely the various types of regressive answers and the progressive answer. There are not so many—I believe six or eight answers, on how to answer these questions. Each person answers the questions of life in his particular way. Of course there are individual variations which are infinite, and which are different for every person. But at the same time there are some big categories of answers.

We have to see that each person's existence is a drama in which he or she gives his or her specific answer to the problem of life, successfully or unsuccessfully. And we have to understand the total answer, which he or she gives. This total answer can be the answer of complete regression to mother's womb, it can be the answer of remaining at mother's breast, it can be the answer of being bound to father's command, it can be the answer of full development of one's own powers. And not only these. There are a number of variations. But it is always a total, structured answer, and this is why I say this is to be looked upon as a hero of a Shakespearean drama.

The answers a person gives to life are not just a little fragment here and a fragment there. They are a totality, always a structure, and you can understand a person only if you understand the total structure of the answers which he gives to existence: How does he try to remain sane? How does he try, and has he tried, to solve the problem of his relatedness to the world? You have to see the total answer, which a person gives. Whether he is psychotic or neurotic, or so-called healthy, this does not make any difference. Everyone gives an answer which is total and structure-like.

From the very beginning one should attempt to see, to understand this total answer. From the first hour, one should begin to ask oneself: "What is the prop of this drama?" and not be seduced to grab this and to grab that, because one is afraid not to understand the whole. I believe every person becomes intensely interesting if one understands his drama. It is not a matter of him being terribly intelligent. The human drama is something extremely interesting provided we understand it, and do not underrate the significance of a particular struggle of a person in his existence, reducing it to trivialities.

Being aware of the own mode of relatedness

I am convinced you cannot separate your mode of relatedness to the patient, your realism as far as the patient is concerned, from your own mode of relatedness to people in general and from your realism in general. If you are naive and blind, to your friends and to the whole world, you will be exactly as naive and blind to your patients. You will pick out certain little things, as you have learned, through your technical training, that this is this, and that is that, and yet you will not really understand the person. To really relate is not a matter which depends primarily on the object. It is a faculty, it is an orientation, it is something in you, and not something in the object. If I am caught in fiction and unreality, as far as people in general are concerned—myself, my wife, my children, my friends, the whole world—then I am just as caught in fiction when it comes to the patient.

This also means that if we really want to understand the unconscious, that is to say that part which exists, and which the social filter, as I call it (cf. 1960a, pp. 99-106; 1962a, pp. 115-124), does not permit to come into awareness, then indeed we have to transcend the frame of reference of our society. I would put it this way: We can understand the unconscious fully only if we are critical and aware of the limitations of our own culture and the patterns of our society. If we are caught in them like everybody else, then indeed we cannot really understand more than those slight differences in which the person dissociates more than, let us say, beyond the call of duty, or social duty. Then we understand the extra little bit of fear, the extra little bit of anxiety, the extra little bit of alienation, but this extra little bit, which is individual, is not quite enough to understand a person fully. The critical understanding and awareness of the fiction in the social pattern in which we live is a very essential condition for the full awareness of the dissociated part of another person. In addition to that it is necessary to understand other societies and other cultures, from the primitive ones to the civilized ones—simply to understand and see other possibilities of structures and experiences, which were conscious for them but which are unconscious for us.

To give an example: The ancestors of the Scandinavians in the early middle ages had a secret society called the Berserker. Berserker means literally the Bear Shirts *(Bärenhemdige)*. The purpose of this society was to transform yourself, if you were initiated, into an animal of prey, into a bear. That was saintly, that was the highest spiritual achievement: going back to the animal, becoming an animal. And the sign of this was the highest degree of rage, a person worked himself into an insane rage. But he did this quite consciously, because in this insane rage he felt he had dropped all that was human and had become an animal and that was his original life. (It is very strange that from the Bear Shirts to the Brown Shirts there are only two thousand years. Actually, if you take a man like Hitler with this particular kind of craziness, these insane rages were one of the most characteristic traits of his.)

I give the Berserker as an example, and of course there are thousands of others. If I want to understand a person with an insane rage, then indeed it helps me a great deal to know something about the Bear Shirts. Because then I can see that the insane rage is not just a peculiar individual thing, which is typical for this person, and I talk about the aggressiveness and destructiveness of his mother, and so on—but that this rage is an answer to life. This is a religion, it happens to be his secret, private religion. The more we know about other forms of experience outside of our own cultural frame of reference, the more we are able to understand in ourselves and in others, to experience that which in our society happens to remain outside of consciousness because it does not fit.

ABOUT THE FIRST SESSIONS

What is the *plan of an analysis?* Do we have any plan beyond the aim of psychoanalysis: to understand the dissociated part of the patient, and to help him to understand it? I think we could do something more even in this general sense: to follow a strategic maxim. It is necessary to engage ourselves, to be in it, to see the patient, to be related to him and to respond to the patient. We can see what we can do, where it leads. We cannot make a long time plan before we have jumped into the situation—and "jumped" means not just to listen, to be interested, but what I spoke of before, to see the patient, to encounter the patient, to be engaged with the patient.

Aside from this very general idea, the first thing one should do is to form *an idea of what this person was meant to be,* and what his neurosis has done to the person he was meant to be. I do not mean that in a religious sense particularly, or in a teleological sense. I mean it in the sense that we are not born as blank sheets of paper. Not only are some of us born as more timid and others as more aggressive, I believe we are born already with a very definite personality, which can be twisted, deformed, changed by our life experience. An apple tree if it grows well will grow good apples, but never pears. And an orange tree will grow good oranges and not apples.

The analyst should have an idea of what this person was meant to be. How would this person be if he had grown in lines of what he was meant to be? How would this person be if his development had not been distorted and neglected? I admit that this is not easy, and I do not mean to claim that one can always do this easily, or perhaps at all. Nevertheless it should be attempted. We should never look only at the neurosis *per se,* and we should not make the assumption which many people make that people are born more or less the same, and that the neurosis is the deformation of the objective pattern of man which is the same for all. It is not. The neurosis is the deformation of that particular person. Thus well-being for him means the restoration of his specific personality.

You may object here, that I am suddenly talking about the uniqueness and specificity of a person, whereas I have been talking before about the fact that we are all the same. Well, I tried to explain that both are true. This is not a play with words, indeed we are all the same and yet we are all completely unique. If we were not all the same, I would not be able to understand the patient, but if I think that because I understand the patient, his growth, his development would make him similar to me, then indeed I understand very little.

We should have a picture of the patient, and *this picture of him must be based on a theory*—on a theoretical model or plan. Otherwise we are lost, because we have no frame of reference. The great advantage of the Freudian theory is that there is a model, that there is a theory. I am advocating that, regardless of what your reaction is to my own theoretical frame of reference: Have one! And do not try to think you can really understand anybody profoundly unless you do it on the basis of a model of man—may it be Freudian or anything else.

The next step is to try to see: what are the *chances* for *profound change?* This depends on factors like vitality, the degree to which the patient suffers, the life circumstances which further or do not further his own genuineness, his gift for honesty, the degree of his resistance. Some people are born with a tremendous gift for honesty, and other people are born with very little of that. I do not mean to say that the latter ones are necessarily dishonest but it is much more difficult for them to be honest. The circumstances have to be much more favorable for them to be honest than for the other ones. You will find that there are people who can live among thieves and murderers and yet they are not in danger of losing their honesty. You find other ones where the margin is so small that even a slight seduction is enough to lead them onto the path of sin. All these things you have to appreciate. Then you have to make a judgment: What are really the chances of analysis compared to other efforts, namely supportive therapy, good counseling, or giving it up.

You must be well aware to make up your mind. Not necessarily the in first session, or in the first week, but you must not wait four years until eventually you realize it by the very simple fact that nothing has happened in those years. You can probe, you can make remarks by which you hit on something, in the second or third session, something which you believe is essential and dissociated. You can do this in an incidental way and you can watch the patient's reaction: There is a flicker of recognition there—very good, if that happens in the third session. Maybe a little smile, maybe a nod. Or, there is a violent reaction and you can judge: Does that have a paranoid quality, or is it just a reaction of the kind that you can cope with, within the next three months? Or is there a blandness by which the patient wishes to say: "Oh, yes, how very wise you are", but you can see that he has not reacted at all. If you do this kind of probing five times, ten times in the first few months, you get a pretty good feeling for what this patient can really react to and what his chances are for analytic treatment.

Another factor is to *appreciate the resistances:* the degree of the main repressions and the main resistances. Then you can decide whether this is really somebody whom you can analyze or somebody whom you cannot analyze. In the latter case the method of symbolic satisfaction is indicated. The patient is really very sick, he really needs satisfaction through motherly help. The analyst gives him satisfaction in one way or the other. Under this condition, the patient can go on existing. If you choose to do that, it is therapy on the basis of analytic understanding, but you also know very well that it is therapy which stops short of the final awakening of the patient, because he or she cannot go beyond a certain level.

In the first place psychoanalysis should begin—and not so rarely I have said this to a patient—with an honest and realistic appreciation. Not just with a phrase like: "Of course, I cannot guarantee that you will be cured by the analysis". This sounds very honest, but it isn't because it implies: "Of course, we cannot guarantee ...". Of course, *but* there is a reasonable chance that we can do it. There is no such reasonable chance.

Therapeutic success can by no means be guaranteed. We cannot say that most people are likely to be helped by psychoanalysis, apart from those who are very sick. I am not saying this as something destructive. I have great faith in psychoanalysis, and the longer I work with this method, the older I get, the more I believe in it. But in this respect analysis is no different from some other methods in medicine. If it is sufficiently important for the patient—in case it is a question of his life—he will eagerly use a method which has a 10% chance or a 5% chance to cure him. But the doctor should be honest with him, because otherwise he does not challenge the forces in the patient which strive for health, as he prevents the patient from seeing the seriousness of the situation.

I now want to bring up some things which I have observed in my experience with supervision and in seminars, as the *main faults I find in students.* In the first place, I find that many young analysts, and there may be some older ones too, are really frightened of the patient, and have every reason to be frightened of him. Here comes a man with a problem which he has suffered from for forty years. It is terribly difficult, we know very little, from our experience, we know it is not the regular thing that we have learned about. And this man believes that we can solve his problem. In addition he pays us, and quite handsomely, sometimes.

It is such a nervous strain, to undertake to promise that we can help him, that naturally we are defensively frightened. I do not suggest we should not do it, but we should be aware of what magnitude this enterprise has and how little we are really prepared for it. We are setting up an adventure for him and for ourselves, and we have no reason to deceive him by taking on an easy attitude, as if this was just a matter of him coming to our office and everything will be fine. If we refrain from doing that, we will be much less frightened of him, because we have not given him the impression that we are so certain.

In this respect we do not imitate the physician in general. If you go to a physician with a broken arm or with an appendicitis or something, and the physician says: "For heaven's sake, I do not know whether I can ever cure you", that would be rather frightening, and you would go to somebody else. We are really not in the position of the average physician, on the contrary, because each time we deal with a most difficult, possibly incurable illness. But if we are aware of this and do not take on the smug attitude of the analyst sitting on this side of the table or the couch, we will already be less frightened of the patient.

Analysts share with Protestant ministers a problem about which there is an unadmitted doubt—the ministers about the existence of God, and the analysts about the unconscious. Officially, the ministers believe in

God, otherwise they could not function, and officially the analyst believes in the unconscious and that the method can be used to uncover the unconscious. But I have discovered that many analysts do not really believe in it. They pretend to, because how would they be able to have patients, and belong to a school, and graduate and so on unless they did not. Just as a minister has to pretend he believes in God, otherwise he would be kicked out of his congregation. Actually, there is a great deal of disbelief, doubt, double—talk, and wiggling out of this whole thing by all sorts of rationalizations.

This leads to a second problem which I think analysts and ministers have in common: an amazing, constant sense of guilt, a) for deceiving oneself, because one does not really quite believe in what one is saying; b) for deceiving the patient because the analyst secretly thinks: "For heaven's sake, I am much sicker than he is, and I never got better" and secondly: "This unconscious I've never really experienced, and yet I have to go on preaching this doctrine of the unconscious and salvation by uncovering the unconscious".

I have sometimes started a seminar by simply asking the question: "Have you ever seen anybody who was cured or essentially helped by psychoanalysis"? It would be really absurd to take a group of surgeons or internists and ask the same question. But I do not think it is absurd at all in our work, because the sad fact is that there are many of our students who have in fact never seen anyone who has been definitely changed by the uncovering of the unconscious, including his own. There is a lot of self-deception, of feelings of guilt, of doubletalk, but this is not analyzing. I think it is very important to analyze this phenomenon.

In analyzing a psychoanalyst, one should pay a great deal of attention to his repression of all the doubts, guilt feelings, and so on that he has about the whole thing. I think he would feel this would be very helpful. Some people might in fact rather be doing something else. Because it is a terrible burden to go on, whether you are a minister who preaches about God and do not believe in him, or an analyst who really do not believe in the whole business about the unconscious. That is very unhealthy for your mind and for your body, and terribly boring too. So I think it is important to analyze to what extent someone really believes in what he professes to his patients and which he claims to be specialized in.

To get out of the conflict, out of this dilemma, liberal ministers talk about God, but God is only a symbol of transcendence. In the same way many analysts say: "Call it psychoanalysis"—but what they do is counseling, they teach the wisdom of living, they give good advice, they are encouraging, they are nice. They do all sorts of things, but all that phrased in analytic words, so that the patient should not notice that they are doing what a counselor does.

I find a great lack of frankness in these matters in people, and a great deal of doubt and all sorts of double—talk and evasions. It is terribly important for the whole analytic profession to see this and to get out of it by putting things on the table, by clarifying things. We should not be dealing with these things in a gentlemanly way and say that of course we all agree that we believe in the unconscious.

ASPECTS OF THE THERAPEUTIC PROCESS

One more thing is the *establishment of the analytic situation.* The analytic situation begins, as Sullivan has so often emphasized, with the fact that the patient wants me to analyze him, and he has to prove to me that he needs it. It is not enough that he comes to my office for some reason or other. To establish an analytic setting it is necessary to have a situation as clean as a surgical room, only in a different sense, namely, from the very first moment, a situation without sham and without fiction. Freud emphasized this very clearly himself. No word and no smile with a patient should be of the easy, conventional, fictitious kind in this situation. The patient must feel when he comes to you that this is another world different from the one he is accustomed to, it is a world not of pretense, it is a world of complete realism in every sense. And it is a world in which two people are related to each other in a central way, and are engaged in each other.

How can we help the patient in his task to make the unconscious conscious, to become aware of dissociated material—to become aware of that which is within him, and which he does not dare to be aware of? In the first place we have to *avoid any kind of intellectualization.* Intellectualization is one of the greatest mistakes we make. The Freudians save themselves from this mistake by not talking. That is a good way of avoiding intellectualization. They just remain silent, often for hours or weeks. But that is no great help either. The non-Freudians do just the same, they go on talking, which is not any better. So you talk about grandmother, and what happened there, and why you feel this and so on—all of it sensible talk, which in fact only helps the patient to do what he has done all his life, to intellectualize his so-called problems a little more and not to experience them. Obviously, the task of analysis is that the patient *experiences* something and not that he *thinks* more. That is so not only for an obsessional patient but for everybody, including the analyst. The function of the analyst from the very beginning of the process is to avoid on his part any kind of aid and comfort, or the tendency to intellectualize and to substitute the experience with words, ideas, concepts.

Secondly, I think it is very important in general that *when the analyst sees something, he should say it,* in full clarity. Truth has a peculiar quality. The truth, since it represents reality, touches a person where the half-truth does not. If you are in real relatedness to another person, really with him, in him, and you say something which is a reality for him, it is very difficult for that person to hang on to his resistances. If he is very sick, he may, of course—I mean there is no doubt about it. But the person who is not that sick, will, if you are in full contact with him and say to him: "Look here, what I see is this ...", usually find it very difficult to wiggle out and give you a lot of rationalizations and ideas which lead to nothing.

If you tell the patient half the truth, because you think he cannot take it all (as you think he is not ready, when in fact the one who is not ready is usually the analyst), then the patient is indeed untouched. Just as the phone does not ring when five of the digits in the phone number are right, but not the sixth one. You do not touch him. On the contrary, the patient feels unconsciously that he is fooled because in a way he knows better. He thinks that if you are so careful in formulating this, it must be something terrible, you must think it is terrible. The patient again gets into an atmosphere of unreality and half-truth and double-talk which he is already so accustomed to, as most people are, from childhood on, and you destroy the whole situation.

Let me give you an example, which I see very often in supervision. The analyst says to a person: "Well, it seems to me that you feel *as if you were* a child of five. The fact is, however, that *you are* a child of five, affectively and emotionally, while intellectually and socially you are a man of forty". Now if I just say to the patient: "You feel like a child of five", I do not quite hit it. Because he is that child of five. Of course, I have to add: "Indeed, you are also something else". But this "as if" or "like" already leaves the door open. And the patient says, "Well, I do not *feel* like a child of five", and maybe he does not, but he is! What I mean is, there is nothing good short of the most complete directness and reality with regard to what I see in the patient. Now, I realize that there are situations and people where you have to weigh your words carefully, for instance in cases of intense anxiety, in pre-psychotic states, and so on. But the majority of our patients are not that way.

I often hear the discussion among students: "Well, isn't it too early", or: "Can the patient take that"? I usually find that funny. I can say for myself, that if I think I understand something and if I have no special reason to think that this will harm the patient, or that what I am saying is so foreign to the patient that he would not understand it at all, I am very happy to tell him exactly what I see. I think it is rather ridiculous to talk about the problem *as if* it were in general, *as if* our most important and difficult problem were to utter our great insights. Because our great insights are by no means so frequent and we are very happy when we understand something.

If you really understand something about the unconscious, you have to make a decision. You have to make the decision that this is there in spite of common sense, in spite of the common sense of the cultural pattern, and stick your neck out. You have come to the conviction that this is there, this is what you see, in spite of the fact that all evidence and all common sense seem to speak against it. To give a very simple example, which we come across again and again. Let us say that the patient has a mother who seems to be very nice, and everybody says she's nice. According to conventional standards, she is then a very nice woman. But actually, she's a murderess. I am not saying that you are so quick in being impressed by the fact that somebody is a murderess, but at one point you will be in a particular case. Then you say: "Well, it seems to me your mother is a little aggressive sometimes". What you really do, is you do not take the responsibility for making a judgment, for deciding what you see.

Many of us have a wish to live as comfortably as possible. A surgeon has to make a decision on the spot and sometimes a very responsible one, about life or death. He cannot say: "Let us wait for two hours, and I will think about it". He has to make the decision right here and now. Analysts seem to be in a position in which they feel they do not have to exert themselves at all. Now, if I say "analysts", I am talking as an analyst and I know all of what I am talking about from my own past. I have been practicing analysis for thirty years, I have gone through many failures, and there is not a single thing, a single criticism which I have uttered so far or which I shall utter, that I do not know from my own experience. I think it is dangerous to choose to be comfortable and not to risk making a judgment which is against common sense, against conventionality, and which you think will make the patient very angry.

Another very important aspect of the analytic process is *cutting through the resistance.* This is one of the things one has to do systematically—cutting off one way of retreat after the other until the patient is driven into a corner. There he cannot run away by means of rationalizations, there he is forced to experience something—or he may stop the treatment and never come back again. What sounds like such a shocking method or cruel method, is actually not so cruel at all, because I can drive the patient into a corner if I am with him, and if he knows that. If I am with him he really feels the solidity and the reality of my relatedness to him and our communication.

One could define analysis, a) by telling the patient what one sees and therefore stimulating him to dare to see himself, and b) at the same time by systematically cutting off the ways of resistance, ways of retreat, until the point where the patient is confronted with himself and has to feel something or to stop coming.

What happens when the patient has got in touch with something that was dissociated? He has a sense of increased vitality, of exhilaration, of joy, quite regardless of whether the thing was most embarrassing or not. He has simply got in touch with a piece of reality within him. If we have any reason to believe that the basic concept of Freud's is right, namely that the uncovering of dissociated material leads to health, or frees our innate tendencies for mental health, then indeed this experience to me is most convincing, and we see again and again in both our patients and in ourselves.

Once something within us has really been touched, there is an increase in energy. Then we usually see that this is like a fog which goes and comes, that three days later the fog sets in again, and you have to work on it again, and you have to attack the resistance again. This is a process—you might call it *working through*—which takes quite some time. But actually, the symptom of an analytic discovery is never intellectual: "Oh, that is right, Doctor! I can see that you are right". If the patient says that you are right, and then adds—if he is intelligent enough—some more intellectual twists to the theory, he has not really achieved anything. But if he goes away with a feeling of exhilaration, of increased vitality, and if he leaves us with the same feeling, then we know indeed, that something of a true analytic nature has been accomplished.

There is only one criterion for whether a session is satisfactory or not, one minimum criterion: that the session is interesting. If a session is boring, either for the patient or for myself, something was certainly wrong. I remember very well the sessions during my transition from Freudian methods to other methods, when I was so bored that I could hardly wait till the end of the session. I listened dutifully and I made every effort, and yet I was just waiting for the session to end. This was actually the reason why I felt there was something fundamentally wrong in my way of going about it. I know my teachers were awfully bored too, because many of them fell asleep during the analysis, and I remember how shocked I was when I heard one of my teachers say at a party that he had found a new tobacco which helped him to keep him from falling asleep. Another one said falling asleep was not so bad because he had dreams about the patient and this was the best insight yet. (I fell asleep once or twice, but I had a tendency to snore, so I did not dare, really, to push that very far. But I do remember I was terribly bored).

Since quite a number of years, even if I am tired, it happens only in the exceptional case that I am bored. And that for me is the first criterion for evaluating an analytic session, whether I am bored or the patient is bored. If the patient is bored, it is just as bad, and in fact you cannot even keep it apart; if the patient is bored, I am bored, and *vice versa.*

Factors Leading to Patient's Change in Analytic Treatment

Erich Fromm

CURING FACTORS ACCORDING TO SIGMUND FREUD AND MY CRITIQUE

When speaking about factors leading to analytic cure, I think the most important work written on the subject was Freud's paper *Analysis, Terminable and Interminable* (1937c), which is one of his most brilliant papers, and, if one could put it that way, one of his most courageous papers, although Freud never lacked in courage in any of his other work. It was written not long before his death, and in a way it is Freud's own last summarizing word about the effect of analytic cure. I first shall summarize briefly the main ideas of this paper and then, in the main part of this lecture, try to comment on it and possibly make some suggestions in connection with it.

First of all, what is interesting in this paper is that Freud presents in it a theory of psychoanalysis which had not really changed since the early days. His concept of neurosis is that neurosis is a conflict between instinct and the Ego: either the Ego is not strong enough, or the instincts are too strong, but at any rate, the Ego is a dam; it is not capable of resisting the onrush of instinctual forces, and for this reason neurosis occurs. This is in line and consequent with his early theory, and he presented it also in its essence without trying to embellish or modify it. What follows from that is that analytic cure consists essentially in strengthening the Ego which in infancy was too weak, enabling it to cope now with instinctual forces, in a period in which the Ego would be strong enough.

Secondly, what according to Freud is cure? He makes it very clear, and I may quote here from *Analysis, Terminable and Interminable* (1937c, S. E., Vol. 23, p. 219): "Firsts the patient"—provided we speak of cure—"shall no longer be suffering from his [former] symptoms and shall have overcome his anxieties and his inhibitions. There is another very important condition. Freud does not assume that cure of the symptoms, disappearance of the symptoms per se constitutes cure. Only if the analyst is convinced that enough unconscious material has been brought to the surface which would explain why the symptoms have disappeared [naturally in terms of the theory]—only then can the analyst be convinced that the patient is cured, and is not likely to have repetitions of his former symptoms. Actually, Freud speaks here of a "taming of the instincts" (cf. loc. cit., p. 220). The analytic process is a taming of the instincts or, as he also says, making the instincts more "accessible to all the influences of the other trends in the Ego" (loc. cit., p. 225). First, the instincts are brought to awareness because how can you tame them otherwise?—and then in the analytic process the Ego becomes stronger and gains the strength which it failed to acquire in childhood.

Thirdly, what are the factors which Freud mentioned in this paper as determining the results of analysis—either cure or failure? He mentions three factors: first, "the influence of traumas"; secondly, "the constitutional strength of the instincts"; and thirdly, "the alterations of the Ego" in the process of defense against the onrush of the instincts (Cf. loc. cit., p. 225).

An unfavorable prognosis, according to Freud, lies in the constitutional strength of the instincts, plus or combined with a modification, an unfavorable modification of the Ego in the defense conflict. It is well known that for Freud the constitutional factor of the strength of instinct was a most important factor in his prognosis for a patient's cure in an illness. It is a strange thing that Freud throughout his work, from the early writings on until this very latest of his writings, emphasized the significance of constitutional factors, and that neither the Freudians nor the non-Freudians have done more than paying lip service at the very most to this idea which for Freud was very important.

So, Freud says one unfavorable factor for cure is the constitutional strength of the instincts, even, he adds, if the Ego is normally strong. Secondly, even the Ego modification, he says, can be constitutional. In other words, he has a constitutional factor on two sides: on the side of the instincts and on the side of the Ego. He has a further factor which is unfavorable, and that is that part of the resistance that is rooted in the death instinct. That, of course, is an addition that comes from his later theory. But naturally, in 1937, Freud would consider also that as one factor unfavorable to cure. What is the favorable condition for cure according to Freud? This is something which many people are not aware of when they think of Freud's theory, namely, that according to this paper of Freud's, the stronger the trauma the better are the chances for cure. I shall go into the question why this is so and why I think this was so in Freud's own mind, although he does not talk too much about it.

The person of the psychoanalyst is the other factor that hopefully is favorable to the cure. Freud makes here, in this last paper, a very interesting remark on the analytic situation that is worthwhile mentioning: The analyst, he says, "must possess some kind of superiority so that in certain analytic situations he can act as a model for his patient, and in others as a teacher. And, finally, we must not forget that the analytic relationship is based on a love of truth—that is, on a recognition of reality—and that it precludes any kind of sham and deceit." (S. Freud, 1937c, S. E. Vol. 23, p. 248.) I think that is a very important statement Freud made here very clearly.

One last word about Freud's concept here, which he does not put explicitly but which is implicit and which goes through his whole work if I understand it correctly. Freud always had a somewhat mechanistic view of the process of cure. Originally the view was, if one uncovers or discovers the repressed affects, then the affect by becoming conscious gets out of the system, so to speak; this was called abreacting, and the model was a very mechanical one, like getting pus out of an inflamed spot and so on, and it was supposed to be quite natural, quite automatic, that this happened.

Freud and many other analysts saw that this wasn't true because, if it were true, then the people who act out most their irrationality would be the healthiest ones because they would get the stuff out of their system—and they don't. So, Freud and other analysts gave up the theory. But this was replaced by the less explicit idea that the patient has insight, or, if you use another word, becomes aware of his unconscious reality, then his symptoms simply disappear. One has not really has to make a special effort, except the one to come, to free associate, and to go through the anxieties which this necessarily involves. But it is not a question of the patient's particular effort, particular will—he will get well provided one succeeds in overcoming the resistances, and the repressed material comes to the fore. This is by no means as mechanistic as Freud's original abreacting theory was. But it is still somewhat mechanistic, as I see it. It contains the implication that the process is a smooth one, in the sense that, if one uncovers the material, then the patient will get well in this process.

Now I want to make some further comments on, some additions to and some revisions of these views of Freud on the causes that effect cure. First of all, I want to say that, if one asks what is analytic cure, then I think that what unites, or what is common to all psychoanalysts, is Freud's basic concept that *psychoanalysis can be defined as a method which tries to uncover the unconscious reality of a person* and which assumes that in this process of uncovering the person has a chance to get well. As long as we have this aim in mind, then a good deal of fighting among various schools would be somewhat reduced in importance. If one really has that in mind, one knows how very difficult and treacherous it is to find the unconscious reality in the person, and then one does not get so excited about the different ways in which one tries to do that, but one asks which way, which method, which approach is more conducive to this aim, which is the aim of all that can be called psychoanalysis. I would say that any therapeutic method which does not have that aim may be therapeutically very valuable, however it has nothing to do with psychoanalysis, and I would make a clear-cut division right at this point.

As to Freud's concept that analytic work is like reinforcing a dam against the onrush of the instincts, I don't want to argue against this point, because I think many things can be said in favor of it. Especially, I believe, if we deal with the question of psychosis as against neurosis, then we really deal with the brittleness of the Ego and the strange thing that one person does and another person does not collapse under the impact of certain impulses. So I'm not denying the validity of the general concept that Ego strength has something to do with the process. But nevertheless, with this qualification, it seems to me that the main problem of neurosis and cure is precisely not that of: here come the irrational passions and there is the Ego which protects the person from becoming sick.

There is another contradiction, and that is the battle between two kinds of passion, namely, the archaic, irrational regressive passions as against other passions within the personality. I shall be a little more explicit to make myself understood. I mean by the archaic passions: intense destructiveness, intense fixation to the mother, and extreme narcissism.

By *intense fixation* I mean the fixation which I would call a symbiotic fixation, or which in Freudian terms one would call the pre-genital fixation to the mother. I mean that deep fixation in which the aim is really to re-turn to the mother's womb or even return to death. I should like to remind you that Freud himself in his later writings stated that he underestimated the significance of the pre-genital fixation. Because in his whole work he put so much emphasis on the genital fixation, he therefore underestimated the problem of the girl. While for the boy, it is plausible that all this should start with the erotic genital fixation to the mother, with a girl it doesn't really make sense. Freud saw that there is a great deal of pre-genital—that is to say, not sexual in the narrower sense of the word—fixation to the mother, which exists both in boys and girls and which he had not paid sufficient attention to in his work in general. But this remark of Freud's also got lost somewhat in the analytic literature, and when analysts speak about the Oedipal phase and the Oedipal conflict and the whole business, they usually think in terms of the genital, not of the pre-genital fixation or attachment to the mother.

By *destructiveness* I mean not destructiveness that is essentially defensive, in the service of life, or even secondarily in the defense of life, like envy, but destructiveness in which the wish to destroy is its own aim. I have called that necrophilia. (Cf. E., Fromm, 1964a, which deals precisely with this problem of what are the sources of, and what is really severe pathology.) [Strong mother fixation, necrophilic destructiveness and extreme narcissism are malignant passions]—malignant because they are related to, they are causative of severe illness. Against these malignant passions you have also the opposite passions in man: the passion for love, the passion for the interest in the world—all that which is called Eros, the interest not only in people, but also the interest in nature, the interest in reality, the pleasure in thinking, all artistic interest.

It is fashionable today to talk about what the Freudians call Ego-functions—which I think is a poor retreat and the discovery of America after it has been discovered for a long time, because nobody ever doubted outside of Freudian orthodoxy that there are many functions of the mind that are not the result of instincts in the sexual sense. I think by this new emphasis on the Ego, one has done some retreat from that which was the most valuable part in Freud's thinking, namely, the emphasis on the passions. While Ego strength in a certain sense is a meaningful concept, the Ego is essentially the executor of the passions; it's either the executor of malignant passions or of benign passions. But what matters in man, that determines his action, what makes his personality, is what kind of passions move him. To give an example: It all depends on the question whether a person has a passionate interest in death, destruction and all that is not alive, which I called necrophilia, or a passionate interest in all that is alive, which I call biophilia. Both are passions, both are not logical products, both are not in the Ego. They are part of the whole personality. These are not Ego functions. These are two kinds of passion.

This is a revision I would suggests with regard to Freud's theory: that *the main problem is not the fight of Ego versus passions, but the fight of one type of passion against another type of passion.*

BENIGN AND MALIGNANT NEUROSES—
WITH A CASE HISTORY OF A BENIGN NEUROSIS

Before I go on to the question: what is analytic cure or what are the factors leading to analytic cure, naturally one has to consider and to think about the question: what kinds of neurosis are there? There are many classifications of neurosis and many changes in the classification. Dr. Menninger has recently suggested that most of these classifications have no particular value, without really suggesting a new one that has one and that he recommends as an essential classifying concept. I would like to suggest the following classification—this is a very simple one in a way—and that is the difference between benign neurosis and malignant neurosis.

A person suffers of a benign or light neurosis, if he or she is not essentially seized by one of these malignant passions, but whose neurosis is due to severe traumata. Here I am entirely in agreement with what Freud said, namely, that the best chances for cure lie precisely in those neuroses where the patient suffers from the most severe trauma. The logic is that if a patient survives a severe trauma without becoming psychotic or showing forms of sickness which are exceedingly alarming, then indeed he or she shows that from a constitutional standpoint he or she has a lot of strength. In those cases of neurosis in which what I like to call the nucleus of the character structure is not severely damaged, that is to say, is not characterized by these severs regressions, these severe forms of malignant passions, I think there analysis has its best chances. Naturally, it requires work in which whatever the patient has repressed has to be clarified, has to come to consciousness; that is to say: the nature of the traumatic factors, the reactions of the patient to these traumatic factors—which have, as is very frequent, denied the real nature of the traumatic factor.

I want to illustrate a *benign neurosis* with a short case history of a Mexican woman. She is unmarried, about 25 years old, her symptom is homosexuality. Since the age of 18 she has only had homosexual relationships with other girls. At the point where she comes to the analyst she has a homosexual relationship with a cabaret singer, goes every night to hear her friend, gets drunk, is depressed, tries to get out of this vicious circle, and yet submits to this friend, who treats her abominably. Nevertheless, she is so frightened to leave her, she is so intimidated by the threat of the other woman to leave her, that she stays on.

Now, that's rather a bad picture: a case of homosexuality, but very much characterized by this constant anxiety, light depression, aimlessness of life, and so on. What is the history of this girl? Her mother was a woman who has been the mistress of a rich man for a long time. All the time she was the mistress of the same man, and this was the offspring of the relationship, the little daughter. The man was quite faithful in a way, always supporting the woman and the little girl, but he was not a father in evidence, there was no presence of a father. The mother, however, was an utterly scheming mother who only used this little girl to get money out of the father. She sent the girl to the father to get money out of him, she blackmailed the father through the girl, she undermined the girl in every way she could. The mother's sister was the owner of a brothel. She tried to induce the little girl into prostitution, and actually the little girl did, twice—she wasn't so little then—appear naked in front of men to be paid for it. It probably took a lot of stamina not to do more. But she was terribly embarrassed because, you can imagine, the children of the block, what names they called her, being quite openly not only a girl without a father, but also the niece of the owner of the brothel.

So the girl developed until the age of fifteen into a frightened, withdrawn girl, with no confidence in life whatsoever. Then the father, in one of his whims, sent her to school, to college in the United States. One can imagine the sudden change of scenery for this little girl, coming to a rather elegant college in the United States, and there was a girl who kind of liked her and was affectionate to her, and they started a homosexual affair.

Now there is nothing amazing in that. I think it's quite normal that a girl so frightened, with a past like that, would start a sexual affair with anyone, man, woman or animal, who shows real affection; it's the first time that she gets out of a hell. Then she has other homosexual affairs and she goes back to Mexico, goes back into that same misery, always with uncertainty, always with a feeling of shame. Then she hits on this woman I have spoken about who kept her in a state of obedience—and that's when she comes to the analyst.

What happened in analysis was—I think in the course of two years—that she first left this homosexual friend, she then stayed alone for awhile, then she began to date men, then she fell in love with a man, and then she married him and she isn't even frigid. Obviously, this was not a case of homosexuality in any genuine sense. I say "obviously"—some may disagree with me—but in my own opinion this is as much homosexuality as probably most people have as potential.

This was actually a girl who—and one can see that from her dreams—was simply frightened to death by life; she was like a girl who comes from a concentration camp, and her expectations, her fears, were all conditioned by this experience. In a relatively short time, considering the time usually required for analysis, this patient develops into a perfectly normal girl, with normal reactions.

I give this example just to indicate what I mean by, and what I think Freud means by, the strong role of trauma in the genesis of neurosis as against the constitutional factors. Of course, I am aware of the fact that when Freud talks of trauma he means by this something different from what I would mean: he would look for a trauma essentially of a sexual nature; he would look for the trauma happening in an earlier age. I believe that very often the trauma is a prolonged process in which one experience follows another and where, really, you eventually have a summation, and more than a summation, a piling up of experiences—sometimes in a way which I think is not too different from war neurosis, where there comes a breaking point when the patient gets sick.

Nevertheless, the trauma is something that happens in the environment, which is a life experience, a real-life experience. This holds true for this girl and of these kinds of patients with traumas, where the nucleus of character structure is not basically destroyed. Although the picture can be quite severe on the outside, they have a very good chance to get well and to overcome the reactive neurosis in a relatively short time because constitutionally they are sound.

In this connection, I want to emphasize that in the case of a benign or reactive neurosis the traumatic experience has to be quite massive to be an explanation for the genesis of neurotic illness. Is the trauma seen in a weak father and a strong mother, then this "trauma" does not explain why

a person suffers of a neurosis because there are many who have a weak father and a strong mother and don't become neurotic. In other words, if I
want to explain neurosis by a traumatic event then I have to assume that
the traumatic events are of such an extraordinary nature that it is unthinkable that there a cases with the same traumatic background who are perfectly well. Therefore I think in those cases, when one hasn't more to show
than a weak father and a strong mother, one has to think of the probability
that there are constitutional factors that are at work. That is to say, factors
that make this person prone to neurosis and in which the role of the weak
father and the role of the strong mother could become traumatic only because the constitutional factor tended to neurosis. Under ideal conditions
such a person might not have become ill.

I'm not willing to accept the assumption that one person becomes
very sick and that all my explanation is one which holds true for so many
others who didn't become very sick. You find a family of eight children
and one is sick and the rest isn't. Usually the rationale is: "Yes, but he was
the first one, the second one, the middle one, God knows what..."—that's
why his experience was different from the experience of all others. That is
very nice for those who like to comfort themselves that they have discovered the trauma, but to me it is very loose thinking.

Naturally, it can be that there is a traumatic experience that we
don't know, that is to say, which hasn't come up in the analysis. If the analyst will have the skill to find that truly and extraordinarily strong traumatic experience and can show how this was essential for the development
of neurosis, I am very happy. But I cannot simply call that a traumatic experience which in many other cases turns out not to be a traumatic experience. There are quite a number of traumatic experiences that are really extraordinary. That's why I gave this example.

There is one other instance, which I just want to mention, which is
a very modern phenomenon, and a very hard question to answer. How
sick, really, is modern organization man: alienated, narcissistic, without relatedness, without real interest for life, with interest only for gadgets, for
whom a sports car is much more exciting than a woman. Now, how sick is
he then?

In one sense one could say he's quite sick, and therefore certain
symptoms would follow: he is frightened, he is insecure, he needs constant
confirmation of his narcissism. At the same time, however, one might say
a whole society is not sick in that sense: people function. I think for these
people the problem arises how they succeed in adapting themselves to the
general sickness, or to what you might call the "pathology of normalcy."
The therapeutic problem is very difficult in these cases. This man indeed
suffers from a "nuclear" conflict, that is to say, from a deep disturbance in
the nucleus of his personality: he shows an extreme form of narcissism and

a lack of love of life. And yet to cure him he would in the first place has to change his whole personality. Besides that he would have almost the whole society against him, because the whole society is in favor of his neurosis. Here you have the paradox of having in a way a sick person theoretically, but who is, however, not sick in another sense. It's very difficult to determine what analysis could do in this case, and I really find this a tough problem.

To speak of what I call the benign neurosis, there the task is relatively simple, because you deal with intact nuclear energy structure, character structure; you deal with traumatic events which explain the somewhat pathological deformation. In the atmosphere of analysis, both in the sense of bringing out the unconscious plus the help which the therapeutic relation to the analyst is, these people have a very good chance to get well.

What I mean by the idea of *malignant neurosis* I have already said. These are neuroses where the nucleus of the character structure is damaged, where you have people with either extreme necrophilic, narcissistic or mother-fixated trends, and usually, in the extreme cases, all three go together and tend to converge. Here, the job of cure would be to change the energy charge within the nuclear structure. It would be necessary for cure that the narcissism, the necrophilia, all the incestuous fixations change. Even if they do not change completely, even if there is a small energy charge in what the Freudians call the *cathexis* of these various forms, this would indeed make a great difference to the person. If this person were to succeed in reducing his narcissism, or in developing more of his biophilia, or in developing an interest in life and so on, then this person has a certain chance to get well.

If we speak of analytic cure, in my opinion one should be very aware of the difference of the difference of the chances for cure in the malignant cases and in the benign cases. One might say that is really the difference between psychosis and neurosis, but it isn't, really, because many of what I call here malignant character neuroses are not psychotic. I am talking here about a phenomenon that you find in neurotic patients with or without symptoms, who are not psychotic, who are not even near psychotic, who probably would never become psychotic, and yet where the problem of cure is an entirely different one.

What is different is also the nature of the resistance. You will find in a benign neurosis—after all the resistance born out of hesitancy, some fear and so on—that, since the nucleus of the personality is really normal, the resistance is relatively easy to overcome. If you take, however, the resistance of what I call the malignant, the severe neuroses, then the resistances are deeply rooted, because this person would have to confess to himself and to a lot of human beings that he or she is really a completely narcissistic person, that he really cares for nobody. In other words, he has to fight against insight with a vigor that is much greater than that of the person who suffers from a benign neurosis.

What is the method of cure in severe neurosis? I do not believe that the problem is essentially the strengthening of the Ego. I believe the problem of cure lies in the following: that the patient confronts the irrational archaic part of his personality with his own sane, adult, normal part and that this very confrontation creates conflict. This conflict activates forces which one has to assume if one has the theory that there exists in a person—more or less strongly and, I think, again that is a constitutional factor—a striving for health, a striving for a better balance between the person and the world. *For me the essence of analytic cure lies in the very conflict engendered by the meeting of the irrational and the rational part of the personality.*

One consequence for analytic technique is that the patient must travel on two tracks in the analysis. He must experience himself as the little child, let us say, of two or three he is unconsciously, but he must at the same time also be an adult responsible person who faces this part in himself, because in this very confrontation he acquires the sense of shock and the sense of conflict and the sense of movement which is necessary for analytic cure.

From this standpoint the Freudian method would not do. I think we find here two extremes: the Freudian extreme is that the patient is artificially infantilized by the situation of the couch, the analyst sitting behind and so on, the whole ritualism of the situation. Freud expected, and René Spitz explained this in an article, that this is the real purpose of the analytic situation, to artificially infantilize the patient so that more of the unconscious material comes up. I think this method suffers from the fact that in this way the patient never confronts himself with this archaic or infantile material; he becomes his unconscious, he becomes a child. What happens is, in a way, a dream, but in a waking state. All this comes out, all this appears, but the patient isn't there.

But it is not true that the patient is a little child. The patient (let us assume for the moment he is not a severe psychotic) is at the some time a normal, grown-up being, with sense, with intelligence, with all sorts of reactions which fit a normal being. Therefore, he can react to this infantile being in him. If this confrontation doesn't take places as it usually doesn't in the Freudian method, then indeed this conflict doesn't appear, this conflict isn't set in motion. In my opinion one of the main conditions for analytic cure is lacking.

The other extreme from Freud is that method of psychotherapy that is sometimes also called analysis and in which the whole thing degenerates into a psychological conversation between the analyst and the grown-up patient, where the child doesn't appear at all. Here the patient is addressed as if there were none of these archaic forces in him, and where one hopes by a kind of persuasion, by being nice to the patient and telling him: "Your mother was bad, your father was bad, but I'm going to help you, you'll find yourself secure," that this will cure him. A neurosis that is very light may be cured that way, but I think there are shorter methods than five years. I think a severe neurosis is never cured unless you have, as Freud said, unearthed or uncovered sufficient unconscious and relevant material.

What I am proposing here is simply that the analytic situations both of the patient and in a sense of the analyst, is a paradoxical one, that the patient is neither only the child and the irrational person with all sorts of crazy fantasies, nor is he only the grown-up person with whom one can converse intelligently about his symptoms. The patient must in the same hour and at the same time be able to experience himself as both, and therefore experience the very confrontation that sets something going.

The main point as far as cure is concerned is for me the real conflict that is engendered in the patient by this confrontation. This cannot be done in theory and this is not done just by words. Even if one takes a simple thing, as when a patient says: "I was afraid of my mother," what does that mean? That is the kind of fear we are all accustomed to; we are afraid of the schoolteacher, of a policeman, we are afraid that somebody might hurt us—that is nothing so world-shaking. But maybe what the patient means when he says he was afraid of his mother can be described, let us say, in these terms: "I am put into a cage. There is a lion in that cage. And somebody puts me in and closes the door, and what do I feel?" In dreams, this is exactly what comes up, namely, the alligator or the lion or the tiger trying to attack the dreamer. But to use words, "I was afraid of my mother," that falls short of the necessity to cope with the patient's real fear.

CONSTITUTIONAL AND OTHER FACTORS FOR CURE

I come now to some other factors, some favorable, some unfavorable. First of all, the constitutional factors. I indicated already that I believe the constitutional factors are terribly important. In fact, if you had asked me 30 years ago about the constitutional factors and I had heard something I am saying I would have been very indignant; I would have called this a reactionary or Fascist kind of pessimism which doesn't permit changes and what not. But in quite a few years of analytic practice I have convinced myself—not on any theoretical basis, because I don't even know anything about the theory of heredity, but by my experience—that it just isn't true to assume that we can account for the degree of neurosis as simply proportional to the traumatic and environmental circumstances.

It's all very nice if you have homosexual patients and you find out that the patient has a very strong mother and a very weak father, and then you have the theory that explains homosexuality. But then you have ten other patients who have just the same weak father and strong mother, and they don't turn out to be homosexual. You have similar environmental factors that have very different effects. Therefore I really do believe that, unless you deal with extraordinarily traumatic factors in the sense I was talking about before, you cannot really understand the development of a neurosis if you do not think of constitutional factors, in the sense that, either alone, because they are so strong, or at least in cooperation with certain conditions, certain constitutional factors make environmental factors highly traumatic and others do not.

The difference, of course, between the Freudian view and my own is that Freud thinks, when he talks about constitutional factors, essentially about instinctual factors, in terms of libido theory. I believe that constitutional factors go much further. I cannot try here to explain this any further right now. I think constitutional factors cover not only factors, that are usually defined as temperament—be it in the sense of the Greek temperaments or in the sense of Sheldon (1942), but also factors such as vitality, love of life, courage, and many other things That I don't even want to mention. In other words, I think a person, in the lottery of the chromosomes, is already conceived as a very definite being. The problem of a person's life, really, is what life does to that particular person who is already born in a certain way. Actually, I think it's a very good exercise for an analyst to consider what would this person be if life conditions had been favorable to that kind of being he was conceived as, and what are the particular distortions and damages which life and circumstances have done to that particular person.

Among the favorable constitutional factors belong the degree of vitality, especially the degree of love of life. I personally think that one can have a rather severe neurosis, with a good deal of narcissism, even with a good deal of incestuous fixation, but if one has love of life then one has an entirely different picture. To give two examples: One is Roosevelt and the other is Hitler. Both were rather narcissistic, Roosevelt certainly less than Hitler but sufficiently so. Both were rather mother-fixated, probably Hitler in a more malignant and profound way than Roosevelt. But the decisive difference was that Roosevelt was a man full of love of life, and Hitler was a man full of love of death, whose aim was destruction—an aim which wasn't even conscious, because for many years he believed that his aim was salvation. But his aim was really destruction, and everything that led to destruction attracted him. Here you see two personalities where you might say the factor of narcissism and the factor of mother fixation, while different, were markedly present. But what was entirely different was the relative amount of biophilia and necrophilia. If I see a patient who might be quite sick, but I see lots of biophilia, I am quite optimistic. If I see in addition to everything else very little biophilia but a good deal of necrophilia, I am prognostically quite pessimistic.

There are other factors that make for success or failure which I just want to mention briefly. They are not constitutional factors, and I think they can be tested pretty much in the first five or ten sessions of the analysis.

(a) One is whether *a patient has really reached the bottom of his suffering.* I know of one psychotherapist who only takes patients who have gone through every method of therapy that it is possible to find in the United States, and if no other method has worked, he accepts the patient. That, of course, could be a very nice alibi for his own failure—but in this case it is really a test, namely, that the patient has gone to the bottom of his suffering. I think it's very important to find that out. Sullivan used to stress this point very much, although in slightly different terms: the patient has to prove why he needs treatment. By that, he didn't mean the patient has to give a theory of his illness, or anything like that. Obviously, he didn't mean that. He meant the patient must not come with the idea: "Well, I'm sick. You are a professional who promises to cure sick people, here I am." If I were to put anything on the wall of my office, I would put a statement which says: *"Being here is not enough."*

Thus, the first task of analysis is very important: to help the patient be unhappy rather than to encourage him. In fact, any encouragement that tries to mitigate, to soften his suffering, is definitely not indicated; it is definitely bad for the further progress of the analysis. I don't think anyone has really enough initiative, enough impulse, to make the tremendous effort required by analysis—if we really mean analysis—unless he is aware of the maximum suffering which is in him. That is not at all a bad state to be it. It's a much better state than to be in a shadowy land where one neither suffers nor is happy. Suffering is at least a very real feeling, and is a part of life. Not to be aware of suffering and to watch television or something is neither here nor there.

(b) Secondly, another condition is that the patient acquires or has *some idea of what his life ought to be*, or could be—some vision of what he wants. I have heard of patients who have come to an analyst because they couldn't write poetry. That's a little exceptional, although not so rare as one might think. But many patients come, because they are not happy. It's just not enough not to be happy. And if a patient were to tell me he wants to be analyzed because he is unhappy I would say: "Well, most people aren't happy." That isn't quite enough to spend years on a very energetic and troublesome and difficult work with one person.

To have an idea of what one wants in life is not a matter of education and also not a matter of cleverness. It might very well be that the patient never had a vision of his life. In spite of our overwhelming education systems people don't get in it many ideas of what they want in life. Nevertheless I think it is a task of the analysts also in the beginning of the analysis, to test whether the patient is capable of having some idea of what else life could mean except being happier. There are many words patients in the big cities of the United States use: they want to express themselves, and all that—well, this is just phraseology. If somebody dabbles in music and likes hi-fi and this, that or the other—these are just phrases. I think the analyst cannot be, must not be satisfied with these phrases, but must get down to reality: what is really the intention of this person—not theoretically—but what does he or she really want, what is he or she coming for.

(c) Another important factor is the *patient's seriousness*. You find many narcissistic people who go into analysis solely for the reason that they like to talk about themselves. In fact, where else can you do that? Neither one's wife nor one's friends nor one's children will listen by the hour to one's talking about oneself: what I did yesterday, and why I did it, and so on. Even the bartender will not listen that long because of the other customers. So one pays thirty five dollars, or whatever the fee is, and one has a man who listens to my talking about myself all the time. Of course, I have to catch on, as a patient that I have to talk about psychologically relevant topics. So I must not talk about pictures and paintings and music; I must talk about myself, and why I didn't like my husband or my wife, and why I did like him or her, or what not. Now, that also must be excluded, because that is no sufficient reason for an analyst, although it's a good reason to make money.

(d) Another factor very closely related to this one is *the patient's capacity eventually to differentiate between banality and reality*. The conversation of most people, I think, is banal. The best example I could give of banality are the editorials of the New York Times, if you'll forgive me. What I mean by banality here, in contrast to reality, is not that something is not clever, but that it is unreal. If I read an article in the *New York Times* about the Viet Nam situation, it is so banal to me. Of course, it is a matter of political opinions—simply because it's unreal, because it deals with fictions, even to the degree that suddenly American ships fire at unseen targets and nobody knows what there was. And then all this has to do with the salvation from communism and God knows what. Well, this is banal. Similarly, the way people talk about their personal lives is banal, because they usually talk about unreal things: My husband did this or did that, or he got a promotion or he didn't get a promotion, and I should have called my boy friend or I shouldn't... This is all banal because it doesn't touch upon anything real, it touches only upon rationalizations.

(e) Another factor is *the life circumstances of the patient.* How much neurosis he can successfully get by—that depends entirely on the situation. A salesman may get by with a form of neurosis with which a college professor might not get by. I don't mean because of a difference of cultural level, but simply because a certain type of highly narcissistic, aggressive behavior wouldn't do in a small college, they would throw him out. But if he's a salesman he may be extremely successful. Sometimes patients say: "Well, doctor, I just can't go on with that," and my standard answer to that gambit is: "Well, I don't see why you can't. You have gone on with it for 30 years and many people, millions of people go on with that until the end of their days, so why you can't I can't see. I could see why you wouldn't want to, but I need some proof why you don't want to or that you don't want to." But "You can't" is simply not true; that's also phraseology.

(f) The point that I want to stress most, is the *active participation of the patient.* Here I come back to what I said before. I don't think anybody gets well by talking, not even by revealing his unconscious, just as little as anybody achieves anything of importance without making a very great effort and without making sacrifices, without risking, without going. If I could use symbolic language which often appears in dreams: through the many tunnels which one has to pass through in the course of life. That means periods when one finds oneself in the dark, periods where one is frightened, and yet where one has faith that there is another side of the tunnel, that there will be light. I think in this process the personality of the analyst is very important, namely whether he is good company and whether he is able to do what a good mountain guide does, who doesn't carry his client up the mountain, but sometimes tells him: "This is a better road," and sometimes even uses his hand to give him a little push, but that is all he can do.

(g) This brings me to the last point: *the personality of the analyst.* One could certainly give a lecture on that, but I just want to make a very few points. Freud already made one very important point, namely, the absence of sham and deception. There should be something in the analytic attitude and in the analytic atmosphere by which from the very first moment the patient experiences that this is a world that is different from the one he usually experiences: it's a world of reality, and that means a world of truth, truthfulness, without sham—that's all that reality is. Secondly, he should experience that he is not supposed to talk banalities, and that the analyst will call his attention to it, and that the analyst doesn't talk banalities, either. In order to do this, of course, the analyst must know the difference between banality and non-banality, and that is rather difficult especially in the world in which we live.

Another very important condition for the analyst is the absence of sentimentality: one doesn't cure a sick person by being kind either in medicine or in psychotherapy. That may sound harsh to some, and I am sure I will be quoted for utter ruthlessness towards the patient, for lack of compassion and authoritarianism and what not. Well, that may be so. It's not my own experience of what I'm doing or my own experience with a patient, because there is something quite different from sentimentality, and that is one of the essential conditions to analyze: to experience in oneself what the patient is talking about. If I cannot experience in myself what it means to be schizophrenic or depressed or sadistic or narcissistic or frightened to death, even though I can experience that in smaller doses than the patients then I just don't know what the patient is talking about. If I don't make that attempt, then I think I'm not in touch with the patient.

There may be some people who have idiosyncrasies towards certain things. I remember Sullivan used to say that an anxiety-ridden patient never came to his office a second time because he just had no sympathy nor empathy for this kind of thing. Well, that's perfectly all right. Then one just doesn't take this kind of patient, and one is a very good therapist for those patients with whom one can feel what they feel.

It is a basic requirement of analysis to feel what the patient feels. That's the reason why there is no better analysis for analysts than analyzing other people, because in the process of analyzing other people there is almost nothing which is in the analyst that doesn't come up, that isn't touched, provided he or she tries to experience what the patient experiences. If he or she thinks: "Well, the patient is a poor sick guy because he pays" then of course he remains intellectual and he never is convincing to the patient.

The result of this attitude is that indeed one is not sentimental with a patient, but one is not lacking in compassion, because one has a deep feeling that nothing that happens to the patient is not also happening in oneself. There is no capacity to be judgmental or to be moralistic or to be indignant about the patient once one experiences what is happening to the patient as one's own. And if one doesn't experience this as one's own, then I don't think one understands it. In the natural sciences you can put the material on the table and there it is and you can see it and you can measure it. In the analytic situation it's not enough that the patient puts it on the table, because for me it's not a fact as long as I cannot see it in myself as something which is real.

Finally, it is very important to see the patient as the hero of a drama and not to see him as a summation of complexes. Actually, every human being is the hero of a drama. I do not mean that in any sentimental fashion. Here is a person born with certain gifts, and usually he fails, and his life is a tremendous struggle to make something out of that which he is born with, fighting against tremendous handicaps. Even the most banal person in one sense, looking at it from the outside, is exceedingly interesting once you see him as that person, as that living substance which was thrown into the world at a place not desired by him nor known to him, and is fighting in some way his way through. Actually, the great writer is characterized precisely by the fact that he can show a person who is banal in one sense and yet who is a hero in the sense in which the artist sees him. Just to take one example, the figures of Balzac—most of them are not interesting and yet they become terribly interesting by the power of the artist. We are not Balzacs, so we cannot write these novels, but we should acquire the capacity of seeing in a patient a human drama, or, for that matter, in any human being in whom we are interested, and not just a person who comes with symptom A, B, C, D.

In concluding, I want to say something about *prognosis*. I believe that in what I call the benign neuroses there is a very good chance of cure, in the malignant neuroses the chances are not very good. I won't go into percentages now because in the first place that is a professional secret or trade secret, and in the second place one would have to talk a lot about it. Nevertheless, I think it's a common experience that the chances for the cure of severe, malignant neuroses are not too good. I don't think there's anything to be ashamed about that. If you have in medicine a severe sickness and you have, let us say, a five percent chance of cure with a certain method—and I think the chances in analysis are even a little better— provided there is no better method and this is all that the physician can do, everybody—the physician, the patient, his friends, his relatives, everybody will make the greatest effort to achieve health, even though there is only a five percent chance. It is wrong not to see the difference between a benign neurosis and a malignant neurosis and to be in a kind of honeymoon mood in the beginning and to think: "Well, analysis cures everything." Or, if the analyst tries in some way or another to kid himself, in looking at the patient, that things are not as severe and with as little hope as they sometimes are. Even in those cases in which a patient may not get well, at least one condition is fulfilled in a good analysis, and that is that the analytic hours, if they have been alive and significant, will have been the most important and the best hours that he ever had in his life. I think that cannot be said about many therapies, and that at least is a comfort to the analyst who struggles with patients who often have indeed a very low chance of cure.

In the non-malignant neuroses there is a much better chance. I would suggest to consider that among the light forms of neuroses many might be cured, but by methods much shorter than two years of analysis, that is to say, by having the courage of using analytic insight to approach the problem very directly, and possibly to do in twenty hours what one feels obliged to do, as an analyst, in two hundred hours. There is no reason for false shame to use direct methods when they can be used.

PART II

RELATIONSHIP
AS DIRECT MEETING

Direct Meeting

Rainer Funk

As I rang the bell at the entrance to the apartment building "Casa La Monda" in Muralto near Locarno, Switzerland on September 1, 1972 and took the tiny elevator to the fifth floor, I had no idea that this first personal encounter with Erich Fromm would be the beginning of a unique relationship for me.

Everything that I had been taught up to that point and everything that I had learned, tried out, and experienced myself in the previous twenty-nine years had been centered on education and thought. I was absolutely convinced that this was the way to supremely master life, even my personal, social, moral and religious life. To comprehend and to intellectually safeguard the human was my educational goal. I was equally certain that, after an experience like Auschwitz, we could only place our hopes in humanity if it were protected against failure by something which ensured and transcended man. Fromm's humanistic justification of ethics was dubious—too trusting and naive. In my initial letter to him, of August 1, 1972, I had already intimated that his humanism would clearly be "the starting point for a constructive debate."

The elevator finally arrived on the fifth floor. When the doors opened I looked straight at Erich Fromm. He was standing in the doorway to his apartment, and looked at me in a friendly and expectant way. I took two steps toward him and greeted the seventy-two-year-old stiffly with the formal address "Professor." He shook hands with me and facing me, replied: "*Guten Tag, Herr Funk.*"

Fromm invited me to join him in his study. My first impression was the breathtaking view of Lake Maggiore from the window. Fromm had positioned his desk—strewn with books and manuscripts—in front of the picture window extending across the room so that his gaze always fell on the water and its dramatic interplay with light. On the opposite shore the peak of Mt. Gambarogno was visible in the sunny haze of the late summer afternoon.

Not until later did I become aware to what a degree a person's relationship to nature instinctively creates a sense of trust in me. Here I had apparently encountered another human being who shared my affinity. Fromm offered me a chair next to this desk, facing the room. The bookshelves were overflowing, and manuscripts and handwritten drafts and notes were piled on every conceivable surface. This rather chaotic environment became obscured, however, as he seated himself and focused on me with an expression in his eyes that is difficult to describe.

FROM FACE TO FACE

Fromm looked at me in such a straightforward way that my attempts at polite conversation abruptly ceased and any role-specific behavior became unnecessary. Although we had only met face-to-face a few minutes before, a dimension for the relationship had already emerged, allowing closeness and trust, but no longer allowing the evasion of a question or topic that had been broached with clever remarks. Somehow Fromm's eyes, encircled by wrinkles, and scrutinizing me intently, managed to initiate a conversation that appeased my anxieties and made it possible for me to concentrate intently.

The initial focus of our meeting was by no means my questions about his works and thoughts. Fromm inquired about my professional situation and why I was interested in his body of thought, particularly his ethics. Above all, he asked which aspects of psychoanalysis, religion and theology interested me. He even wanted to know my stance on Germany's *Ostpolitik*, my opinion of the Bavarian-born politician Franz Josef Strauß, and my assessment of Konrad Lorenz's theory of aggression. However, it wasn't his intention to discern my political or ideological orientation as quickly as possible. The questions—as it became clear to me through our conversations over the following eight years—were intended to reveal my deepest concerns and preoccupations. Fromm wanted to understand my innermost being: if and what I loved and hated, valued and sought, critically assessed and rejected, what appealed to me, encouraged, stimulated and angered me, delighted or thrilled me, what made me feel anxious or guilty or what frightened me. He was curious about my feelings, my needs, my interests and passions.

This was something entirely new to me. It was not my "head," my thoughts or my intellectual and argumentative abilities, that interested him, but—to continue on the same metaphorical level—my "heart." What motivated me, fascinated me, passionately moved me, what was behind my values and compelled me—this is what he wanted to learn. Thinking, the art of argumentation, brainwork, knowledge—all of these were at most means for arriving at what really drove people.

Fromm's undivided interest was directed toward coming into contact with inner strivings and feelings and understanding them not as obstacles but as bearers of energy. Even if the emotional powers were less than flattering and prevented thought and action in line with reality, it was crucial to make contact with them and meet them with understanding. Only in this way could the hidden meaning of intense feelings of jealousy or a paralyzing sense of inferiority, for example, be recognized, and the energy bound there be released for a rational or loving approach. The result was a school of thought, in which 'head' and 'heart' were linked and which strove for cognitive insights *carried by feelings*. Consequently, it comes as no surprise that particular emphasis was placed on the fundamental role of feelings.

Through his interest and questions Fromm wanted to get in touch with my inner world, my rational and irrational, overt and covert strivings. To do so, he utilized eye contact. Since infancy we have all learned to express our inner state—our affects, feelings, wishes, needs as well as our inner reactions—through eye contact.

Naturally, at the time, I was incapable of comprehending this fully. What I did sense, however, was that he had a special way of approaching me: it had a great deal to do with his gaze, which one could hardly evade. The pupils of his blue, myopic eyes behind the rimless eyeglasses appeared to be diminished in size, causing his look to seem almost penetrating. His gaze corresponded to his way of being interested in my inner life, my soul.

But there was something else about the way Fromm looked at me, spoke to me and focused the conversation. Despite the directness and bluntness with which he approached uncovering my soul, I did not at all feel interrogated, cornered, judged, unmasked or exposed. I quickly sensed that he was dealing with me in a pleasant way, with understanding and warm-heartedness, and that I had no inclination to justify or to conceal myself. He reached out to me and, through his sincere interest in what concerned me, let me sense that there was no reason to fear oneself or one's inner world. Every look and every word conveyed a sense of solidarity and kindness.

This type of human encounter was an entirely new experience for me: this way of conversing, of being with the other, of venturing into that world of feelings and passions which is at work behind our thinking, together with the assurance of a well-meaning glance from the other person, making small talk or pretences at concealment superfluous. Initiated by Fromm, it signalized the beginning of a new intellectual approach for me.

LETTING SOMEONE SENSE: "THIS IS YOU"

The Frommian philosophy has its roots in experiences which Fromm himself had in therapeutic relationships. Approximately twenty years later, as his literary executor, I was preparing a number of Fromm's unpublished manuscripts for publication, when I came across the transcript of a lecture he had held at the William Alanson White Institute in New York City in 1959. There precisely this experience of solidarity was described:

"The feeling of human solidarity is one of the most important therapeutic experiences which we can give to the patient, because at that moment the patient does not feel isolated any more. In all his neuroses or whatever his troubles are, the feeling of isolation, whether he is aware of it or not, is the very crux of his suffering. There are many other cruxes, but this is the main one. At the moment when he senses that I share this with him, so that I can say, 'This is you,' and I can say it not kindly and not unkindly, this is a tremendous relief from isolation. Another person who says, 'This is you,' and stays with me, and shares this with me.

"I have had the experience increasingly through the years that once you speak from your own experience and in this kind of relatedness to the patient, you can say anything and the patient will not feel hurt. On the contrary, he will feel greatly relieved that there is one man who sees him, because he knows the story all the time. We are often so naive, to think the patient must not know this, and the patient must not know that, because he would be so shocked. The fact is the patient knows it all the time, except he does not permit himself to have this knowledge consciously. When we say it, he is relieved because he can say: 'For heaven's sake, I knew this always.'" (1992g [1959], pp. 178-9.)

What Fromm says here about the therapeutic relationship also held true for him in general. In every type of relationship there should be a "direct" meeting with the other person, a face-to-face encounter; the face reveals the inner world of the other. A face-to-face encounter goes beneath the surface, making a "central relatedness" possible:

"I can explain the other person as another Ego, as another thing, and then look at him as I look at my car, my house, my neurosis, whatever it may be. Or I can relate to this other person in the sense of being him, in the sense of experiencing, feeling this other person. Then I do not think about myself, then my Ego does not stand in my way. But something entirely different happens. There is what I call a *central relatedness* between me and him. He is not a thing over there which I look at, but he confronts me fully and I confront him fully, and there in fact is no way of escape." (Ibid., p. 174.)

Such a direct encounter means to be interested:

"We are interested in another person, we listen attentively, we listen with interest, we think about the person, and yet the

> other person remains outside...We should try to be aware of
> the difference between lack of interest, interest and what I call
> the direct meeting with the other person, not only with regard
> to our patients, but with regard to everybody." (Ibid., p. 178.)

What distinguishes this "direct" meeting with another person from interest in another person? The "direct" meeting facilitates coming into contact with the feelings and passions of the other in order to be able to experience him or her as a whole person. For Fromm, there was one definitive characteristic of this kind of direct encounter with the other: "If you really see a person...you will stop judging provided you see that person fully." (Ibid.) No matter how often we are forced to pass judgment on what we want and what we resist in the course of living and in safeguarding our existence, in a "direct" meeting, in a direct encounter with the other, we must refrain from judgment, if we truly want to see him or her. "If you see yourself, whatever you are, you will stop feeling guilty, because you feel: 'This is me.'" (Ibid.)

Significant in the "direct" meeting is the direct encounter:

> "At the moment when you see yourself or another person
> fully, you do not judge because you are overwhelmed with the
> feeling, with the experience: 'So this is you', and also with the
> experience: 'And who am I to judge'? In fact, you do not even
> ask that question. Because in experiencing him, you experi-
> ence yourself. You say: 'So that is you' and you feel in some
> way very plainly: 'And that is me too'...If I see the other per-
> son—what happens is not only that I stop judging but also that
> I have a sense of union, of sharing, of oneness, which is some-
> thing much stronger than being kind or being nice. There is a
> feeling of human solidarity when two people—or even one
> person—can say to the other: 'So that is you, and I share this
> with you.' This is a tremendously important experience. I
> would say, short of complete love, it is the most gratifying, the
> most wonderful, the most exhilarating experience, which oc-
> curs between two people." (Ibid., p. 178.)

AN EXHILARATING EXPERIENCE

I vaguely perceived Fromm's capability for the face-to-face encounter when I met him personally for the first time on this first of September in Locarno. Exactly thirty-three years earlier the Second World War had begun with the invasion of Poland. Fromm, a Jew by birth, was able to avoid persecution and genocide by emigrating to the U.S.A. in 1934. Sadly, although he had done everything in his power from New York City to try to arrange for the emigration of relatives, whom he cared for deeply, he was only able save a few from deportation to concentration camps and subsequent murder there.

Evidently, Auschwitz did not, however, deter Fromm from seeking the face-to-face encounter with the other. Nor did he need transcendental authorization or a justification beyond man in order to have "the most exhilarating experience" "which occurs between two people." The practice or utilization of the capacity for the direct encounter necessitates neither a rational proof nor a special justification. In the course of its realization it proves itself to be morally right and good. The only question is what prevents one from actually doing this—the capability to encounter oneself and others directly can be limited, neutralized or even thwarted by fears, prejudices, biases, illusions, inhibitions, irrational bonds, etc. For Fromm, to put it concisely, it wasn't the head that made decisions but the heart, through emotional and psychic drives. These drives determine to a great degree whether our thinking is rational and reality-oriented and whether our feeling is loving and solidaristic—or not. This is why Fromm generally spoke of the capacity for reason and love instead of that for the "direct" meeting. The practice of reason and love is what ultimately makes "exhilarating" experiences possible.

During our first personal encounter I merely had the impression that the arguments with which I had intended to dispute Fromm's humanism had become obtuse and unessential. The way he approached me was totally "disarming." With my intellectual "weapons," that is logical, argumentative thought, I wanted to challenge, not concede something. I wanted to be right, not rational. I was seeking a confrontation, and Fromm was offering me a face-to-face-encounter.

I accepted his offer and noticed how both encounters during my initial visit invigorated me. I left Locarno highly motivated and energized. The following weeks, I formulated the sections on Fromm's social psychology and his theory of character orientation for my dissertation, and visited him in Locarno again in the summer of 1973. The following summer Fromm—who had only spent the summer months in Switzerland until then and otherwise lived in Cuernavaca, Mexico—decided not to return to Mexico, but to reside in Locarno year-round. This is how he came to ask me to be his research assistant, while he was writing the book *To Have or to Be?* (1976a). I lived in Locarno for some time; later I worked for him while based in Tübingen, visiting him regularly in Locarno as well as in Hinterzarten and Baden-Baden, two spas in the Black Forest, where he and Annis spent the hot summer days together.

Above all, the almost daily contact with Fromm in 1974 and 1975 gave me the opportunity to develop a comprehension of his philosophy by observing and reflecting on its effects, although we rarely discussed this specifically.

Our conversations revolved in part around topics which I had researched for the book *To Have or to Be?*, for example, the conception of "activity" in Aristotle, or oral traditional studies on the Sermon on the Mount in the New Testament, or the concept of the Godhead in Meister Eckhart. The other part of the conversations—usually continuing for three or four hours—focused on specific passages and chapters of the book in progress, *To Have or to Be?* (1976a), which Fromm had given me to read as soon as Joan Hughes, his British secretary, had typed the handwritten version from the yellow legal pads. What distinctly characterized these conversations were Fromm's elucidations from his vast reservoir of historical and political events as well as his personal experiences and encounters with important figures in politics, society and psychoanalysis. Equally unforgettable: his boundless trove of jokes from the Jewish and psychoanalytic scene. It was extraordinarily difficult for Fromm to refrain from telling a joke that suddenly came to his mind.

But it wasn't actually the topics under discussion which caused me to notice the effects of his philosophy, as interesting and entertaining as these were. It was the face-to-face encounter which—regardless of the subject matter—he made possible with clearly perceptible effects on me. Particularly conspicuous were my heightened attentiveness and ability to concentrate; our interpersonal communication did not consume strength but released energy instead. During our countless discussions, I never experienced a feeling of exhaustion nor a decline in attentiveness. I was wide-awake and on some evenings worked on my dissertation far into the night after our meeting, the time spent together with Fromm having been energizing and stimulating. Equally striking was that I often lost all sense of time. Frequently it seemed as if I had arrived half an hour earlier, although three or four hours had actually elapsed.

Only in retrospect did the impact of the encounter with Fromm become clear to me; his contact with my emotional realm and my driving forces apparently had initiated a process of personal growth, although in all those years I never experienced Fromm in a therapeutic setting. (Since according to Fromm, the most significant therapeutic factor is the capacity of the therapist for a *direct meeting*—a face-to-face encounter with the patient—and not a setting defined as 'therapy,' it is not surprising that I observed typical therapeutic effects outside the therapeutic setting.) Nor did we ever discuss the following observations.

As a result of my contact with Fromm, I began to sense and seek a relationship to nature again. During childhood I had always known whether the moon was full, or waxing or waning, or new at a particular moment. Now I had rediscovered the lunar phases and was captivated when the full moon was reflected in the lake and illuminating the snow-covered peaks. On January 4, 1975, the first red bud of the camellia in front of my window in the Via Mondacce burst into bloom, and before long there was no mountain peak on the horizon that I hadn't scaled.

My decision to stop smoking in the spring of 1975 made life exceedingly difficult for me. Over an extended period of time, cigarettes had supported and stabilized something within me. I was oriented on "having" the cigarettes and on the nicotine-related effects of smoking. But who was I without the cigarettes? As a nonsmoker? The intense daily work on the manuscripts for *To Have or to Be?* was not without consequences. Freeing myself from this "having" mode of existence became a moment of truth: whether I chose only to intelligently discuss the alternative "having" vs. "being" or whether I dared to put the theory to practice, i.e. dared to try to *be* without a crutch of *having*. The withdrawal symptoms were intense, and it took me several months to consciously and fully realize that the alternative to the "having" mode of existence is not the "not-having" mode of existence but the "being" mode of existence. The "being" mode of existence, as I learned, had much to do with becoming aware of other things in oneself and in one's social context as well as with allowing and pursuing new interests.

This was *terra incognita* for me, which I trod on with a wish for professional reorientation. I wanted to discover—in a more exacting and professional way—what really motivates and drives me and others; I wanted to familiarize myself with approaches to the human unconscious, both my own and that of others. At the same time I became aware that what interested me and what sparked my interest in scholarly work was changing considerably. To determine the morally right, the morally demanded and the morally favorable, that is, the morally good, and its justifications is undeniably an important and challenging question. However, it became increasingly clear to me that another question preoccupied me much more, namely, why people who recognize something as being morally right and good do not act in accordance with these insights in their concrete actions and decision-making. What hinders their utilization of the faculty of reason? Which irrational forces lead to their failure to act rationally?—I wanted to undergo training in psychoanalysis and leave the fields of theology and ethics, which I consequently did in 1977, after completing a doctoral dissertation on Fromm's ethics (see R. Funk, 1982) and having been accepted in a psychoanalytic training program in Stuttgart.

ENCOUNTERING THE FOREIGN

How crucial the direct encounter with the self is and what consequences it can have were phenomena which I initially observed with Fromm himself. Hardly a day went by when he did not actively seek this direct encounter with himself. Fromm usually allotted an hour in the late morning for "his exercises." What he meant were physical and contemplative exercises which he had described in *The Art of Being* (1989 [1974-75]) as exercises promoting attentiveness and self-perception, sensory awareness exercises, Tai Chi as well as self-analysis. He concentrated on his body movements, on his breathing, attempted to become totally empty and to meditate. He also tried to become aware of what resounded in him emotionally or pre-occupied him mentally: for example, a feeling of uneasiness that persisted after an interview, or the impulse to write a letter to the editor for *The New York Times*. Whenever he could remember a dream from the night before, he tried to decipher its message, in order to be able to confront his own un-conscious strivings, fantasies, emotional powers, and conflicts.

The effects of these exercises seeking the direct encounter with the self were clearly apparent, not only to Fromm himself but to those around him as well. The most impressive example for me was the opening address Fromm gave at a symposium in Locarno-Muralto in May 1975. Together with the Gottlieb Duttweiler Institute in Switzerland, I had organized this symposium in honor of his seventy-fifth birthday. During the preceding weeks Fromm had been considerably incapacitated by a broken arm, and for a long time it had been uncertain whether he would be able to hold the opening address. He ultimately spoke extemporaneously for two hours on "The Meaning of Psychoanalysis for the Future" (1992h [1975]). Afterward I asked him where he had found the concentration and energy for the lecture, and he replied, without any pretensiousness whatsoever: "Well, this morning I spent twice as long doing my exercises."

Someone who practices the direct encounter with himself or herself can draw on powers also serving the direct encounter with other people, facilitating his or her total absorption in a topic and in the other person. The opposite is also true: Someone who practices the direct encounter with others draws on experiences facilitating the encounter with the foreign and the other within himself or herself.

That Fromm was versed in both and consequently able to be with himself and with the other could readily be seen in his facial expression. After his death, I found a series of photographs of Fromm, taken with the assistance of a photographic innovation (a battery-powered rewinding mechanism) allowing an entire series of photographs to be shot within a few seconds. On the strip of developed negatives there was one photograph that showed Fromm with his eyes shut next to another photograph in which he was looking directly at the photographer. In the course of these sequential images Fromm must have closed his eyes for a split second and been photographed in the process. On closer scrutiny this photograph depicts a face concentrated on the inner self, a face totally immersed in itself. The adjacent photograph of Fromm with his eyes wide open gives the impression that his eyes are totally focused on the observer. In the first, he is totally with himself, in the second, he is totally with the other.

These portraits reveal how intensely Fromm must have practiced the direct encounter to learn to be with himself and with the other. At the same time, they also illustrate the significance of the practice of the direct encounter for the successful realization of humanity and of social existence. Regardless of the type of relationship in which the direct or face-to-face encounter is carried out, in the relationship to others, in scholarly or scientific work, in artistic or therapeutic endeavors, in dealing with nature or in dealing with one's own inner powers, the direct encounter always releases energy for direct encounters in other areas of life.

The experience drawn from the practice of the face-to-face encounter inspired Fromm's development of the concepts of the "productive character orientation," "biophilia," and the "being mode of existence." "The person who fully lives life is attracted by the process of life and growth in all spheres," writes Fromm in *The Heart of Man* (1964a, p. 47). In *To Have Or to Be?* (1976a, p. 103) he summarizes the exponential effect of the direct encounter as follows: "Genuine love increases the capacity to love and to give to others. The true lover loves the whole world, in his or her love for a specific person." While for the "having" mode of existence it holds that every instance of sharing and every use of what is had leads to its consumption and its consequent loss, sharing and using—by a person in the "being" mode of existence—lead to the experience of an abundance in sharing and to the growth of the individual's own powers in using them.

Whenever I wanted to more fully comprehend what Fromm actually meant by "productivity," "reason and love as [one's] own powers," "biophilia," or the "being mode of existence," I found it helpful to recall the effects of the face-to-face encounters with him.

Fromm's capacity for the face-to-face encounter finally explains why his writings have a special appeal for many people, particularly those who have difficulties reading and comprehending highly conceptual, abstract theories. In an interview conducted by Hans Jürgen Schultz (1974b, p. 105), Fromm confessed: "I have no gift for abstract thought. I can think only those thoughts that relate to something I can concretely experience." This is why Fromm also sought a direct encounter with the issue or problem under consideration in his written work. Before beginning to write, however, he had to find a mental but not totally unemotional approach to what others had written on the same question. When reading a primary text it was vital that he could directly relate to what he was reading. With certain authors this was regularly the case—above all Sigmund Freud and Karl Marx, Baruch Spinoza and Meister Eckhart. With a number of other authors this was rarely the case—for example, Georg Wilhelm Hegel, Martin Heidegger, Theodor W. Adorno and most of the sociologists.

Fromm spent much more time reading than writing (perhaps twenty or thirty times as much). When he finally did start to write, he generally put his ideas on that specific topic on paper in one sitting—by hand, preferably with a fountain pen or ball point pen. The following day he read what he had written the day before and sometimes started over from the beginning, if he had been unable to express what concerned and interested him and what he wanted to say. He then made another attempt until he felt that he had become one with the topic. While writing, Fromm also sought the direct encounter, namely, with a topic, with concepts, arguments and ideas; not until this encounter in his opinion had been correctly conveyed in the written text did he give the handwritten text to his secretary, so that she could prepare a typewritten manuscript, which he could then give others to read.

Because Erich Fromm's writings arose out of a direct and inwardly perceived encounter with the works of other writers and with a topic, and were not the outgrowth of abstract thought and conceptual-logical thought processes, many readers feel addressed by them and are able to enter into an inner dialogue with what they read. Fromm lived and felt what he said and wrote. Teachings and life were closely interconnected in Fromm's person and works because both involved the practice of direct encounters.

From Couch to Chair

Marianne Horney Eckhardt

I think of Erich Fromm as a member of my extended family. He belonged to the circle of my mother's (Karen Horney) friends. I probably met him first around 1930, when I was 16 or 17 years old, but my own contact with him started only with his accepting me for analysis when I came to New York for psychiatric training in 1937. My mother suggested him as an analyst. Their collaboration and friendship had continued to be close. The analysis lasted three years on a three-times-a-week basis with some interruptions due to Fromm's health. At the time, I was not a candidate in psychoanalytic training and knew little about psychoanalysis apart from my mother's writings. She had just published *The Neurotic Personality of Our Time* (K. Horney, 1937.)

The analysis was ended at my request. I felt a surge of wishing to proceed on my own, coupled with a novel sense of self-confidence. I felt a need for freedom from self-examination. self-consciousness had plagued me all my life. Fromm—and this is important—ungrudgingly went along with my decision, though he had little to go on which would reassure him that I really was or would be functioning in a better mode. I had changed from a very detached, though reasonably competent, person with a minimal personal life and much anxiety, to a person with new urgent stirrings, who wished to break out of her shell. I am ever grateful for his respecting this inner urge.

In retrospect, my decision still feels right, as it did then. I remember the summer after this graduation as being one of the most enjoyable summers of my life. I was reaching out and was responded to. That fall I met my husband; we were married the following year. The analysis freed me to grow. Much was still to be outgrown, but it enabled me to learn from outer and inner experiences.

It is my belief that no other analyst could have been so profoundly helpful. For a long time, this belief rested less on Fromm's skill as an analyst, than on the fact that he knew my mother as a close friend and also knew my older sister, a striking talented and successful actress, who, nevertheless, was also the bane of my existence. This inside knowledge gave him a perspective that proved vitally helpful to me. He appreciated their talents and fame, but was well aware of the personality aspects that had impacted my life.

This, however, cannot be the whole story. Much of his philosophy of the "being"-mode, which Fromm later developed in his books, to which I have come to feel a great kinship, must have been atmospherically present in those years. At the time, Fromm was writing his first book *Escape from Freedom* (1941a). He was just beginning to formulate his own beliefs and develop a style of his own. Except for the last six months, I was still on the couch during our sessions. The shift from couch to chair, to talking face-to-face and conversing in a meaningful dialogue made a notable a difference to my sense of Self. I felt addressed as a person and not as a patient. He was kind and went out of his way to accommodate my ever-changing schedule as a Payne Whitney resident.

Nonetheless, our relationship remained distant. Transference feelings remained an enigma to me, including my occasional sudden eruptions of anger, which took us both by surprise and were beyond my or his comprehension. He was, then, not at his best in dealing with transference reactions. Still, it seems this distance was my contribution.

About ten years or more later, having experienced analyses from the therapist's point of view, it occurred to me what a non-satisfying patient I had been and that he could not possibly have any idea how much he had helped me. I wrote him a long letter to which he responded. From that time on, we developed a fond friendship. I had opportunities to see him in Washington, D.C., in Mexico, and in Locarno, Switzerland.

Awakening the Patient

David E. Schecter

Erich Fromm was the most fully alive and awake man I have ever met or can imagine. These qualities were contagious. To be truly with him one felt fully alive and awake.

As a teenager in 1941, I read his book, *Escape from Freedom* (1941a), and I found my orientation to man and life. The book also helped explain to me the barbaric holocaust and how the sadist needed the masochist, as much as the reverse, in order to achieve what Fromm—way back then—called symbiosis.

I was determined to leave Canada and study with this man at the White Institute. To my shock, in 1951, I found he had moved to Mexico. But this cloud had a silver lining: he would come back to New York City 3-4 months each year, during which times I arranged to work with him in intensive supervision—2-hour sessions, four times a week for four years.

If I ask myself why the supervision with Fromm lifted my spirits so high, it undoubtedly has to do with the fact that Fromm saw each supervisory and psychoanalytic session as a dramatic search for truth. He was above all a truth-seeker who knew that an essential part of the analysis was to shed sham and illusion.

His face would brighten with expectation when he asked, "What are this man's passions?" Moreover, in almost every supervisory session, Fromm would ask in all seriousness, "Well, what did you learn about yourself in this session with the patient?" He was not simply asking about counter-transference in the narrow sense, but about what new questions and experiences I had encountered. For Fromm, every session was meant to be a meaningful encounter. He showed his boredom with following trivial byways. It became clear that Fromm himself intended to learn something from every supervisory session. His attitudes transformed my attitudes with patients since our work together. I now always look for the yearnings, the cravings and desires of the patient and the fears he has associated with these.

A brief clinical vignette will demonstrate Fromm's aliveness and passion in our work together. After I described how the patient told of his father hiding the best food in the house when company came to visit, Fromm warmed with excitement. He asked all kinds of detailed questions about the father's behavior and then launched into a talk about the hoarding character which he fully described in *Man for Himself* (1947a). When he felt he was becoming too distant for the patient's experience, he would often say "Forgive me for indulging in some theory but it's relevant here." He went on to talk about hoarding as an anti-life trait.

One day I told him about a patient's fantasy of living inside the underpants of Marilyn Monroe. His face brightened and he made the observation that Freud did not take the Oedipus complex seriously enough. This patient was trying—according to Fromm—to recreate a symbiotic relation to the woman. The patient's craving had little to do with genital sex. With excitement Fromm went into his idea of every patient having a private religion with a central passion that motivates his whole life. These were heady pre-Oedipal concepts in the 1950s and needless to say my excitement after such a supervisory session ran high and carried itself into my psychoanalytic work which became filled with a new sense of drama. Fromm was most generous in his supervisory work. He shared his private associations not only through direct interpretation but through jokes, parables and stories from his own life.

In the summer of 1957, Fromm organized a conference on "Zen Buddhism and Psychoanalysis" with D. T. Suzuki, who was his house guest. I was thrilled to be invited to participate in the dialogue with Suzuki, Fromm and others. It was clear that Fromm loved and admired the then 86-year-old Suzuki. Fromm was especially interested in the experience of becoming one with the object of perception—for instance a flower—and giving up one's Ego boundaries in the process. Suzuki not only taught about this experience but lived it and Fromm wanted to learn from Suzuki. Next to the Zen Conference, I was presenting a case of a severely obsessional man to a group of about seven of us—all graduates of the Institute—including Ernest Schachtel, Edward S. Tauber and Maurice Green. The Seminar began at 2 p.m., when we saw Suzuki intently absorbed in watching Fromm's kittens at play. At 5 p.m., when we adjourned, Suzuki was still thoroughly entranced by the kittens' play. Fromm marveled at Suzuki's power of intense absorption in which Western clock hours seemed to be of little relevance. Fromm told the following story: Suzuki had commented that a stone Japanese lantern would look beautiful in the garden and that he would find one for Fromm. Years passed; Fromm forgot about the promise. Almost ten years later, two weeks before Suzuki's death, a beautiful Japanese lantern arrived with a brief note: "This is the one."

Fromm was an independent worker who sought help only from experts from specialized fields. When we visited him in Cuernavaca, he excused himself for lessons he was getting in neuro-anatomy and neuro-physiology for his book on *The Anatomy of Human Destructiveness* (1973a). With a chuckle he explained the barter system: for each lesson he received he would offer an hour of psychoanalytic supervision to his teacher. He was already 72 years old and completely open to learning about areas that were relevant to his work but foreign to his background.

Fromm was a disciplined worker. He explained that he would not be available from 10 a.m. to 3 p.m. (he was in his early seventies) since that was his time for reading and writing. He confidently expected us to entertain ourselves. After the evening meal and ensuing discussions—in which he avidly listened to our mother-child research—he would finally say, "Children, it's time to go to bed." On one occasion, he visited our bedroom and with great tenderness tucked in our blankets and wished us pleasant dreams.

Fromm was a man who liked little celebrations. On his birthday in March of '73 he opened a bottle of champagne, clasped our shoulders in a circle and began to sing a Hassidic chant, his face and body beaming with pleasure as he swayed back and forth. In 1974, Paul Lippmann and I visited him in Locarno. Upon hearing that it was Paul's birthday, he organized a steamer trip from Locarno to Ascona where he treated us to a festive lunch. It was clear that he was tired. The physical fatigue seemed to be transcended by his spirit of friendship and solidarity.

The last time I saw Fromm, he looked terribly frail. However, his voice and eyes were full of life. He described a group of doctors entering his room and instead of asking how he felt they told him he was well because his blood chemistries were normal. They talked about their yachts to each other during their bedside visit to him. Fromm was forever an avid observer and analyst of human social functioning. I remember his musing over how one's own narcissism is the most difficult trait to overcome.

One of the most exciting ideas that grew out of our case discussion was Fromm's thesis that the neurotic seeks the solution for his life in a system of private religious worship. [...] Fromm presented his thesis this way: Man attempts to solve the dilemma of his existential separateness and isolation by taking two pathways. He may take the *regressive* way, refusing "to be born," returning to the womb, the breast, the lap or hand of mother; or to seeking the security of father's command. [...] The second kind of solution available to the existential dilemma of our separateness is a *progressive* one: the drive to be born psychologically. This leads toward growth and individual freedom and away from incestuous ties. [...]

Thus, when Fromm saw a patient he asked himself two questions: (1) What is this patient's private religion? What does he see as his way of salvation? And, (2) What can I as an analyst do to help him achieve a progressive solution toward growth?

In response to the latter question, Fromm saw the analyst as having the function of awakening the patient to his dilemma and confronting him with a clear vision of the two alternative solutions to his life, i.e. towards life or towards death.

One of Fromm's greatest clinical talents was his ability to delineate in a relatively short time the central strivings and issues in the patient. He also converted the chronically depressed or obsessively complaining situation into an acute crisis in those circumstances where he felt the individual patient had the capacity to take it. I have been struck by Fromm's faith in the reserve capacity of the human in time of crisis when the best in him can be mobilized. It reminds me very much of converting Selye's biological Stage of Exhaustion into an Alarm Reaction by undergoing a new stress. Although one has to be sure that the patient has the reserve, Fromm felt that most analysts erred in the opposite direction and sold their patients short by undervaluing their capacities, largely because of the analyst's compromising solution in his own life. This phase of Fromm's work I believe must be understood carefully in the light of each patient and the stage of his analysis, and not practiced flamboyantly and without responsibility as a firecracker technique.

Fromm's capacity to dramatize the patient's life situation was also a dangerous weapon. In application, the dramatization must be felt in an utterly sincere way; otherwise the patient will rightly feel the sham of playacting and playing with his life. [...]

Fromm felt strongly that the relationship of analyst to patient should be the model of direct relatedness if the patient was ever to overcome one of his severest problems, namely that of alienation. It would be an interesting subject for further discussion as to how much of the cure in analysis occurs through the processes of the patient's identification with and/or inspiration from the analyst. It is my belief that these two processes may be necessary for growth in some analyses but are not sufficient in themselves, especially for resolution of the transference. As Fromm saw it, the goal in communication was, what he called "core-to-core penetration." This involved the analyst's giving up his professional and social facades, as well as having a responsible and loving attitude toward the patient. This does not mean that he ceased to be questioning or even suspicious of the patient's motives. However, this type of questioning lacks a paranoid distrust of the patient.

I would like to enumerate briefly some specific techniques which Fromm saw as helpful in achieving greater directness with the patient.

(1) He attempted to present the patient's situation from an entirely new perspective, either by the use of symbolic stories, humor, or even references to himself. He felt it was most important for the analyst not to fall into the atmosphere of the usual heavy grimness that the patient would bring to a session.

(2) Sessions were held face-to-face. Fromm attempted to speak to the pa-

tient in as concrete a way as possible. Thus, he tried to avoid such words as anxiety, dependence and guilt which he felt were abstractions that served only to block inner feelings. Instead of saying, "you are insecure because of your over-dependency on mother," he would be likely to say, "mother is everything to you; you worship her and are afraid of her as we saw in this recent episode…" The former example is an intellectual, causal relationship which has the danger of "explaining away" the solution rather than provoking it into further depth. The second quotation is a more accurate description of the patient's feelings which helps to further sharpen and associate to them. (This is why I believe the reliving of certain childhood episodes allows us to recapture an emotional set which is much more alive and concrete because it was less well defended against in that period of life.)

(3) Fromm believed it would be disastrous to be sentimental with one's patient. He defined "sentimentality" as the presence of feeling for an object to which we are not really related. This is so often the patient's problem—that he summons up more feelings of pseudo-love for the beggar on the street than feelings of real love for his wife. The therapeutic relationship should be in bold contrast to any such make-believe or sentimental feelings.

(4) The analyst attempts to contact the dissociated parts of the personality through transference, fantasy, dreams and free association. Fromm advanced some provocative ideas on how free association could be cultivated so that it does not deteriorate into a sterile ritual. He likened free association to what the Chinese call, "belly thinking," and contrasted this with "thinking about" a dream, for example. These are some of the methods he suggested for revitalizing free association (cf. 1955d):

    (a) "Tell me what is in your mind right now;" the 'now' signifying the urgency of the situation.

    (b) "Concentrate on the picture of your father and tell the first thing that comes to your mind," in contrast to, "tell me about your father."

    (c) "Assume your telephone rings and you are told that I have died. What comes to mind?"

    (d) "Imagine a white blank movie screen; when I say 'now' tell me what goes on in your mind."

    (e) "Try to form the experience 'I' and say what comes to mind at the very moment when you try to feel 'I'." (These last two examples are taken from the teachings of Augusta Slesinger.)

    (f) "What comes to mind when you think of the thing you like least in yourself—the thing you are most ashamed of—most proud of?"— All of these are attempts to heighten the immediate reality and concreteness of the situation.

(5) In order to achieve contact with the core of the patient's Self, Fromm saw the necessity in helping the patient to strip away the layers of character defense and neurotic avenues of escape. As he put it at the Zen seminar in 1957, "the patient must burn his bridges behind him before he can go forward." This approach in therapy is very similar to the so-called "cornering process" of Zen where all the usual and typical character solutions are denied to the Zen student. In fact, we are told that some Zen masters provide different koans to suit different character types.

(6) As has been described previously, Fromm attempted to convert a chronic or alienated life situation into an acute crisis in the here and now, between the patient and analyst.

Conveying Hope to the Patient

Dale H. Ortmeyer

My introduction to Erich Fromm was reading his book *Escape from Freedom* (1941a) in 1948. The book was on a great books reading list for a Sociology Theory course taught by Joseph Gittler at Iowa State College. I had been discharged recently (1946) from the U.S. Army after serving in combat in Europe and in occupation troops in Japan. Coming from a pacifist family, being in combat in the Infantry in World War II caused me extreme inner conflict. *Escape from Freedom* (1941a) gave me reasoned thinking about the necessity of fighting Hitler and the Nazis. He correctly stated that Hitler and the Nazi administrators were rigidly authoritarian and completely indifferent to human life. Later, he called them "necrophilic" (consumed with death rather than life). They had to be contained if not eliminated. I never dreamed at that time that I would be presenting in psychoanalytic case seminars chaired by him at the William Alanson White Institute in New York City a decade later.

My memories of Erich Fromm's psychoanalytic theory and work date back to 1957 through the 1960's when I was first a candidate, and then on faculty at the William Alanson White Institute of Psychiatry, Psychoanalysis and Psychology. Fromm was a highly respected founder, analyst, supervisor, teacher and mentor for several of us at White. Reading his many books has also been a rich source for memories. Over the many years of analytic work, I have read most of Fromm's books. I chaired the Memorial Service for Fromm at White in 1980; chaired a 50th Anniversary at White of senior analysts who had been supervised, analyzed or taught by him; and taught courses to candidates at White on Fromm's ideas and clinical work. I have internalized his teachings, which have guided me in my analytic work and in my life (cf. D. H. Ortmeyer, 1997).

While a candidate, I had lengthy supervision with Anna Gourevitch and Ed Tauber. Each was mentored by Fromm, and acknowledged that Fromm was the major influence in their own analytic work. Let me describe two vignettes of patients in my own practice, while in supervision with Ed and Anna that hark back to Fromm's teaching.

In supervision, one of Ed's inquiries was if my supervised patient could relax and enjoy events in her life, such as dining out or going to the beach. It became clear that her doom forecasting of events was so pervasive that she could not find pleasure or satisfaction in any moments in her life. Unravelling the doom-forecasting of future events so that she could live in the moment became one major undertaking of my work with her, mentored by Ed. Ed told me that Fromm had taught him the art of play in his work with patients. By play, Ed meant, not unlike Winnicott, to help patients to experience pleasure, desire and love in the moment. Such experience builds self-regard, self-esteem and hope.

In supervision with Anna, she kept challenging me to think aloud about my ongoing therapy sessions with my patient. As I was slowly able to do so, I found that I was also sharing my thinking aloud with my patient, and slowly my patient was doing the same. Anna said that Fromm had taught her to actively think about her patients' lives; and to express her thinking to her patients at appropriate times in the analytic work. Patients would let her know if she was wrong.

In her own contribution included in this volume, Anna Gourevitch quotes Fromm's own words that he first adhered strictly to Freud's approach and that he expected to hear from the patient that which was in accordance with the theory. He related that he came to realize that he did not know the patient as a person, and he became bored with the work. He began to see the necessity of learning as much as he could about the whole patient, an individual in his society.

This view of "the individual in his society" led him to develop the concepts of "social character" and "social unconscious" as important psychoanalytic concepts for the treatment of patients. I have discussed the clinical relevance of social character and social unconscious in another publication (D. H. Ortmeyer, 2002). To briefly summarize: "Fromm was aware that characteristic interpersonal views of Self and significant others, and the accompanying linguistic-emotional style are the warp and woof of the social character, the internalized patterns commonly held in the culture, not idiosyncratic to the individual." (Ibid., p. 5.) The unconscious needs to be rendered conscious in order to live a loving, humanistic life.

His view of "the individual in his society" was remarkably important to me with my patients. As a clinician practicing in Manhattan, I saw patients who recently came from many other cultures and languages, although the majority of my patients came from urban America. Even those of my patients who were born and raised in the urban Eastern United States often had immigrant parents who maintained much of their "home" culture in their families. It was vital to find out and deeply appreciate the "culture" of the family that patients had internalized. I saw patients from Pakistan, India, Australia, several Western and Eastern European countries, Japan, China, and varied Hispanic backgrounds, to name some of the places of origin. Of course, their reasons for migrating to the U.S, and their internalization of urban U.S. culture were also important cultural events in their individual lives. Level of education achieved and urban or rural family environment make for differences in the psychoanalytic work in all cultures. Fromm discussed such differences in case seminars and their importance to the analytic work of the therapist-patient dyad being presented.

Fromm often led clinical seminars and gave Society lectures when candidates presented on-going therapy sessions with patients they were treating. When he moved to Mexico in 1950 and became Director of the Mexican Psychoanalytic Institute, he would come to New York one or two months of the year, and spend much of his time at White.

He was unusually creative in his insightful remarks about analysts' presentations of their clinical work. He liked to discuss with the presenter to understand what was "going on" between the therapist and his/her patient. He could be quite free with his appreciation as well as his critique of what was transpiring. He worked similarly with patients. His remarkably inquiring mind led to an active interchange with his patients. He could be confronting when faced with repressed difficult emotional-linguistic patterns. At other times, he could be gentle and supportive of repressed positive talents of his patients. He had a good sense of humor that could often relax his patients. He also had a remarkable memory for passages from the Old Testament and sayings of prominent European Rabbis, and would give such comments to illustrate a point.

Boredom, he said, should not be part of the analytic experience. When asked if patients were never boring, he said, of course they were. It was a major defense, a resistance, to avoid active involvement. The analyst had the responsibility of interpreting it to the patient. There was no reason for the analyst to be bored if he/she was fully involved in the relationship. The analyst could always have an active mind, wondering, questioning, thinking and feeling even if he was quiet.

When asked if he would present a case study of his work with a patient, he declined to do so. He went on to explain that others might try to copy his clinical approach rather than develop their own clinical skills in concert with their own personalities. Each analyst should use his own creative abilities to develop his individualistic style of working with patients. No two analysts were alike. Furthermore, no two patients were alike. It was better to develop clinical skills that were tailored to each therapeutic relationship. He was in agreement with the interpersonal point of view. He believed that the give-and-take of interpersonal therapy was the skill we develop rather than an intrapersonal frame that the analyst interpreted to the patient. Back in the late nineteen-fifties, his view of analytic work was highly criticized, particularly by the Freudians of the day.

He was very much in favor of a patient internalizing the changes wrought by the analytic work as soon as possible. He suggested that with neurotic patients, the analyst begins treatment at three times a week. The analyst needed to give the patient as much freedom as possible to internal-

ize change. He was willing to try changing sessions to more or less frequency per week if the patient was too resistive or becoming too dependent
in the transference upon the analyst, i.e. too idealizing of the analyst. Patients, he said, were very diverse in their needs for time and space for internalization of changes.

He thought that people had the greatest capacity to change when
they were in crisis. At that point, their resistance to insight was less because their external reality necessitated changing. Patients were more
likely to give thought to their difficulties in living and to their mental-
emotional health.

Hope, which implies a positive view of the future, was fundamental to his view of life, and it was conveyed to his patients during sessions.
He suggested that patients had often repressed a positive self-image of
their talents and abilities, just as they had repressed difficulties in their relatedness and in their living. Each needed to be brought to their conscious
mind.

Fromm was emphatic that in order to have a healthy mind, one
also had to have a healthy body. His spending years in a sanitarium in
Switzerland to overcome tuberculosis no doubt left him convinced of the
necessity of a healthy body. Clara Thompson, Director of [the William
Alanson] White [Institute] when Fromm was Chair of Faculty, strongly
agreed. She had Charlotte Selver, who approached neurosis through body-
sensory awareness, give courses at White (R. Spiegel, 1981). Fromm
would actively inquire of patients as to their body awareness, their ability
to relax, medical history, their type and frequency of exercise, sports they
played, their food habits, and intake of alcohol or drugs. He might readily
suggest that they learn how to relax their body, have a physical exam, or
exercise; perhaps even to see a trainer for exercise or a dietician for their
food habits.

He could be very warm, supportive and solicitous of severely disturbed patients, but usually referred them to someone else who had more
time at their disposal than he did. Similarly, in supervisory seminars, he
could be warm and supportive of analysts who were working with severely
disturbed patients. I presented a case to him of a disturbed young woman
who was in the oldest profession, and I was quite caring in helping her
manage her chaotic life. He was most supportive of my work with her; but
also asked what my goal was in therapy with her. I stumbled as I had not
thought beyond management. He asked me to think about it now. I said I
hoped she would be able to lead a better life. He gently recommended that
once management was not so crucial, she needed to ask herself and think
about what her own goals might be.

Fromm thought that *self-analysis* needed to be integrated into
one's conscious existence; just as care of the body needed conscious atten-

tion throughout one's life. self-analysis included dream analysis, the realization of one's potential, and thinking about one's inner free associations and outer behavior. Personal analysis, to him, was only the beginning of a lifetime of self-analysis. I have published an article on "Self-Analysis, Learning and Literature" (D. H. Ortmeyer, 1997) elsewhere so will not repeat it here. In it, I tried to portray my own internalization of mentors who help to guide my inner discourse.

I will close my view of Fromm's clinical work with a quote from Funk: "Shortly before his death Fromm said in an interview: 'It is a strange thing, most people believe that in order to live a good life, one has not to practice.' For Fromm, life was not to be taken for granted but also a task assigned. For him, it was not always an easy task. The art of living demands daily practice, using one's inner life force. This art is to be discovered both within oneself and in interaction with reality—often resisted by the 'pathology of normalcy' disguised as 'common sense.'" (R. Funk, 2000, p. 164.)

Directness in Therapy

Harold B. Davis

My experience with Fromm was a limited one, primarily as a student, hearing him lecture, and reading most, if not all, of his works. Despite the limited contact, he had a strong influence on my development as a psychoanalyst. My first memory of Fromm was hearing him speak at the New School for Social Research in 1957. I was immediately struck by the presence he expressed through his bearing, his directness, and his message. He spoke like he wrote. I do not recall the content of the lecture except that he was challenging, if not critical, of psychoanalysis as it was currently being practiced. I recall bringing one of his comments into a therapy session, and so he served as means of expressing my own criticism of my therapy at that time. However, beyond this personal reference, I was struck by his capacity to challenge the assumptions of our field.

During my doctoral studies at Michigan State University (1957-1961), I was able to have contact with Fromm since he was a faculty member for the four years I was there, coming for two intensive weeks in the fall and spring. I took a course with him the first year he taught there and sat in on the course in subsequent years. He also held regular office hours and was readily available during those times. He clearly enjoyed engaging people in discussion and learning from them as well as communicating his views. When Fromm discovered that one fellow student who met with him was a survivor of the Warsaw Ghetto, Fromm was intent to learn from the student's experience. When several students invited him to their house, he readily accepted. He was surprised that a group of students could afford to rent a house.

My recollection of him is of a man who spoke directly to the other. This directness was challenging especially in the Midwest of that time and perceived as insensitive to the self-esteem of the other, if not hostile. Even today when Fromm is discussed his clinical approach can be criticized as insensitive to the self-esteem of the patient. His style of confrontation was consistent with his directness. My sense is that Fromm took each person at his worth and never talked down to anyone. He made an assumption that patients and others did not need to be protected from what was necessary for them to hear, speaking to their strengths rather than perceiving them to be too weak to hear what he had to say. While the patients might feel shaken up, they were not devastated.

In class, he related a clinical example of a well-known Hollywood writer who consulted him regarding his inability to write something significant. Fromm asked him how he spent his days. The writer said he woke up, sat by his pool, took a swim, had breakfast, relaxed, etc. Fromm reported saying to him, "My God man, how do you expect to write anything significant living that way?" He reported that the writer was energized and quite taken by his comment, which Fromm felt, was a positive sign. This challenge could be perceived both as a criticism of the writer's life and a challenge to a higher level of living. Whether it was a criticism depended upon the relationship and the tone or manner in which it was stated. Fromm was sensitive to his impact; he said that if he felt annoyed or angry he wouldn't say anything since it would not come out right. I understand that a number of analysts who followed Fromm's style of confrontation found their patients stopping treatment, perhaps because the analysts were not able to be direct in a non-critical way. Fromm may also have minimized the transference his patients had to him so that a patient would hear from him what he might not hear from another analyst. I have found that at times, with certain patients, a simple direct statement that confronts the patient with his self-deception is a most powerful and meaningful analytic intervention.

When I was a graduate student, I was asked to present a patient to Fromm at a public forum. It was quite an experience. While some felt I was being criticized and offered support, I felt in his directness he was challenging not only me but also the approach which I was being taught in Michigan at that time. I had experienced this type of challenge from Hebrew schoolteachers and from my father, who was born in the late 1880's, so it was not foreign to me. But an important lesson I learned from Fromm was the way in which the interaction in the session expresses the transference and the importance of not only what one says but also how one acts. In presenting to him, I could not approach a clinical presentation from a traditional viewpoint. So when I read from the file and included the word "borderline," he held me accountable for the use of the word, even if it was not originally mine. In all probability the patient fit the diagnosis, but Fromm's challenge and opposition to this diagnostic term were instructive. I should think of a person and not of a diagnosis and I should think for myself.

Fromm was aware that he was perceived as critical for being unsentimental. Fromm stated that one characteristic of an analyst was "…the absence of sentimentality." He went on to say:

> "That may sound harsh to some, and I am sure that I will be quoted for utter ruthlessness towards the patient, for lack of compassion and authoritarianism and what not. Well, this may

be so. It's not my own experience with a patient, because there is something quite different from sentimentality, and that is one of the essential conditions to analyze: to experience in oneself what the patient is talking about. ... And if I don't make that attempt [to experience in smaller doses the patient's psychological state], then I think I'm not in touch with the patient." (1991c [1964], p. 38.)

The keywords here are, experience in oneself and touch i.e., to be in touch with one's own and the patient's emotional state and experience. His directness was a means of being in touch with a person without physically touching; the essence of empathy.

He told the story of a cancer patient who had an obsession that she left the gas on when she left her house, and would return to find her house on fire. She was compelled to return to her house and check that there was no fire. Fromm said her anxiety was connected to her anxiety about her cancer returning. However, he clearly stated that the patient had passed the five-year period where a return of the cancer was unlikely. If she had only been free of the cancer for two years, he would not have made the interpretation since she needed the symptom. It would have been cruel to take it away. (Cf. 1991d [1974], p. 66.)

I have selected these two examples because I believe they are what remain with me clinically from my limited experience with Fromm. They indicate that the essence of his approach was the relationship and the analyst's sensitivity as a rational authority. His approach has influenced me ever since I gave a talk entitled, "Technique: A Questionable Concept" that incorporated some of these ideas many years ago. While a technical approach to a patient was foreign, if not an anathema to Fromm, he was not insensitive to the self-esteem of the patient as the example with the cancer patient indicates. Some of his manner was in keeping with other European analysts of his generation with whom I have had contact.

Space does not permit me to indicate the many ways in which Fromm's writings and the many opportunities I had to hear him speak have influenced my thinking. Briefly, Fromm's analysis of social character and its impact on individual development coincided with my background in political science. An example of his political perceptiveness: in *The Sane Society* (1955a), he decried the political process in an alienated society where television was used to create political personalities that are sold to the public. He referred to a statement by a Republican Party member who suggested that they get a candidate who would represent the party, which for Fromm was like selling soap. The personality, aided by television, would be an endorsement of the party. The former president [George W. Bush] was sold as "a compassionate conservative". Another aspect of Fromm's writings that influenced me was his insistence on ethics, although he de-fined it differently from the usual cultural definition.

What also remains with me from my experience with Fromm was his sense of hopefulness about psychoanalysis despite his criticism of the way it was being practiced. He could see the possibility for growth in a person who had been severely damaged. He also recognized the power of the analytic setting, and said that some people had their best moments in the analytic hour. Therefore, as long as the analyst felt he could work with a person and as long as the person wanted to come, the process could be maintained. While he was critical of an endless analysis, the possibility for any one person to come for a significantly long period is an indication of the worth he placed upon an individual's life.

PART III

ERICH FROMM'S
THERAPEUTIC PRACTICE
IN THE MIRROR OF SUPERVISION

"There Is Nothing Polite
in Anybody's Unconscious"

Ruth M. Lesser

To attempt to specify 'Frommian therapeutic practice' is paradoxical when Fromm rejected any prescriptive ideas. To him, the classical emphasis on technique implied a mechanical, routinized, 'doing-to' approach, that aborted the uniqueness and vitality of 'being with' an individual patient. Furthermore, Fromm believed no two people were alike any more than two sets of fingerprints; there were *no* routine cases. Thus, the analyst could achieve understanding only through allowing herself/himself to be "soaked with" (1960a, p. 112) the individual patient's feelings and being aware of her/his own capacity for similar experiences. The analyst's self-awareness and careful observation of the particular patient took precedence over any standardized set of practices.

For Fromm, the primary goal of psychoanalysis was to enable the patient to become individuated and autonomous, with courage to transcend irrational, constricting cultural values. Since character was in large part shaped by these same values, achieving self-direction in a warped society was a difficult task that was best accomplished through an authentic encounter between analyst and patient. Fromm rejected any dogma, ritualized procedure, or a priori theory-based interpretations that denied the uniqueness and complexity of the individual patient and violated the potential for a singularly vital encounter. He was critical of existing theories, which he believed encouraged adaptation through conformity rather than self-direction, active choice and responsibility.

My understanding of Fromm's clinical approach is derived from my work with him in supervision and seminars from 1964 to 1968, when I was a candidate at New York University's Postdoctoral Program in Psychoanalysis and Psychotherapy. Fromm was living in Mexico at the time, and came to New York to teach and supervise twice each year for about a month. The seminars were held at a dining table in his home, where, on Sundays, he supplied not only edification but also bagels, lox and coffee. Over a period of four years, my individual supervision took place almost daily during his stays in New York. We sat face-to-face, in his small, sparsely furnished home/office. As we worked, there was a gracious European formality in his manner. He was always 'Dr. Fromm' to me and I was 'Dr. Lesser' to him. Yet his face was that of a gentle man. His eyes were extraordinarily expressive. At times they seemed piercing, reflecting his wish to cut through any deceit or evasion. At other times they twinkled with impish humor. At still other times they could communicate a deep warmth and tenderness (see also J. Silva García, 1989).

CASE ILLUSTRATION

In one seminar, and in my individual supervision, I presented my psychoanalytic training case, a man I had already seen for two years. Dr. Fromm had requested that the case presented in his seminar be one of a patient who reported dreams, since he enjoyed working with dreams, and felt they were more honest and revealing than other material. I was particularly eager for Dr. Fromm's guidance because the patient's persistent lateness, cancellations, and no-shows had not yielded to either my patience or my interpretations about his fears of closeness or need to control. We were deadlocked, and I was becoming increasingly bewildered, frustrated, and losing confidence in myself as an analyst. Dr. Fromm dealt with my concerns with interest and respect, requiring only an honest presentation of the material and of the interaction between the patient and me. I presented an account not only of the difficulties in the analytic relationship but also the patient's history, socioeconomic and cultural background, dreams, fantasies and symptoms.

I told Dr. Fromm that my experience with 'Stanley' had begun well. He was an articulate, intelligent, educated, Jewish professional, who espoused conventional liberal values that I shared. He seemed to be a near-perfect psychoanalytic patient, presenting dreams, fantasies and other ostensibly rich symbolic material, along with a multitude of interesting, obsessional symptoms. Consciously, I saw him as troubled and suffering, an innocent victim of his compulsions. I took his self-presentation at face value, and although I was irritated by his lateness, it did not seem directed at me. After all, he was late everywhere, including work. I did not seriously question the sincerity of his apologies. We were both very civilized and earnest. When we did meet, he treated me with seeming respect, nurturing a wishful vision of myself as a benign, well-intentioned authority.

Stan had sought treatment because he was "hamstrung by compulsive habits." He engaged in endless rituals including repeatedly checking his closet to see whether any dust had settled on his clothes; using Saran Wrap to cover pocket change and torn, dirty papers lying on top of his dresser; carefully folding his filthy handkerchiefs, having "the neatest dirty laundry in town," etc. He complained that it often took him two to four hours to leave his apartment. Fromm later characterized him as "King of the Closet."

He had had a lifetime history of superficial, detached relationships with people. There were very few girlfriends from adolescence on. Those he did have were uneducated Gentiles whom he had held in contempt. He also never had any real friendships with boys or men. He tagged along after high school athletes (also non-Jewish) who came from a lower socio-economic class, and had no interest in education or any intellectual pursuits.

Embarrassed by his scholarly achievements, he played them down and willingly did the boys' bidding by running their errands, and getting drunk with them. Later he flunked out of graduate school in his eagerness to be included by the gang. Still later, when he was stationed in Germany after World War II, he was a hanger-on with former Hitler supporters. He even offered himself as fodder for their anti-Semitic jokes.

When I began working with him, he reported a fantasy: "There was a fire. I was trying to impress you. I rescued you and the two children. You had a 6-year-old boy who was almost overcome by smoke, and there was a 9-month-old in the crib. The boy was on my back and I held the baby with his legs around me. Only you suffered any injury. Then I came to visit you in the hospital. The children were alright. I was aware of being a hero. Your gratitude was effusive. Your children weren't there, but your husband was. He was cool like a mannequin. You suffered burns."

In contrast to the melodrama of his daydream, his reported sleeping dreams demonstrated his alienation, deadness and passivity. In one, he followed orders given by a machine—a radar tower radioing Voice of America messages. In another he wondered about who was in political power. He also dreamed that his girlfriend had given him a long list of impossible demands to relay to the cleaning lady. (In reality, the girlfriend had sent him to the clinic because of his obsessional behavior.) He ostensibly complied with the instructions rather than directly revealing his objections. His dreams depicted a dehumanized, impersonal world.

With this data, Fromm developed a formulation of what he called the basic, unconscious character orientation, which in Stan's case was anal sadistic. However, unlike Freudian analysts, he did not use this term to indicate libidinal fixation at a particular developmental level. Rather, Fromm was describing a person who related to the world in terms of overt and covert power operations through which he dissociated his enormous sense of helplessness and rage. This was evidenced in Stan admiring and ingratiating himself with powerful aggressors throughout his life.

Fromm pointed out that Stan continually betrayed himself. He denied his Jewishness, his intellectual achievements, and any need for relationships of substance. He never took a stand that would alienate him from those in power, even though he consciously pictured himself as a fervent supporter of the oppressed. While espousing liberal values like honesty, peace, productive work and responsibility, he reported good times with former Nazis. Fromm further observed that this man had no real concern for anyone, including me. He believed that Stan's passivity and eagerness to follow the gang could allow him to become a fascist in a different society.

It was a struggle for me to absorb Fromm's observations because I had been so taken in by Stanley's self-description, and his apparent trust in me. Although I knew intellectually that his lateness expressed his need to control and that I had occasionally felt hurt, I hadn't allowed myself to fully experience his hostility. Once Fromm had articulated his perceptions, I realized that Stan's apologies and sheepish looks were a disguise for his underlying scorn and contempt for me. As I continued to work with Stan, it became more and more apparent that Fromm's view was largely accurate. However, while Fromm was skeptical about Stan's ability to change his patterns of relatedness, or become more autonomous, I felt Stan might have more capacity for genuine compassion and feeling than Fromm saw.

Fromm believed the main thrust of the analysis should be an examination of the contradictions between Stan's view of himself as a moral, courageous rescuer (as in his fantasy about saving me), and his unconscious alliance with evil power—the good boy versus the angry sadist. The first task was to communicate to Stan in a direct, authoritative—but not authoritarian—way my perceptions of his character. All further inquiry should be guided by the goal of helping Stan become aware of his orientation, his 'secret plot', as we had formulated it, and the deleterious consequences for his sense of well-being. Every opportunity should be taken to contrast discrepancies and contradictions of his verbal communications with his basic feelings. Fromm recognized that his contrite, apologetic demeanor could easily instill in me a sense of experiencing myself as a vicious sadist, and suggested that the quality of confrontations could be lightened by using humor to express skepticism. He saw a raised eyebrow, or a chuckle, along with a statement such as, "Do you really believe that?" or "Is that so?" as useful. However, rather than prescribing specific interventions, Fromm encouraged me to use my own individual resources and style.

Fromm also cautioned me that historical data or fantasies ('false dreams') did not accurately represent Stan's unconscious values and feelings, since as conscious formulations they were greatly influenced by social norms. He saw Stan's daydream as cheap melodrama, full of banalities and clichés. Thus, in his daydream cited above, Stan achieved a sense of power and benevolence after heroically saving my children from a burning house. However, there was no evidence of any feeling for me (I had been injured), only a need to impress. His underlying scorn and contempt was revealed in his concurrent dream of me as a cleaning lady.

As stated above, Fromm thought I had to communicate directly my perception of Stan's character as soon as possible. Fromm believed this was an essential step in every analysis. It demonstrated the analyst's competence and that the patient had been listened to, understood and taken seriously. Conveying a sense of urgency rather than a notion of embarking on a leisurely "fishing expedition" was also necessary. Thus, I should let Stan know I wouldn't accept his attempts to rationalize, cover up and play innocent.

When I asked Dr. Fromm how to deal with Stan's lateness, he recommended that I delay discussion until I fully understood its meaning. This would defuse my anger and allow a constructive exploration in the context of his core character. Fromm thought my anger (and any strong emotional response by the analyst) represented a failure of understanding, and its expression would be destructive.

Nevertheless, to block Stanley's efforts to maintain power and control, Fromm advised me to confront the manipulativeness of his behavior head on. He told me that he might say to such a patient: "Now look here, we're not playing a game. If you continue to come late I won't see you. We're not playing cat and mouse. Twenty minutes late and that's it." For similar reasons, Fromm advised me to substantially raise Stanley's extremely low clinic fee, relative to his financial resources. Fromm commented that to Stanley it was well worth the paltry sum to miss or come late for an appointment to maintain control and express his scorn and contempt for me and our work.

The patient kept testing me, eventually arriving 18 minutes late. As I became more comfortable about asserting my authority in the interest of our work, I changed the time limit and told him he would only have five minutes leeway. I had to call upon all my strength to stick to this rule, but it served to mobilize his seriousness in attending to his life in a no-nonsense, realistic fashion.

It was difficult for me to maintain a sustained effort to challenge and uncover Stanley's disguised feelings. I had to fight my own tendency to slip back and collude with his conscious view of himself as an innocent victim, a champion of the underdog. I did not want to be aware of his sadistic qualities. However, by challenging his evasions and rationalizations and blocking any routes of escape, as Fromm had recommended, Stanley was forced to address his basic issues. Initially, I hardly noticed the change, which was first manifested in the quality of his descriptions of his experiences. Instead of the melodrama, his reports became more sincere and matter-of-fact. As we continued the work, it became clear that his need to impress, kowtow or defy me or others significantly diminished. He became noticeably less anxious and more aware of who he was.

My work with this patient continued for several years. The major task was to explore how his way of relating to others led to the sacrifice of his integrity. We also explored how his interest in securing power through manipulativeness and identification with powerful others often resulted in feelings of helplessness, loneliness and alienation. As time went on, Stan seemed more vital, rebelling against conventional powers in a constructive fashion and making significant contributions through his work. His capacity for engaging with others improved, most clearly in his loving relationship with his children. When he became highly anxious his compulsive symptoms would flair up to some extent, though never as dramatically as when I first worked with him.

THE ANALYTIC RELATIONSHIP

Fromm's view of the analytic situation radically differed from classical ideas. He disagreed with Freud's focus on etiology, reconstruction, and promotion of the transference regression. The latter, he thought, encouraged a childlike dependency on the analyst, antithetical to the primary psychoanalytic goal of fostering the patient's autonomy in the present.

Further, according to 1964 and 1965 seminar notes, he believed that a priori theoretical constructions impeded understanding because they obscured the individual's unique life experience. The analyst's goal was to help the patient discover his/her true identity through shedding conscious illusions, thus releasing repressed potential.

Fromm felt it important to address the adult, mature aspects of the patient. To this end, he abandoned the use of the couch in favor of a face-to-face encounter where each participant could be fully seen by the other. Analytic anonymity, even if possible, was not in the interest of understanding the patient or advancing analytic goals. Fromm acknowledged that this required a great deal of courage in the analyst—courage to allow herself/himself to be fully known and to take an independent stand even in the face of the patient's anxieties or anger.

For Fromm, the analyst had to be aware of her/his own feelings. Cognition alone did not suffice, and, in fact, could be misleading if one sought genuine contact with another. This did not mean analysts had to share their private lives or feelings. Fromm certainly discouraged countertransference confessions, because he was concerned about their seductive and/or manipulative motivations. He did, however, believe that questions about public aspects of the analyst's life should be answered unhesitatingly. Fromm saw the conventional insistence on 'analyzing' such questions as trivial and a waste of time.

Further, Fromm was clearly convinced that analysts should openly support humanistic values both inside and outside the consulting room. He himself publicly participated in important social causes. I remember telling him about my anxiety when I met a young woman patient at a peace march. As a more traditionally-trained analyst, I was worried that being seen outside the consulting room would hinder the process. Fromm said, on the contrary, that this was a fortunate event. Because the patient saw me stand up for my beliefs she might be able to muster her courage to rebel and separate from her very conventional, controlling mother.

Fromm was also convinced that patients know more about the analyst than either acknowledged. Therefore, his answer to many personal questions about himself would be, "If you wanted to know that, you could." He seized every opportunity to encourage patients to be observant and to express their observations of the analyst. He would actively inquire about their views of him, and recommended that patients' accurate perceptions be validated and that congratulations might well be useful. He also considered carefully any observations that might pertain to aspects of himself that were out of his awareness.

Fromm had a complex view of the analyst's subjective responsiveness to the patient. On the one hand, he saw the analyst's consciousness of her/his emotional life as essential for the purpose of fully experiencing the patient's experience. The knowledge thus gained facilitated the patient's awareness of her/his own dissociated inner life. On the other hand he, like other analysts of his day (from Freud to Sullivan, and Horney), believed that the analyst's role was properly that of an expert—a 'trained instrument'. It followed that Fromm conceptualized countertransference as an 'unfortunate' result of the analyst's incomplete understanding of the patient and/or her/himself (R. I. Evans, 1966). Thus, he cautioned his supervisees to be alert to the influences of their biases and blind spots. Even before the inception of treatment, when deciding whether to work with the patient, the analyst must ask whether the patient was of genuine interest or was simply an income-producing or status-enhancing object; whether the analyst's stake in the outcome was greater than the patient's; whether the analyst was promising more help than she/he could deliver; whether her/his own character orientation would impede the process with a given patient.

Unlike many analysts, Fromm believed that the analyst as participant could not be entirely clear about the nature of her/his participation, and so cautioned against a focus on the analytic relationship as a primary source of data or interpretive interventions. He believed that analysts too often used transference interpretations defensively, to avoid their own anxiety or to avoid an authentic encounter with the patient. Data from the patient's daily life was less likely to be contaminated by the analyst's subjectivity.

Given these considerations, the optimal analytic attitude, according to Fromm, was that of a rational, mature authority, who was an 'observant participant'. I believe that he would have disagreed with those, including some of his closest associates (e.g., E. S. Tauber, 1954), who advocated the use of countertransference as primary data for understanding the patient. The analyst's emotional reaction was her/his own responsibility and should not be attributed to the patient's provocation. Nor, as indicated above, would Fromm have approved of communicating strong emotional reactions to the patient.

Recent attempts to find similarities between Fromm's ideas and other theorists (D. Burston, 1991; M. Bacciagaluppi, 1989) obscure essential differences in perspective. His aversion to any ingenuousness on the part of the analyst would rule out attempts to use empathy as a technical device (e.g., H. Kohut, 1971). Similarly, he would object to the idea of the "analyst ... [having] to seem to want to give what [was] really only given because of the patient's needs." (D. W. Winnicott, 1947, p. 203) He would also object to conceptualizing the analyst as parent, since this would not only be inauthentic, it also infantilized the patient. Most important, Fromm's social concerns and attention to socioeconomic factors in the formation of character and in everyday life were distinctive and crucial. No other psychoanalytic theorist has contributed as significantly to a systematic examination of these issues theoretically or clinically.

People have sometimes characterized Fromm as confrontational and judgmental in both his supervisory and analytic stance. This is perhaps understandable because unlike more cautious, traditional analysts he always focused directly on what he saw as the patient's core orientation and/or the supervisee's difficulty. There was no waiting for just the right moment, no hesitation about articulating his judgments, and no equivocation about just the right dosage of truth. With good-humored irony, he noted, "There is nothing polite in anybody's unconscious," including the analyst's. One of his most characteristic phrases after hearing some story from a patient or supervisee was, "Now, look here...," after which he would explain what he observed about the patient's character (see R. I. Evans, 1966; A. H. Feiner, 1975). These words, out of context, may convey an impression of a moralistic authority. Yet, as I sat with Fromm, I heard a sense of urgency. Time was precious. He once said that a surgeon who sees a tumor on the lung moves swiftly to excise it. He was profoundly committed to the task he took most seriously, which was, as Tauber so eloquently described, "to grasp life, to search and to dare uncertainty" (E. S. Tauber, 1959, p. 10). His directness, then, was not condemnation but an expression of hope and faith that speaking honestly and clearly to the healthy, striving adult in the patient would foster awareness and ultimately the freedom to fulfill unexplored potentialities.

CONCLUSION

Several authors have said that Fromm had intended to write a book about technique (see, for example, M. Bacciagaluppi, 1989; and B. Landis, 1981). My own experience leads me to doubt it. He rarely procrastinated. Matters important to him were always given a high priority. For example, during the 1968 presidential campaign, he dropped all prior commitments, supervisory appointments and seminars to participate in Eugene McCarthy's campaign, and to write *The Revolution of Hope* (1968a) so as to inspire public criticism of the Vietnam War.

In our supervisory contacts, he showed no interest in codifying a 'Frommian' technique, whether in book form or in directives to me about how to conduct my work. Fromm encouraged me to use my own judgment to express observations and to be confident in my own beliefs. His respectful attitude toward me (as well as toward my patients) allowed me to talk about significant personal conflicts without shame or fear of being judged. His responsive understanding helped me become more profoundly aware of both unused potential and dissociated limitations. It was an exhilarating experience to know him and be known by him. As an analyst, I began to feel a little less anxious more of the time.

However, I take issue with Fromm's advice to me that the primary focus of the analytic inquiry be on data outside the relationship. I invite and value a less hierarchical, more personally expressive collaboration with patients because I believe the analyst and patient must articulate and examine their experience of each other both as vital information and as a precondition for change. Correction for the analyst's subjectivity can and must be found by listening carefully and respectfully to the patient's perceptions, and seeking corroboration in the patient's daily life. In retrospect, the work with Stan would have been more vital had we more directly addressed his contempt, hostility and attachment to me as well as my response to him. On the other hand, I agree with Fromm that the analyst's emotional response is by definition subjective. Therefore, it must be used cautiously.

Whatever the differences in our views, during the last 28 years Fromm has been a crucial influence on my work. Following his suggestions to take seriously patients' observations and to encourage mutual directness in the analytic relationship, I have the good fortune to be reanalyzed in almost every session. Also, when difficulties and disappointments occur in the psychoanalytic engagement, I remember Dr. Fromm's statement about his own analytic work: "I never promise to cure anybody. But I try to provide a few rich hours."

"What Have You Learned about Yourself from Your Patient?"

Robert U. Akeret

Our first two-hour session was scheduled to begin at 10:00 A.M. on a Monday. That morning I was up at 5:00, had dressed and breakfasted by 6:00, and was out pacing Riverside Park and talking to myself by 7:00. The case I planned to present was Seth's, and to that end I had brought with me most of my records on him as well as tape recordings of two of our therapy sessions and a rather heavy reel-to-reel tape recorder-player. [...]

Physically, Fromm was hardly an imposing figure. Rather short and somewhat plump, he was modestly dressed in open shirt, tweed jacket, and dark trousers. His thick, still dark hair was combed straight back from his squarish face, and he wore rimless bifocals that seemed to emphasize the bushiness of his eyebrows. The man's famed intensity—his highly focused energy—was instantly palpable. I felt it in the powerful intelligence that shone through his eyes, yet it also seemed to radiate from his entire face; for lack of a better term, I would say that Erich Fromm had a robust aura.

Once inside Fromm's small, book-strewn office, I remained standing, searching the walls for a socket in which to plug the recorder. Fromm watched me for a moment, looking rather bemused, and then said, "Tell me, Dr. Akeret, what do you know of narcissism?"

I stared back at him, the recorder still in my hand. My God, it was a test! If I didn't pass, he would surely turn me right back out the door to make room for a better-prepared student. "Yes, narcissism," I fumbled. "Self-absorption, a total immersion in one's own ..."

"Let me tell you a little story." Fromm interrupted, his eyes twinkling. "When I was a young man studying in Frankfurt, I was constantly worried that I would make career choices that would set me on the wrong path and I'd never be able to get back on track again. I could be quite obsessive and obnoxious on this subject. Well, one day I said to my uncle, 'What will become of me?' and my uncle instantly replied, 'You, Erich? You will become an old Jew!'"

He burst into laughter, and in a moment I was laughing with him. Then he gestured to the chair beside his desk. I set down the tape player and sat, my head spinning. What had just happened here? In a single little anecdote Fromm had shown me the folly of trying to impress him with my preparation and earnestness. I was here to learn, not to be his star student. He had managed to tell me this in a self-effacing, humorous story without a hint of direct criticism. What's more, in laughing together, we had made immediate emotional contact. Thus began my training with Dr. Fromm.

I proceeded to tell him about Seth, his presenting problem, his background, and my work with him to date. Fromm listened enthusiastically, nodding his head, shaking his head, smiling, frowning, and hitting the edge of his desk with his open hand. He reacted as if he had never heard such a bizarre and compelling story in his life, although I knew very well that he had literally heard thousands of similar stories in his professional career. But of course, that was the point: No two stories—no two persons—are the same. One must always focus on the patient's individuality, not see him as a 'type' or as an example of a particular psychological syndrome. Again Fromm was not offering this to me as a lesson; he simply believed that this was so and was acting accordingly.

When I finished my presentation, he said, "What a battle you have on your hands, Doctor. I wish you great strength."

He turned in his chair and gazed for a moment out the window onto the Hudson. It was early April. The sky was bright; the trees in the park were just budding. Then he turned back to me.

"Sadism is always so sad, don't you think? Such a sad attempt to compensate for powerlessness. A sad attempt to transmute impotence into omnipotence. Your patient must have lived a painfully curtailed life with this monstrous mother of his. I see it everywhere I look in the world—a will to destructiveness as the result of an unlived life."

I wanted to reach in my pocket for my pen and notebook so that I could jot down his words and study them later, but I knew that that was not the way Fromm wanted me to learn from him. The ideas were important, but the immediacy of our responses to each other was more so.

"What really strikes me about Seth's fantasies is how mechanistic they are," Fromm went on. "A bloodletting *machine*, an orgasm *machine*. In his fantasies he is an object, not a living human being. It is so thoroughly necrophilic; the man is trying to objectify himself out of existence."

A couple minutes later he asked me, "Do you think in his core he truly wants to escape from this mother fortress of his?"

"Yes, I really believe he does," I said, then added, "That's just my feeling, of course."

"*Only* your feeling, Dr. Akeret?" he laughed. "Tell me, what else do we have to go on in our work—signs from God?"

A moment later he said, "Your patient knows that it all begins and ends with this terrifying mother, doesn't he? He knows it, and *yet* he doesn't know it at all."

"Exactly," I said.

"It is not easy," Fromm said, shaking his head back and forth. "Sometimes telling a patient that he is angry with his mother is like telling Hamlet that he is not fond of his stepfather. The patient has to feel it in his blood to really know it."

Fromm asked me about Seth's dreams, and I automatically reached for my records. Seth was a prolific dreamer with great recall, and I had carefully recorded all the dreams he'd told me. Fromm made a dismissive gesture with his hand.

"Just one that you remember," he said.

I recounted the most recent dream Seth had told me. It was just a snippet, really. In the dream, Seth struck his mother with all his might, but she didn't feel a thing. After a couple more of these hits, the mother turned to Seth and said, "That's wonderful, darling! Show your anger! Do it more!"

"Marvelous!" Fromm cheered. "What do you make of it, Dr. Akeret?"

The dream's meaning seemed eminently clear to me.

"It shows how powerless—how impotent—he feels in relation to his mother. Hard as he tries, he can't make a dent in her," I said.

"But what about *you*?" Fromm asked. "How did you fare in this dream, Dr. Akeret?"

I gazed back at him, perplexed. I didn't see myself in this dream anywhere.

"Oh, she's very clever this woman, even in his dreams," Fromm said. "This business of 'Show your anger! Do it more, darling!'—why, it's a devastating parody of psychotherapy itself. A parody of *you*! She's mocking you, Doctor. She still has all the power over him, and she knows it. And so, obviously, does Seth."

He leaned toward me in his chair.

"The battle lines are drawn very clearly, Dr. Akeret," he said. "It's like the wager God made with Satan for the possession of Job's soul. And the devil always starts with an advantage—the advantage of not being restricted by moral considerations."

A few minutes later I glanced at my watch for the first time since I'd entered Fromm's office. It was eleven forty-five. I only had fifteen minutes left, and there was a question I needed to ask.

"Do you think Seth could become really dangerous?" I asked. "Act out his fantasies and actually hurt someone—his wife perhaps?"

"Yes, that's a real possibility, I'm afraid," Fromm answered seriously.

"My God, what can I do?" I blurted.

"Help him choose life," Fromm replied quietly.

We both remained silent for a moment. It was time to leave. Fromm smiled warmly at me.

"So, Doctor," he said, "what have you learned about yourself from your patient?"

I thought I had misheard him.

"About him?" I fumbled.

"No, about *yourself,* Akeret. What you learn about him follows from what you learn about yourself."

For some reason unknown to me, my dream of a few nights earlier suddenly popped back into my consciousness. It was, I thought, the most transparent dream I'd had in years, and when I'd awoken, I was pretty sure that it had been stimulated by my recent sessions with Seth. In the dream I rowed a dinghy across a stormy channel to a little one-room weather-worn cottage on an island. Inside, in the middle of this room, was a large, soft bed, and lying in it was my mother in a nightgown. She motioned for me to join her in the bed, and in great excitement I dove under the covers with her.

When I told the dream to Fromm, he clapped his hands together enthusiastically.

"Wonderful! I do believe you will be able to help this poor fellow," he said. "You are already swimming together in the same waters."

"The Oedipal waters," I said, smiling.

Fromm became intensely serious again. "There is a portion in the Talmud that speaks of such dreams," he said. "It says that a man who dreams of watering an olive tree with olive oil has incestuous desires. But a man who dreams of sleeping with his mother is seeking after knowledge."

At noon I walked out into the sunshine feeling positively high. I was so bursting with energy that rather than head directly home, I walked over to the park and, tape player still in hand, bopped along the path, grinning like a schoolboy.

"What Is this Patient Really After?"

George D. Goldman

The following is an account of a case presented to Erich Fromm for supervision in July of 1958. I had recently graduated from the William Alanson White Institute and was anxious to work on a case with Dr. Fromm.

Dr. Fromm was seen in his New York home on Riverside Drive 180. He was on a long visit from his permanent residence in Mexico. He was very open and did not display any strong need for anonymity and neutrality. Sessions would extend through his lunch hour, at which time he would have his maid bring his lunch, which he would casually eat without apology or explanation, or allowing extra time. He would also answer telephone calls during our session. Two other details stand out in my memory. He was quite casual in attitude and dress; at no time did he wear a jacket. The other detail concerned my awareness of his experiencing physical (stomach) discomfort at times during the sessions, which he verbalized.

First my overview of his *theoretical framework for treatment*: He felt if the real person YOU, could make contact in reality with the core of the real OTHER, then and only then could therapy take place. Timing, theoretical frame of reference, developmental theory, one's readiness to hear, the potential of the confrontation, and stirring up resistance were all dismissed. If you knew something about the patient, you didn't keep it secret. The patient was more often than not ready to hear it. The countertransferential acting-out dangers seemed to be minimized by him, although he did focus a lot on the therapist. Perhaps I realized with bitterness that some of the bad habits I have exhibited in the past, like answering the phone during sessions, I learned from him. I justified them by saying that this authority on 'exploitation' did not consider what he did to be exploitation, so why should I? I have fought my own tendencies to act-out as he did during supervision since then and have, I hope, controlled them.

THE CASE

The patient was a 28-year-old, single, white Jewish male, born and raised in a nearby metropolitan area. He was employed as a marketing consultant for a Madison Avenue management firm. He had an older, married sister, age 30, and a younger, single brother, age 24. The patient's father was described as a small man, lacking in ambition, initiative, and responsibility. His one asset was that he was a warm person. The patient's mother was the stronger parent. She was gregarious, active in the synagogue sisterhood and in local politics, and the one who made the family decisions.

The following interpersonal events, which the patient had labeled as the "white bread incident" and the "towel incident," were presented to Dr. Fromm with the above brief history. The white bread incident occurred when the patient was 13 years old. He was sent to the store on a Sunday night to buy a rye bread. The bakery did not have any rye bread; the delicatessen next door did not either. He brought back a white bread. The patient's mother then "blew her top," telling him he was stupid, inept, and in general berated him for bringing white bread when he knew the family never ate white bread. The story was supposed to illustrate how his mother never gave him a chance to use his own judgment but tried instead to dominate him completely.

The second incident occurred when the patient was 23 years old and living at home. He asked his mother for a large bath towel to wash his car. She said a small one would be sufficient. He again asked for a large one. She came all the way out to the car with the large towel but, before handing it to him, tore it in half and gave him the two smaller pieces, saying she was sure this would be enough.

The case was presented to Dr. Fromm to help clarify what could be done with long-term dependency. Dr. Fromm said,

"Why would the patient call these 'incidents'? They seem to be ordinary life experiences. He seems to be collecting further proof that he is innocent. Saying, 'See, it's all my mother's fault. If you can help, OK, but what can one do?' This historical exploitation is a nice rationalization to continue his lack of responsibility. It reminds me of Freud's life. When he was seven years old, he wet the rug in his parents' room. His father said to him that he was a no-good boy who would never amount to anything. Freud then used this 'trauma' to explain his ambition. But looking back to the time when Freud was two years old, there was an earlier experience where Freud, the very young child, wet his father's bed and when admonished said, 'Don't worry, when I am older and wealthy, I will buy a new big, red bed! So the father's wrath at Freud, age seven, was only a secondary reaction to his son's contempt. Freud was the complete favorite of his mother. He was not a harmless little boy, but a little dictator.

"Analysts can be much too uncritical of their patients. Why didn't the boy bring home rye bread? Could it really be possible that there was no rye bread available in town? He knew the family did not eat white bread. What was he trying to do by so innocently bringing white bread? This is nonsense. This boy is tied and was tied to his mother. He was her favorite, the crown prince who roared for the reins of government. The weak father protest is not the case. Be careful in assessing the infant. Were the parents so bad? Or, was the patient so innocent? And, were these incidents so traumatic? What lies behind them?

"The patient and analyst should never enter into a gentlemen's agreement that says to the patient, 'you are right and you are a fine young man.' The patient will feel safe, feeling his parents were wrong, since he, then, does not have to take responsibilities. The behavior of the patient could be provoked. In analyzing present behavior, the analyst should ask himself: Why is this behavior still continuing? Present behavior can be a repetition of childhood traumas, but often many things have changed. This patient has succeeded in talking of his mother all the time."

Dr. Fromm didn't believe that this was the patient's real problem (that the mother was so controlling). "The patient had the idea he had to be the greatest hero in the world. Then his mother's 'promise' would be fulfilled. This, and his competition with men (tied in with his contempt for his father), are the sources of his great ambition. He sets ambition to be everything. When he does this, his relations with others can only have this driven quality. But this doesn't explain why he has been sick all this time. He holds on by his continued talking. He hates anyone who stands in his way on the path to the good life that was 'promised.'

"The historical method is fine for pinning down the patient's anger. But you can best feel the peculiar quality of it in the present. Watch for what in the patient's story is tricky. What is he hiding? The patient is not so innocent. He did not live up to his obligations. He still doesn't. He pleads his innocence through many incidents. He fooled you. He wanted to. But he also wants to get well. He resents it terribly that you could be fooled. He will not forgive you."

I asked Dr. Fromm about tracing back the 'pattern' of fooling a significant authority. Dr. Fromm said, "The patient succeeded in fooling you. That is enough. That is a fact. Why go back? It is also a fact that while he did all he could to seduce you, he resents it that he could. This is a very frequent situation that I see as I supervise analysts. They enter into a secret gentlemen's agreement with their patients. Both fool the other. Both pretend that all is going well until one of the two explodes."

I discussed my theory of psychoanalysis. This, in summary, is: No child is born bad, mean, etc. Behavior that is now uncomfortable and getting the patient into difficulties with people was learned in order to cope with a situation that once existed for this patient. If one can delineate what the patient is doing, what he learned it for, and with whom, it can be seen to be unnecessary. Then, as the situation which called it forth no longer exists, the patient with courage to change can, with help, evolve a new pattern.

Dr. Fromm agreed in general with this, but added, "If after five years the patient is still in treatment, the method is not being successful. You should ask yourself, 'What is this patient really after?' He wants admiration, to be superior to other men; he wants to find people who will cater to him, feed him, follow his every whim. He tries to manipulate people into this role. Aside from being pampered, he wants very little. To accomplish this, he is charming but utterly insincere. He doesn't really give a damn for anyone else. He isn't so innocent. He is tricky. It comes out in his story of the incidents. To do what he did, he has to be tricky."

Dr. Fromm suggested that if the patient called me a fool, I should say, "I have been a fool, but where do we go from here? You have been splendidly manipulative. It must have been more important to prove me a fool than to get better." Dr. Fromm felt this was part of the patient's pattern of showing up men:

"In her 'promise' that she would protect him when ill or weak, understand him when he was troubled, etc., the mothering one gave to the young child, she was also asking him to be everything for her. The father would be seen as ineffectual if he did not protect his son from a mother like this. This boy was under her power and today continues to fall under the power of a woman. He wants to be better than other men so that he will be keeping his part of the bargain. If he succeeds, he will find someone who will be glad to take care of him. He does try for this through trickery and charm, but he is utterly unrelated. Everything is by bluff.

"What is the reason? Is it that his mother was so strict? This is nonsense. He and his mother, both, probably worked well in belittling the father. She didn't do enough for the patient, he felt. You fell for the patient's sob story. What a tragedy it is to be 28 years old and tell of this as illustration of your life. This might be something to tell the patient."

Dr. Fromm felt that if this was said, the patient would have to come to grips with his problems: "Now the patient is making a lot out of nothing. All I see *in* the 'incidents' is the patient and his mother arguing about who is right, about the triviality of who is right. You as an analyst should ask yourself, 'Why should a man of his age spend his time with all this bullshit?'"

I then presented the first *dream* of the patient to Dr. Fromm: "I walked into a room and two men were wrestling on the floor. Suddenly, one man got on top of the other and took a knife and slit the other man from crotch to belly button. I yelled, 'What is happening?' The man underneath said, 'Don't worry, we are only playing.' Then I noticed he didn't have a penis."

The man underneath, according to the patient's associations, was the husband of a woman with whom he had had an affair. The knife was one with which his mother had threatened to kill him when the patient was five years old and naughty. The patient and I agreed that the dream demonstrated the patient's competition with men and need to belittle them, transforming them into women, being contemptuous of them so he could feel superior.

Dr. Fromm said, "The theme is his competition with other men. To sleep with a married woman is always a sign of a deep competitiveness with other men. He always had the desire to be superior to other men. He made the other man small by making him into a woman. "In analyzing his dream, the patient starts with the realistic present situation (the affair with the married woman). He then associates to his mother and the knife. This is the family situation. The mother and he are allies. Again, there is a different slant on his relationship with his mother. What has gone on is a deep alliance between this boy and his mother. Yet when she did not give him enough (all that he wanted), he felt cheated. This is the opposite of what he gives consciously.

"One other important factor. This is all play—yet one man is mutilated in a gruesome way. This is life for this man. There is a great fear of reality breaking in. This is the main fear of people who have not detached themselves from their mothers. Life is still the child's world. Nothing that happens will not be taken care of by the mother of the child if the child keeps his promise and is what his mother 'wanted him' to be. Many of these mother-dependent people keep this attitude throughout life. Life remains a charmed world. Nothing is really serious. 'Life cannot touch me' is their attitude. They have never really thought of questions of their powerlessness and helplessness in terms of the inevitability of death, etc. Their only feeling is that they will be protected if they are 'good.' They do not ever take the responsibility of being adults. The only time that reality ever breaks in is when something real comes up that cannot be averted by this fantasy world, such as a girl they love leaving them, inevitable illness, or death. This shows the patient how unprotected he is and can become a really positive event. This seems to have happened when his girl left him.

"Analysis can, if one is not aware of what is happening, increase this sense of unreality (in these mother-dependent people). The analyst now protects him from reality. In father-centered people, there is more reality orientation because of the father's role as the disciplinarian. If they do well, they are praised; if they do poorly, they are punished. In reality, this boy was the apple of his mother's eye. She wanted him to be a success so she could be proud of him. Because of her 'promise' of protection, he has never left the closed shelter of his unreal world. For such a person, when reality breaks in, the mother could not protect him. With all his charm, he cannot change this. Then is when he felt his first real panic.

"As an analyst, you should never participate in this protective atmosphere. If after analyzing a patient such as this for one year, you see that nothing happens, you tell him of this quite bluntly and then say if no progress is seen at the end of a second year you will quit. The patient must accept responsibility for change. This is reality.

"If you could have said all of this to the patient after his dream, since he was aware that reality could break in, the patient could change. Under the threat of reality breaking in, a patient can change considerably. Analysts often make the mistake that great changes don't take place unless there is a great inner change. In reality, a great threat can make for great change. This person, regardless of his age, had protected himself from reality all his life. Everything in life had gone according to his charming manipulations. Panic for him is the feeling: 'I am on my own and utterly unable to handle it.' This is so often true in mother-attached people. For them, no feeling is real; happy or sad, life remains unreal."

Dr. Fromm asked me a question about the patient's ex-girlfriend. I could not answer it fully. Dr. Fromm said, "If you hear a story, provided you listen at all, the story should become as clear as if you had been there. You should never be left with the feeling that you don't fully understand anything the patient says. If you don't, there will just be a lot of accumulated misunderstandings. You should keep this as a basic rule. Do not fail to question unless, in listening, it becomes so clear that you feel you were actually there."

The patient had had the following *dream* three months before: "I dreamed that I was dreaming about having intercourse with my girlfriend. (This made me sexy the next day.) In my dream's dream, I had satisfactory intercourse, and in the dream, I had a nocturnal emission. My father came into the room. (In reality, when I lived at home, my father would be the one to awaken me.) To do this, he tried to take the covers off. I didn't want him to see the wet pajamas. He grabbed the blankets and pulled. I screamed, 'Daddy, don't.' I woke, but went back to sleep and continued dreaming. My mother then came in. Although she was curious about what was going on underneath, she didn't pull the covers off."

The patient's associations were: "The dream's meaning is obvious. Sex is bad. I'm ashamed, guilty. I see my parents coming in as a fear of being caught." Dr. Fromm asked to hear all about the patient's girlfriend and the patient's relationship with her. He wanted to know her social class, religion, background, and appearance. He then said,

"I have heard his associations, and it is all trash, just words. Why not say this to him? The main problem is to engage the patient, to listen and really react, to get into a situation where he cannot kid himself. Say to him, 'You say your mother did not respect you. You have no self-respect. How can anyone respect you?' Wake him up to a reality instead of prolonging the fiction. 'Sure you have no self-respect, but it is not because of your mother.' One engages oneself, and one sees. We do not know what will be the outcome. The analyst must feel faith in this man becoming alive. If you believe this, you must engage him. Force him by your attitude to talk of something real, in a way that is real. That is all I know when I am analyzing someone. I don't know if I will cure him, or what will come next. I am as utterly real as I can be. I forget I am an analyst. I am like him, a person. I talk with authority because I talk with myself being expressed. I talk of my own reactions. If the patient talks with this very intelligent talk, we are not engaging one another. Try to engage him by making real comments, by reacting to him. It doesn't matter if you are right or wrong as long as it is the real you reacting. I feel the dream means: He says that he is afraid of sex, that it is evil. He says he is afraid his folks will expose him, that his father is worse. This doesn't fit.

"They are showing him he is still a little boy. 'You are a little boy who still wets the bed.' He sees himself not as a man. His father has been rougher. He wants to eliminate the father. The mother is much more understanding. She would say that it is all right to sleep with a girl as long as you do not love her. Actually, his problem with his girlfriend is that he acted like a demanding pampered little boy. In the dream, he senses he is a little boy, and so when he has an affair he can only act like a little boy. This is much more than 'sex is evil.'

"If the analyst can't feel what the patient is feeling, the patient can't feel him. If the analyst talks, then it is he, the authority, talking *to,* not talking *about* the patient. An analyst is the opposite of a mechanic working on a car. You are not the doctor and he the patient. You are not normal and he the patient. You are both people. An analyst can be as crazy as hell, but he must have the faith that people (he and the patient) can emerge.

"We are in the only field where an experienced and well-trained doctor like yourself can legitimately say that he has never, and does not know of anyone who has been, really cured by the method he uses. This puts an analyst in a fraudulent and guilty position. Thus, in turn, it makes for the analyst being encouraging or 'hopeful.' It is not any wonder that a patient feels better with this encouragement. An analyst must feel for and with, without identifying with a patient. One must participate vividly in the other's life, feel and see the patient as someone real. But do not identify with them. We are them, and still ourselves. We are all exactly like everyone else, yet perfectly unique.

"I would like to make a few general remarks on man. For an animal, life is no problem; life is automatically regulated by instinct. Man is different. Life poses the question: 'What can an animal do who can reason?' Man must overcome his sense of powerlessness, weakness, and apartness. If he does not: insanity. How can we answer these problems? Either regressively or progressively.

"*Regressively*—we can return to mother's hand or womb, or father's bed. This attempt would end up in tragedy. Being born as a man, you must progress. *Progressively*—develop one's independence, love actively, develop. Be oneself, yet related. This latter is the ideal of 'mental health.'

"In the history of man, you can find relations of a regressive type. Man worshiping trees, animals, trying to return to nature and primitivity. Or of a progressive type, where man moves forward toward being himself, such as Zen Buddhism. The sick man of our day is afraid to move forward. Unfortunately, in our society, man can move regressively and still find happiness in social acceptance. Resistance is a violent defense against leaving the charmed land of certainty and moving into the world of reality. This is a great fear.

"The analyst has to see every person as a hero of a drama. If we see a patient in terms of one problem—like his girlfriend left him—you could become bored. But if you see him as a human being, he becomes like the hero of a Shakespearean drama. This person becomes part of the drama of life, struggling for physical and spiritual survival. This, in itself, is exciting, although the person may not be doing great things. If you can feel this, you will be able to make the patient exciting to himself. If you can see the patient like this, and the patient can also, then he can have an exciting interest in himself as a human being struggling along. The life of an individual is as exciting as the history of man. We cannot see man as, first, someone with symptoms trying to get adjusted. Psychoanalysis must be a study of existence. In the history of man, there are only five or six plots possible, but the exciting thing is to discover the plot, the drama, what has become of this piece of life? What was this man meant to be, and what of this has he used? Questions every analyst must ask himself regarding every patient."

I asked Dr. Fromm what he meant by his concept of "meant to be." He said, "The physical and psychic are always together. The facial expression or the whole body tells us something of this man. We are born with much more potential, personality-wise, than Kretschmer (E. Kretschmer, 1921) or Sheldon (W. H. Sheldon, 1942) ever thought. We, as analysts, start out with the idea that all a person is is due to his experiences in childhood. But, we have to realize that these are not experiences on a blank sheet, but on a specific person. We, therefore, must say, 'What was the person meant to be?' Then we can see how circumstances affected this child. For example, a baby born timid and sensitive could develop into a man who is a poet or an artist. But if this child had an aggressive, domineering mother, one strong possibility would be that this baby would be squelched. On the other hand, if this mother had an aggressive baby, the baby's aggression would be accentuated, and the adult would be quite different.

"To get well is to find out what your patient was meant to be biologically, not just psychologically. A person can be born lusty, gutsy, strong and hungry for life. Another can be born quite aesthetic. They should develop, if given the opportunity, into quite different adults. One cannot say that one is better than the other; one must, for his patients' sake, help them find what they were meant to be. I used to feel that this emphasis on the constitution was defeatist and reactionary, but I now feel it is important. Temperament leaves open both positive and negative values. Some people are born with congenital goodness or congenital badness or destructiveness."

I questioned the validity of this statement. Dr. Fromm said, "If as a psychologist, you can accept a trait like intelligence having limits placed upon it by heredity, why not the same thing for goodness or badness? Analysts can do something for their patients if they recognize this and channelize their patients' energies along the proper lines."

I felt this point was very unclear. Dr. Fromm said, "With this patient, you fan the patient out of just talking and into living. By this time, you two pretty well know each other's moves (the gentlemen's agreement). The analyst must break through this complacency and move the patient.

"Your patient says he doesn't know what an adult is in this session you've just read to me. I would say to him, and I would be very sarcastic, 'and how would you know?' He would then say, 'What do you mean?' I'd say, 'You are not part adult.' Bang! Now it would be up to him to react. The analyst with a patient who has been in analysis for this long a time, with this type of deep dependency especially, must get into the arena. You must use an approach of directness."

The patient's most recent appointment was characterized by what I felt was extremely hysterical, histrionic, unreal behavior. The patient talked of wanting to 'fuck' his mother, of fantasizing doing it during the appointment hour, and vividly described his mother playing with his penis and, after it was all over, slapping him in the face.

I treated this fantasy as though the patient were acting out something in the transference that was unclear, and kept the focus on the present analyst-patient relationship to find out what the patient was saying symbolically.

Dr. Fromm said, "You have to decide: Is he real or not? I feel he is real, or at least a good deal of it is. He cannot forgive his mother or any other girl for not being very close and everything to him. If this was not an act, you would have deprived him of a very meaningful experience if you treated it as such. You have the patient on the couch. You encourage him to be free and say anything that comes to mind, and then, when deep unconscious material comes out, you don't deal with it."

I asked, "What do you do with it?" Dr. Fromm answered, "The sexual fantasy with his mother was a defense against his deep passive needs for his mother. He became aware of her 'promise' and how desperately he wanted to be taken care of. He could give in to it and regress back to infancy. If he did, he would go crazy. He is two or three years old and expressing his sexuality to fight his dependency. Yet, he is expressing this within the framework of the mother relationship. The treatment has regressed him back to this point. You wanted to do this. Why is this story insincere? It fits the dynamics. Does it frighten you because it is too Freudian? This would be mutual insincerity.

"Remember the mother could not have given him all he wants unless she was crazy. The primary fear is of dependency. Why fear the sexual act then? If he fucks his mother, in his fantasy, he destroys her as the all-powerful mother and makes her into just any other woman. He was on the verge of being sucked into complete dependency, and, for the sake of his continued sanity, he had to destroy her image. For him, inasmuch as mother is mother, sex is not sex, but is feeding. His interest is not to satisfy and love the woman, but to get relief from his tension.

"This patient has said he wants a strong father. A person who has a weak father wants a strong father. To say his father is weak and you are his mother is to say you are weak. This boy, who suffered so from having a weak father, is very angry that you haven't been strong enough. He has all the fury of his disappointment. A boy threatened by the smothering mother, who would desire to sleep with her so she would possess him completely, wants a strong father, who could have made a man out of him by putting mother in her place. He must have a great deal of resentment and fury towards his father for not having saved him from his mother.

"The patient feels that you let him pull the wool over your eyes, and he feels resentful, for you too are therefore weak. This to me is the main point. Analysts go on fishing expeditions with their patients too often. You make a remark that is a legitimate and correct psychoanalytic interpretation, but wherever the patient has thrown the ball, you have gone. You don't seem to have any goal as to where you felt the ball should have gone that hour. I hear the patient say, 'You are a weak father, and I want a strong one.' I say to myself, 'Any boy would want a strong father to save him from such a mother.' You have disappointed him the same as his father did. I know that this is the important thing that he is saying that has to be opened up.

"You, as his analyst, must say what you know is going on unconsciously, not just say what it might be and just hope that this is relevant. In the seminars that I give, I so often hear analysts ask something, hoping that the patient will say something relevant. Analysts should be a step ahead of their patients and should know and direct patients to that which is important."

I asked about letting patients use their associations, to see where these led. Dr. Fromm said,

"Free association leading to 'the answers' is a myth. One must understand the use of resistance to see this. You must give the patient a lead, one that cannot be misunderstood. For as soon as the patient hears the right thing, he will know. The analyst has the aim of getting at what is in the patient by leading him there. When I say the analyst must lead the patient to the answer, I always mean the answer that is within the patient. Often I hear analysts asking patients a question. I ask the analyst what he expects the answer to be. Quite often the analyst says that he doesn't know. I feel that the analyst should so empathize with a patient that he would know anywhere from one to three possible reactions or answers to any questions. I would not ask the question, for after all, I am a step ahead of him. I should know. If I don't know, he certainly doesn't know. It is, therefore, useless to ask a question, if I do not know the answer. In line with this, the analyst should be more active, not in talking, but in knowing what is happening. This patient needs guidance, he needs a good father.

"The analyst should be like a guide on a mountain-climbing expedition. You cannot carry the patient. You should guide him and, if necessary, should even physically assist him. A good mother's role, just being there, is not enough. This is especially true with mother-dependence."

I asked Dr. Fromm how all of this would apply to the mother-dependent woman. Dr. Fromm said,

"With a girl, the problem is, in one way, very much the same. I have seen women with terrifically strong mother fixations, where it works the same. With a boy, identification with the mother is dangerous; it destroys the sex role. With a girl, she is not thrown off the track, but the danger of being absorbed is still there. I'm not clear, not sure at all of this. I feel one's own sex comes in here. I feel a man can experience what a man can experience, and he can't do this as well with what a woman experiences. Girls who did not have a loving mother try to get a man to be a mother to them. This becomes terrifically frustrating all around. If he is not a man, it will be frustrating to both, no matter what her initial unconscious need. I almost feel men should analyze men. In a girl, if she becomes the man, she can handle the mother and keep from being engulfed.

"In regard to being supportive with this patient, yes, be kind. Prevent suffering that is not necessary, but remember to reach your goal.

There is often suffering. This is inevitable for life. For this patient, the basic situation is one of utter valuelessness and helplessness. How does he then establish his manliness? He must, or he would soon be crazy. He does it, in part, by stabbing out and getting back at every man. By even small defiances, he establishes himself as a man. By defying you and his boss, by being even five minutes late, it is a small ease, a compromise.

"To be a man, then, in summary, he: 1) fucks a girl; 2) makes a fool of other men. But for him, it must always be a hit-and-run affair (his premature ejaculation). Your job is that you must show him that he feels like vermin, dirt. He does this, rebelling, to establish his sense of power and manliness. He has a tremendous need for strong men, as he doesn't and hasn't taken his own responsibilities in his relationship with his mother. He would want a strong father (and you) to help him with his mother. So, because both have failed, he hates you and his father.

"This aggression to you has two sources: 1) he hates all men, as a carry-out of his mother's contempt; 2) he hates his father for failing him. To see what responsibilities he has to assume is a surface step, a small one, though a step in the right direction.

"To get better, this patient must see himself as a vermin or a louse. You must really be in contact with the patient when you say this. You must say it when you feel intimate and loving. If you feel this about him yourself, do not say it to him, then. He must know this self-perception eventually.

"He must see how with feelings like this, no one could live. He must, therefore, reestablish himself: 1) by fucking; 2) by attacking every man. These have been his reactions to the anxiety of any self-awareness. Lastly, he must see how much he would have wanted his father to be a strong father and not a kind mother. If all of this is more than theory, and he and you both know it, then he really will make progress. He must feel it strongly. Without recrimination, he must feel his need of women (mother) being the breast of the world and men (father) being the strong one."

Thus the supervisory sessions ended. It was an interesting and invaluable experience.

"Now, Look here..."

Arthur H. Feiner

Dr. Fromm was always *present.* I'd say something, he'd say something. I'd say something and he'd slap his thigh prefacing a trenchant remark with "Now, look here..." I looked, and picked up his own excitement for the process. It was this excitement and curiosity that he subscribed to, and that was the cause of his consequent joy—all about the plot of a person's life. Dr. Fromm's formulations were keyed to the patient's actual experience, the actual conditions of his life and his idiosyncratic interpretation of events, so that the patient's social practice seemed inevitable. [...]

Many years ago I had the privilege of being in supervision with Dr. Fromm. After an hour of my presentation of work with a patient, Dr. Fromm commented with mild impatience, but evident exasperation, something to the effect that I should stop trying to show him how learned, perceptive and astute I was. He suggested that since I was spending what he called my "hard-earned money" for his counsel, I would profit by showing him my errors, my misjudgments, and my problems with the case. In effect, he said that I would learn more if I were to share with him my difficulties, my inaccuracies, my awkwardness, and my failures.

He said that it seemed that I was fairly good at what I did, and that there was clearly no need for me to impress him. It had been assumed I could become intimate with patients and participate in this profession, since I had been accepted by our Institute and, he noted, it was self-evident that I was considered apt since I would not be in supervision with him were I not. He had been asked by the Institute's training committee to write a report on my work, and, alas, it was reassuring that he had taken no notes, since he had thought of me as a graduate analyst.

Dr. Fromm then made a remark which I did not fully appreciate at that time. I am not quoting his phrasing exactly, but what follows is based on his rhetoric as I remember it. He said that my errors, my failures and my understanding of them, and their rectification, were the keys to learning what the process of analysis was about—they were the keys to "union." I recall that the word "union" was one of Dr. Fromm's favorites. As I understood him at the time, it referred not only to the aspirations, achievements and satisfactions of organized labor—and all social movements as well—but to the basic necessities of individuals in their relationships with each other. I remember I thought Dr. Fromm had used this word as though he considered it a drive—a basic drive in all humans—somewhat at the level of animal life. As I had heard him, "union" sounded as basic to psychological existence as food, water and air to biological existence. [...]

Dr. Fromm had referred to "truth" and "courage" in the context of authenticity. He had a fondness for saying that if a man were going to be a crook, he should be a good crook. I never took this to be flippant, but more as an ironic, paradoxical indication that Dr. Fromm was concerned with consistency—a lack of sham, lack of deceit. This meant to me that the requirement of truth and courage was incumbent on the analyst as well as the patient. By extension, I knew that Dr. Fromm intended this for my relationship with him, and as I recall, that is how it played out.

I had presented to him a patient of Eurasian background whose experiences with men, including her father, her brother, representatives of the British government, her doctor, her dentist, her lovers, and unfortunately, her first analyst, had been abusive and exploitative in various ways. In this she had been unsupported by a self-concerned mother; ignored by a silent, depressed father; intruded upon by a psychotic brother; interned with her family by British authorities; later as a teenager, sexually abused by her gynecologist; then by her dentist and a business colleague; and, as she reported, ultimately exploited by her first analyst. Her needs, her desires, her aspirations, and her feelings were never relevant. They were dismissed. Her dream during analysis, of being kept in a quarry by a figure who looked like Richard Nixon, only to be rescued by a figure who looked like Nelson Rockefeller, was seized by me as a telling, complimenting contrast between previous and current analytic experiences, past and current life.

For me this was an indication of her perception of my benign, beneficent relationship with her. Dr. Fromm simply affirmed that indeed I seemed to be more benign, in a relativistic way, but it was quite clear that the patient felt that her analyst (perhaps the Rockefeller person) was not only astronomically distant by virtue of class, but still met with her in an ambience of unyielding granite. Furthermore, how had it come to be that she had participated in life this way? Her self-definition as derivative of caste, class, race and family experience must have been significant, so why was I not attending to these data?

Dr. Fromm did not intend this comment to be denigrating criticism, although at that time I received it that way. Dr. Fromm was addressing, in a straight-forward way, what was "really real" (another favorite expression of his), and pointing out that I had not considered thoughtfully all of the data, something to which I should be dedicated. And that, to him, was the responsibility of an analyst who was working with patients, and learning with a supervisor. Finally, more than a lesson in what was actually going on with this particular patient, the dialectical notion (Dr. Fromm often used the word "paradox") of the principle of the interpenetration of relativistic and absolutist properties was deeply etched in my mind, never to be forgotten. This was a Marxist notion Dr. Fromm was fond of.

With this particular woman, following Dr. Fromm's critique, the analyst would be moved to look for contributions of aspects of his own behavior, which, from the patient's point of view, would have accounted for the imagery in the dream. If the patient were asking to be rescued, in this derivative way, the analyst would have had to examine the meaning of her asking and anticipating it by examining meticulously her experience of the relationship with the analyst. Had he, in some way, indicated that he would do so? So that she would love him? How was it that she submitted to the Nixon character (pre-Watergate)? Had he too been solicited for rescue only to fail her cynically? Did this figure represent a potential hazard in the analytic relationship and what was it? Because the analyst also wielded power? Behaved similarly? Was an authority, by definition? Why, for example, was the analytic situation symbolized as a granite quarry? Was he cold and unapproachable? Was the analysis conducted in this hard, unyielding, impervious setting, and the analyst a person who presented himself as abundantly affluent, but impenetrably elitist, and distant? The properties of the Nixon character and the Rockefeller character, and their differences, should have been thoroughly explored. Was the Nixon character's implicit opportunism representative of her past? And the northeastern Rockefeller a metaphor for the future? Perhaps an image of her mother's ambition? This exploration would have included their origins, their public and private roles, their differences from the patient, their styles of presentation, as well as the kinds of press each had enjoyed, and how each was recorded by the public. What were their similarities to her? Finally, did the analyst's cautious attempt not to recreate what had happened in her previous analysis serve to defeat the very thing that was necessary—a positive, warm, non-dismissive relationship with a man? Had what was intended as non-invasive become cold and distancing? Had what was intended as an insistence on the patient's relevance become indicative of the analyst's adamantine presence?

The point of all this, of course, is that it would have addressed the issue of how the patient experienced the analyst and the analysis, as well as herself, as homologous to her life's experience and her enshrinement of it. This would have led to a comprehension of the analyst's influence, and with that kind of understanding, the analyst might indeed have responded reciprocally, in terms of what would have been useful for this patient to change. And even then an analysis of how that was being experienced would have been in order. Dr. Fromm was completely open to this kind of exploration—an inquiry, an analysis, and an ongoing analysis of her analytic experience. [...]

Supervision in psychoanalysis has invariably followed several models (E. A. Levenson, 1982): (a) holding or confirming; (b) therapy by the numbers; in which the 'guru' supervisor presents therapeutic principles as abstractions; (c) algorithmic model, or therapy via a series of steps; (d) supervision as therapeutic conduit—in which the 'guru' supervisor analyzes the patient who is being presented by the student, and instructing the student what to say and what to do; and (e) a bootleg, meta-therapeutic psychotherapy in which the technical problems of the student are attributed baldly to his or her counter-transference and the student is told ultimately to "take it back to his analyst"; or a variation in which the alleged counter-transference is analyzed on the spot. This is based on the naive, idealized fantasy that analytic training institutes are like benign, extended families, that simplistically ignores all the inherent power motivations, self-aggrandizing, envy, and competitive relationships.

I believe Dr. Fromm was interested in something else. It seemed to me he wanted to get the error or mistake out in the open, well articulated, not to show it for what it was, a wandering or a straying. For him, an error was part of a gestalt, the whole pattern of the therapy, and I should take myself seriously and think about it that way. The point in this kind of articulation was not the supervisor's correct interpretation, his brilliance, or the airing out of my private psyche, but the reduction of the data from the abstract ideational level to a concrete, total material experiential one, so that I saw clearly that my participation as analyst, influenced in a real, direct way the patient's response (A. H. Feiner, 1991).

With the addition of Dr. Fromm's input as considered possibility, I would have further influence on the presence, contact, and hoped-for change in my patient. She was to achieve a sense of differentiation from me, via my intimate connection with her. The dialectic in this kind of union was to follow the articulation and my experience of union with Dr. Fromm. In the articulation of error, and the play of ideas about struggles in living, the reality of the experience of an intimate way became clear. In my openness to Dr. Fromm, he could say (sometimes slapping his thigh), "Look here ... if you (or the patient) believe(s) that or see(s) things that way, or act(s) that way, of course you (she) feel(s)..." Or, "Let's see," he'd say with a grin, "you're like Rockefeller relativistically but not absolutely, right?"

On one occasion I said that I didn't blame the patient for some feeling or attitude she had (probably in relation to men). I probably meant that I could understand her position, but Dr. Fromm smiled and said, "On Monday you don't blame, but on Tuesday you may. Do you think you are God? Psychoanalysis needs skepticism and inquiry, not judgment." Dr. Fromm then referred to Marx's favorite motto, *"De omnibus dubitandum"* (Of all one must doubt), and favorite maxim, *"Nihil humani a me alienum puto"* (Nothing human is alien to me—cf. 1961b).

Whenever Dr. Fromm spoke of "passion," he considered it as a concept of relatedness, as a dynamic quality of man's faculties. This was a dynamic quality of a person needing to strive for union, i.e., a relationship. And this passion, he was fond of pointing out, was expressed actively, to be described with verbs, not adjectives or nouns. It was not difficult, therefore, for Dr. Fromm to point out that when my patient had dreamed of the Rockefeller character rescuing her from her unyielding, granite-like isolation from men, my error was in failing to discuss what my active contribution had been to her fantasy and how she had participated in her unrewarding relationships with men. This seemed simple enough. But his concept of passion went farther than that. He suggested that the aim of expression of human faculties was to express one's humanity.

Thus, Dr. Fromm pointed out that someone getting lost in a task, perhaps the achievement of some worthwhile goal, or the perfection of some enterprise, was expressing power and establishing boundaries which would illuminate one's identity for oneself. But it could happen that the person used the task, the perfectionism, or the expression of passion to fill his sense of emptiness or to bypass a feeling of worthlessness. In this way, the goal was subverted to self-enhancement. If this were the case, if the task were not enough as a creative expression by a non-alienated Self, the person was prone to do one of two things. He could proceed with his passionate activity only to assume that he was becoming expert, better than all others, with the coincident feeling of grandiosity and arrogance; or he could assume that he was simply not good enough for the task, despite his passionate activity, with the coincident feeling of depression. Either way, Dr. Fromm pointed out, the individual was in the position of alienating himself, by virtue of his need to use the task for his own aggrandisement rather than as expression of his power and passion, as representative of himself.

The analyst's task was a revolutionary one, Dr. Fromm insisted. It was to help the patient transform, that is, change his structure, his self-definition, and consequently his ways of living. He was not to be satisfied with reformation, adjustment or adaptation. That way led to what he called a "pathology of normalcy," which was a denial, a subversion of a human's full potential.

What is it that makes an environment of safety encourage greater openness in safety—a courage to share and play with ideas about oneself and a courage to respond? Does it happen in the contact, the "union" that Dr. Fromm spoke about? Does it make the union? And the articulation, isn't that more than sharing? Surely it involved both of us. There was a feeling of being together, of brothers-in-arms. There was a play of words and concepts. Dr. Fromm and I shared a delight in dialectical thinking. The play on words, the teasing, as evidenced in his remark to me about Rockefeller, brought home my failure to be curious about the self-serving nature of my limited understanding. We played with what I reported, turning it one way and then another, engendering contact—a clean, uncontaminated, reciprocal contact—serious, vivacious, and most friendly. In the brief time we had with each other, he learned a lot about me as I did about him.

It was an exciting, playful, learning experience that expanded once an ambience of safety was established. The play followed effective work, and at the same time intensified it (Ehrenberg, 1990; Feiner, 1990). It came from the union, and facilitated the union at the same time. Of course it was serious. None of my ideas and feelings was dismissed by Dr. Fromm. Nor did I consider any of his not relevant. He was, obviously, more experienced, more expert. His was a rational authority which I found eminently useful, and still do. It is in the atmosphere of play that nothing is warded off, all is considered. Everything can be—the most critical and embarrassing, reflective of ineptitude or personal irrationality. Anything, any image and its appearance could be followed wherever it led.

Play in psychoanalysis surely detoxifies, and may even permit a therapeutically acceptable way of expressing affection and tenderness. It includes possibilities and the comedic as evidenced in double entendres, puns, jokes and ripostes; the willful suspension of disbelief; and a willingness to look at things from all angles, as a try-on or let's see. It is, however, serious in its effect in addressing potential and reducing the forbidding danger of curiosity. And it advances union in its camaraderie. Most important, it is analyzable—as is the response to it. The analyst can always wonder why play is necessarily frowned upon and prohibited, and the patient's reasons can always be explored. As can, of course, the immediate experience.

Most curious to me is that playfulness seems to be rarely reported about in therapy or supervision (see D. B. Ehrenberg, 1990 and A. H. Feiner, 1990; and A. Rothenberg, 1988). The mutual articulation that I experienced with Dr. Fromm was due as much to openness on my part, as it was to Dr. Fromm's response. I was shown who I was, and that was all right, but it was the intimate reciprocity that made the union, so that Dr. Fromm and I became connected and could play with alternatives. I, in my errors, remained myself, as he remained himself. Learning and changing, therefore, could only have been my choice. It was the patient and I that were relevant. And that, after all, was the lesson.

In my experience, Erich Fromm did more to inform my psychoanalytic work with a sense of the dialectic than anyone I know. It was his emphasis on paradox, which I had discerned in his writing that first caught my eye, and his insistence on my grasping the significance of the dialectic in supervision that caught my ear.

PART IV

REMINISCENCES OF ERICH FROMM—
PSYCHOANALYST AND PERSON

Elation and Fortification

Anna Gourevitch

I met Erich Fromm in 1943, half a year after my arrival in the United States, as a result of my fourteen-year-old son giving me *Escape from Freedom* (1941a). Reading this book made me determined to study with Fromm. He was teaching at that time at the Washington School of Psychiatry in the Murray Hill Hotel. The lectures were fascinating and I approached Erich after one of them, wanting to clarify certain aspects of his comments. We pursued the conversation for hours and the tone of the friendship that was established that evening lasted for years. For him, friendship included the sharing of common interests, deep loyalty and also humor. At the end of our first conversation, Erich suggested another meeting the following Friday, but as he stressed, "Five o'clock American time, not Russian time." Whatever the topics we touched upon over the years, we explored their full meaning and importance to us, always picking up where we had left off at our last meeting, so that his move to Mexico later did not interfere with the continuity of our relationship.

I had shared some of Erich's opinions before I met him. Both of us had been trying to come to terms with certain problems concerning psychoanalysis, particularly the conventionality in the orthodox approach and the replacement of the effort to understand the world of the patient with stereotyped interpretations. The problem of the absence of a live approach was familiar to me and I was happy that he could express the total concept of his thinking about this so well and convincingly, things that few people had touched upon previously. Let me quote his own words from an interview published in the German newspaper *Die Zeit* on March 21, 1980:

> "As a student, I remained a good Freudian. True, my doubts increased but I graduated from the very orthodox Berlin Psychoanalytic Institute ... and during the following five or six years, my analyses adhered strictly to what I had learned. I expected to hear from the patient that which was in accordance with the theory ... I finally realized that everything turned out to be as I expected it, never anything new, always well defined conceptions: the Oedipus complex, fear of castration and so on ... Until gradually I realized that I did not know enough of the patient as a person. Also, I became bored by it all. I did not have a living relation to the patient. I did not see him as a human being. And slowly I began to ask myself what it was that

> I really saw and began to see the whole patient ... as an indi-
> vidual in his society." (1977i.)

He used to say that from the shoulders of a giant like Freud one could see farther than the giant himself.

Erich was a multi-faceted, talented man who lived in intense opposition to much of what was conventionally accepted. He had the courage to stand up to many in the profession who were often violently opposed to him. Camus did not say in vain that what characterizes a person is not only what he stands for but what he rejects. Much of what Erich said shook up his colleagues and disturbed them. I was often surprised at the unrest and discomfort aroused in people by his discussions and came to understand that ideas that were different from those of his colleagues were often experienced as an attack.

I remember Erich's straightforwardness and his hatred of stereotypes. He stressed that if you empathized with a person, saying the truth would never harm him. He followed the vibrations of others and had a deep capacity for empathy and a love of his fellow man. His work affected an increasingly wide audience not only because he wrote brilliantly and with erudition, but also because of his exceptional sincerity. Among the things that struck me was his unshakable faith in the future of man. After our encounters, I always felt elated and fortified. We hardly ever touched upon any personal topics in our conversations and yet I felt the daily troubles and problems move away after each meeting. His limitless capacity to appreciate the other and give him full attention filled one with confidence and lifted one's spirits. I am one of the many for whom he will be irreplaceable.

Psychoanalysis:
An Adventure in Learning to Think Critically

Ralph M. Crowley

Erich Fromm's most important contribution to my personal and professional life was encouraging me to be a citizen of the world, a member of the wider and more universal human community, as he was. He did this through his writing, through the many courses I took with him as a graduate psychoanalyst, through my association with him on the faculty of the William Alanson White Institute when he was chairman, and through a year of personal supervision with him in 1946-1947. Just as he was student of the human condition all of his life, I have found my satisfaction in so being.

My acquaintance with Erich came through his first work, *Escape from Freedom* (1941a), which Clara Thompson had recommended to me. Much of what I had learned about people was in general and theoretical terms; this volume and Fromm's *Man for Himself* were most useful in helping me to put his ideas in formulations for patients which surprised them and helped them grow. His discussion of character types and their origin and function made much more sense to me than the Freudian accounts of character.

When Fromm and Horney were teaching together (in 1941) in the newly formed Association for the Advancement of Psychoanalysis, of which I was a member, it seemed we were on the way to a new national psychoanalytic organization which would not embody the rigidities in training inherent in the institutes of the American Psychoanalytic Association. I found it sad when Horney felt that because Fromm was a Ph.D., the same credit could not be given students for clinical case seminars with him as that given for courses taught by M.D.s. While this silliness ended the usefulness of the Association for me, I continued to learn from Fromm. Shortly after (in 1943), he joined the faculty of the New York extension of the Washington School of Psychiatry, soon to become the William Alanson White Institute, of which he was to be one of the founders. During this interim period the Navy stationed me in New York, making it possible for me to take my first course with Fromm in 1943-44 on Character Formation, which helped me to consolidate what I learned from reading.

After leaving the Navy, I joined the faculty of the White Institute, and Fromm became the chairman of the faculty. Faculty meetings were always stimulating; Fromm never let boring trivialities interfere with policy issues, the human issues of learning psychoanalysis. During his regime, the Institute began a low-cost psychoanalytic clinic, the fourth lowest in the United States. Fromm believed intensely in the value of psychoanalysis for everyone, rich or poor, sick or so-called well, functioning or non-functioning, so he promoted this activity at our Institute. After a committee of the faculty approved the plan, the faculty authorized the clinic's beginning on February 8, 1948. The clinic's primary purpose was to serve the community; a secondary purpose was to provide opportunities for research into problems of long-term psychoanalysis; and thirdly to facilitate the training of psychoanalysts.

Fromm recommended a clinic policy in which certain applicants would be given priority based on our ability to provide them with treatment. That policy was embodied in a faculty motion that "the main criterion in selecting patients should be therapeutic worthwhileness, with an attempt to get a cross-sectional group, except for some preference given to people dealing with children." Typical of Fromm, he wished that priority also be given to low-paid professional people such as students, graduate workers, teachers, social workers, clergymen, and those in artistic and creative fields; his aim was to increase their social usefulness, as well as their personal well-being. Here, Fromm clearly showed his ideas as to who in society was most socially valuable to him. The faculty voted against this criterion. We were in no position to determine who was most socially valuable to society.

The other policy for which I remember Fromm most vividly was that of training Ph.D.s. He regarded psychoanalysis, as did Freud, as far broader than a medical specialty. He believed that the White Institute should train psychologists, as well as other Ph.D.s. In 1948, the faculty voted to begin training Ph.D.s, which it has continued doing since. I have never understood why, if the Institute trained psychologists it did not also train social workers, who were recognized in the '50s as having more clinical training, and more experience with patients than psychologists had.

I took advantage of his sojourn at White by having a year of supervision with him. Many have commented that he never wrote specifically on how to do psychoanalysis; both he and Sullivan realized that it cannot be done. All that can be done in a book is to lay down general principles. It is different in supervision. In that relationship, I learned from Fromm his ways of implementing his principles, his philosophy, and his view of human nature, which was well in advance of his time. He was most specific in supervision, never presuming that the supervisee could say or do exactly what he would have done, but offering very specific ideas of what might be said or done.

For example, with my patient, he was most alert to the patient's problem of needing to be in control and thereby controlling others. His advice was a frontal attack on her defense of needing to control. He also called attention to a fault of mine in which I did her thinking for her; that is, I worked overtime trying to think what was wrong with her, when I should have been turning that job over to her. I was preventing her from even thinking that there was anything wrong with her. I fit into her idea that nothing was wrong with her, and that I, as her psychoanalyst, was no good, a pattern manifested in relation to most of the significant people in her life. These themes were repeated throughout the year's supervision, and how Fromm ever stood my not dealing with them more assertively than I did, I shall never know.

At one point he advised my telling the patient in response to her saying that she had learned nothing new, "Yes, you are quite right; you have learned nothing new. Tell me, do you want to learn something?" He continually emphasized in this supervision and the courses I took with him that curiosity and a high level of theoretical interest were essential to becoming a psychoanalyst. The other thing that he emphasized was the ability of the psychoanalyst to arouse this curiosity, often latent in people, by saying something in such a way as to surprise the patient.

He believed that it was part of the psychoanalyst's job to be able to see, from what the patient reported, that which the patient did not see, but was in the patient's mind. From Sullivan one learned something that might superficially be seen to be the opposite. That is, one was not to assume anything without finding out what the patient was thinking or feeling. In my experience, both Fromm and Sullivan were right. One can know from what a patient is saying, more than the patient realizes he has expressed or exposed. On the other hand, it is also true, that words, especially with obsessives and schizophrenics more often obscure than enlighten. It was Fromm-Reichmann's genius, like Fromm, to be able to see through *(diagnose* is the Greek word) to what such patients were communicating.

Fromm felt that psychoanalysis was an adventure in learning to think critically. In no way did he believe that critical thinking was opposed to awareness of one's feelings, to what one enjoys nor to what one finds pleasing, to what one likes or dislikes.

With my patient, Fromm continually stressed that the patient was not really touched by anything; that she did not see any good coming out of psychoanalysis; that she did not know whether she wanted to be psychoanalyzed; and he questioned whether she seriously considered making any changes in herself, out of her need for maintaining her life as safe and comfortable as it was.

In regard to one dream interpretation, Fromm advised my saying this:

"I was thinking more about your dream and here is what I think it says, something more than you let yourself know, or say in any other way. You know yourself better and more thoroughly than you think. This dream is an unconscious insight into your life; that is, your life consists in settling down in a secure and safe place; you have the idea there are exits, but when we come to examine these, they turn out to be illusory exits, that is, only places to look out. By looking out, you get the illusion of having some other life than you have, but you don't really have that. You are uncomfortable but safe— safe even with some luxury—the Venetian blinds. But there is no real way out, just the illusion of getting out from being able to look out, from being able to fantasy what the outside world looks like. Your affairs are like looking through a window; they don't come to anything much. Your life is like that in an air raid shelter, safe, uncomfortable, but with some comfort and no real way out."

In his correspondence with me, he became concerned in the early '60s that the Institute was no longer interested in what he had to teach; that he was not being represented in the curriculum. Where he got this idea I do not know, because as far as I know the Institute has always held his contributions in high esteem and has always seen to it that they were taught one way or another. His views and his writings were and are a dynamic intellectual force in our century. It was a great privilege to be as closely related to this man as I was. There is no way I can forget him or what he taught.

Words are Ways

Edward S. Tauber

I first met Erich in the forties. He was easily friendly, warm and reserved. There was a gentle enthusiasm and liveliness in his manner—nothing forced, yet his amiability was evident.

He was always attentive and serious, but never grim or lacking in humor. As I think and utter these thoughts I feel somewhat uneasy. I don't want my comments to come across as an obituary. Obituaries are too often improved versions of what was—*de mortuis nihil nisi bonum*—this is truly not the case.

My first impressions, gained through supervisory contact were refreshing. He approached therapeutic intervention with a hopefulness and vitality that was new. His formulations were pointed and vigorous. He never missed an opportunity to see what was alive in the patient, but without overlooking the trends that bespoke negation. In the early years his heartiness included good cigars—and good chocolates—which he was happy to share. Erich was never robust or athletic, yet had great powers of concentration and energy for what interested him—his clinical work, current events, social issues, politics, ethical and religious philosophy.

In the middle and later years he expanded his interests to the biological sciences, particularly human evolution and certain aspects of physiology. He showed himself to be open and willing to learn new ideas and to familiarize himself with changing trends in conceptualization of human problems. He could hold to opinions and was neither gullible nor entranced with every alleged break-through. Fromm was a modest person; his forthrightness was not judgmental. He was deeply appreciative of wisdom without being given to hero worship. In a curious way, though, he approached formidable scholarships in alien areas with unflustered confidence that was both startling and touching. He believed that intelligent, genuine people could master the essence of subject matter, no matter how abstruse, if properly presented. One must recognize that Fromm came out of a committed socialist tradition which bespoke an optimistic conviction in man's capacity to search for and discover important human truths. Whatever the shortcoming, this generosity and faith in man's potential to learn and broaden his wisdom served as an inspiration and incitement for others to enter into life experience.

Erich was always a private person. He rarely spoke of personal affairs nor did he encourage one to question him in this respect. He was warm and kindly, but to repeat, he was not sentimental and was unmoved by the sentimentality of others.

[In 1952], I visited him in Mexico shortly after the death of his second wife, Henny. He had invited me to present a paper before his group and to travel with him for several days. It was my first trip to Mexico. We went sightseeing to Mexico City, Cuernavaca, and Taxco. He rarely alluded to Henny's death and bore his mourning quietly. The experience of his company was a rich one for me. He was fascinated with Mexico, its people, its culture and its socio-economic structure. The bull fights interested him. He grasped the symbolism—dear to the Mexican heart—of the concept of the moment of truth. Erich was not a tourist or sight-seer but made it his business to seek out the essence of what was his world—where he made his home for a quarter of a century. In our time together his bereavement was powerfully implicit and yet it was the courage of his spontaneity and responsiveness that remained keenly with me. These latter qualities never left him, even in our last telephone call two weeks before his death.

In the summer of 1957, I spent two months in Cuernavaca. Many of us from New York wished to attend a seminar conducted by Dr. Fromm and Dr. Daisetz Suzuki—followed later by a second seminar conducted solely by Dr. Fromm. Erich had gotten very interested in Buddhist teachings, particularly Zen Buddhism. Contrasting Eastern and Western thought constituted a major part of the seminar. A number of us were asked to formulate what was meant by "cure" and what were the criteria of cure according to the views of some of the outstanding contributors to psychoanalysis—Freud, Jung, Adler and so on. I was asked to present what I understood to be Sullivan's conception of cure. We all found the days together very stimulating. Much of what Dr. Suzuki presented was very new and very provocative for those of us who knew little to nothing about Satori, Haikus and the puzzling Enigmas that the Zen student is exposed to. I recall that Dr. Suzuki was amused and startled by the sense of unholy distress we Westerners exhibit when we are caught demonstrating passive yearning. He said in effect: "It must be very pleasant to rest comfortably in my mother's uterus."

I observed that Dr. Suzuki's comments left some of the more devout participants in a mildly confused state. For us, Suzuki's statement was totally unanticipated. To us, Zen Buddhist doctrines seemed stern, severe and unbending. The Zen master can acceptably respond to his pupil by kicking him down a flight of stairs or belaboring him with his cane if he failed to get the point. Yet for the Zen Buddhist, discussion at certain junctures could only lead one into further meaninglessness. If I understand it correctly, the Zen tradition calls for exorcising endless obsessional verbiage. To them, procrastination and passivity are negations of life; the temptation to escape the challenges of life—to deceive oneself must be transcended.

Thus, Suzuki's response was contradictory and logically inconsistent, but in the Zen sense really not in violation of what could be acknowledged as pleasure. Fromm captured the wisdom of Buddhist thought, and with Suzuki and De Martino wrote one of his finest books—*Psychoanalysis and Zen Buddhism* (1960a)—in which he clarified much of what seemed incomprehensible and contradictory. His profound respect for Eastern thought enriched his sense of man's search for wisdom. Yet, Fromm did not have to "become" a Zen Buddhist. The challenge to growth is enhanced neither by idolatrous worship nor cynical dismissal.

It was particularly heartwarming during the several summers and winter sojourns spent in Mexico to see Erich's interest and enthusiasm for the work I was engaged in at the brain institute directed by Dr. Raoul Hernandez-Peon, Mexico's most illustrious neurophysiologist. In the early '60s, when sleep research had only shortly before become a new and exciting area of scientific investigation, we turned our attention to the origins of dreaming sleep (often referred to as "archisleep" or "paleosleep") in the animal kingdom. In addition to psychoanalytic seminars that I moderated in his department, Erich invited me to present material on sleep studies. He requested Dr. Hernandez-Peon to provide him with personal instruction in modern trends in neurophysiology. For me, the days in Mexico—in the lively inspired climate of Fromm and Hernandez-Peon—were remarkable and never to be forgotten.

As many of you know, Dr. Fromm's interest in social issues began in his youth—historical, ethical and religious themes centering on man were the hallmark of his thinking. These topics were not exclusively academically focused. Where possible, he applied himself conscientiously to taking action. It is not well known that he made numerous and often effective efforts to assist certain persons to be released from iron curtain countries. He made himself actively available to those who sought his advice and support in political areas where he believed humanistic motives existed. For example, he worked tirelessly and intimately with Eugene McCarthy on the campaign trail.

Fromm was deeply concerned with understanding the nature of human destructiveness. Indeed, he published a powerful volume on that theme, entitled *The Anatomy of Human Destructiveness* (1973a). It was clear that when the opportunity afforded itself for extended interviews with Albert Speer, a central figure in the top echelon of Nazi conspiratory war criminals, Erich would have made every effort to explore in depth this man's life history, his system of values over time, and certain unconscious trends reflected in dream material with an eye in part to determining the possibilities for modifiability of destructiveness. Fromm came to the conclusion that this man had changed. In his personal communication to me, he committed himself to this position without qualification. This would seem to be an important conclusion in that the way he conceptualized destructiveness on the basis of clinical experience implied a capacity for modifiability.

In his psychoanalytic work, he dared to present his impressions to his patient. This did not guarantee against a mistaken inference but under favorable circumstances, he could teach a valuable lesson—it is often wiser to hold oneself unambiguously responsible for one's thoughts and feelings than to hedge bets. Fromm's views were presented crisply, which led some to see him as judgmental and incautious. Whatever the shortcoming, he was not inclined to align himself with Addison and Steele who pronounced: "Much can be said on both sides."

A life-long concern with the nature of love, its modalities and its conscious and unconscious acknowledgement for man was central to Fromm's person. As I said before, Fromm was not sentimental nor given to proselytizing. To be able to give and accept love and tenderness should not be taken for granted. These were active processes which represented a reverence for life.

Erich Fromm died quietly in his sleep on the 18th of March, 1980, in Locarno, Switzerland. His wife, Annis, called me from their apartment there that day to tell me of his passing away. Two weeks earlier, I had spoken with Erich on the phone to wish him birthday greetings ahead of time [his birthday was March 23rd]. His voice was soft, showed no signs of discouragement though he had been ill and debilitated for the last two years. In November of 1979, I had flown to Locarno to see him—I knew it would be a last visit. Erich walked about but he was pale and tired. He talked of analysis eagerly. He asked me many questions about my activities and about my sleep research.

In the introductory chapter of our Festschrift volume honoring Fromm *In the Name of Life*, Dr. Landis and I closed with this statement: "We have written of Erich Fromm's commitment to life, his work, and impact. He is a man whose words are ways and whose ways are reason, love and faith in man's possibilities." (B. Landis und E. S. Tauber, 1971, p. 11.) I remember him that way.

His Main Interest: The Human Passions

Jay S. Kwawer

My clearest memories of a case seminar with Dr. Erich Fromm involve a powerful sense of him as passionately committed to truth in the conduct of psychoanalysis, and to absolute honesty with patients. This is appropriate, because we met in December 1973 against the backdrop of the unfolding drama of deceitfulness and moral disgrace of the Watergate era. The one-week seminar took place at Dr. Fromm's New York City apartment; it was sponsored by the Harry Stack Sullivan Society and organized by Jorg Boese. I presented my clinical work with a young man whose family epitomized the national crisis of moral identity of which Watergate was a reflection. In their pretentious, acquisitive, "money grubbing," they represented to Dr. Fromm "the most naked and worst features of American capitalism."

Dr. Fromm's discussion of the clinical data reflected an immense concern for family (and tribal) history and tradition. His portrait of this family's history drew heavily on relations he articulated between character structures and economic systems. Dr. Fromm conceptualized my patient's struggle as an effort to confront the truth about his family's hollowness and emptiness.

Over the course of the week, Dr. Fromm's conviction became increasingly clear that patients know practically everything about themselves even though social convention may persuade them to repress these insights. By speaking the truth, the psychoanalyst assumes a revolutionary position. Fromm's psychoanalytic contract is perhaps best captured in his pledge to the patient, "I only promise I will not lie to you." Dr. Fromm's comments about my clinical work were likewise blunt, direct and unsentimental, and he urged us as analysts to "present the reality in the most precise way."

Dr. Fromm seemed particularly distrustful of institutions, alert to the ways in which psychotherapists' cooperation with institutions betrayed their patients. He spoke eloquently of the need for the analyst to free himself absolutely from such pressures and constraints so as to foster his and his patients' pursuit of the truth.

Congruent with this view, Dr. Fromm regarded universities as apologists for the *status quo,* and as essentially uninterested in the truth. He held the social sciences responsible for perpetuating and rationalizing existing social arrangements, noting that "nothing critical [had] been said

... and there [had] been no revolutions in thinking in the history of the social sciences." He reserved especially acid comments for academic psychology, a discipline that, he believed, ignored human problems.

Dr. Fromm conceived of psychoanalysis as a task aimed at freeing a repressed truth. Dreams were repressed insights that reflected a "peculiar clairvoyant perspective" that provided a glimpse of this truth. He advised us to approach dreams as a Gestalt; from the knowledge of the whole, the parts became clear, and it was unessential to pursue associative elaboration endlessly. Instead, he suggested that we hear the dream as a simple, clear, and truthful statement of character structure.

Dr. Fromm's view of the visionary aspect of dreams, in particular, struck me as a significant departure from the more classical psychoanalytic view that dreams are primarily expressions of the impulse life. His notion of dreams as repressed insights draws more on the cognitive-perceptual functions than does the classical view.

At our last meeting, Dr. Fromm spoke in a more strictly theoretical way than he had before about his image of man, drawing on what seemed like an encyclopedic knowledge of other disciplines. Startling a number of us, he referred to himself as a Freudian, in the sense that his main interest was in the human passions. He sardonically alluded to the "great discovery of Ego psychology that not everything is sexual," and suggested that the concern with "Ego" by American Ego psychologists was motivated by a desire to gain scientific respectability, and that this desire also impelled a shift of interest away from the classical psychoanalytic emphasis on passions and drives.

When You Hear the Word, the Reality Is Lost

Bernard Landis

Erich Fromm's Sunday morning psychoanalytic seminars, which he held at his New York City apartment, began with a fine breakfast of smoked salmon, cream cheese and bagels. In his living room, which faced a peaceful, tree-lined street, the ritual was always the same: Erich would light a cigar, lean back genially in his chair, and call on the student assigned to present a case.

One Sunday morning, a student stumbled. He gave but a sketchy picture of the patient, and the most limited of histories. It was the first time I saw Erich—almost always helpful and supportive—lose his temper. "Please leave," he told the student, "you are totally unprepared." The class sat stunned. Erich reconsidered and allowed the man to stay. I don't recall what followed, but I was struck by the lesson—to be thorough and reliable in one's activities. Those who knew Erich and his work learned from his convictions: courage and responsibility in every action, honesty in relationships, living according to one's volition, resisting the pull of conformity. These are not hard to talk about. Many have written about Fromm's approach to professional engagements and the practice of psychoanalysis, describing his affirming, yet candid, approach to life.

On the occasion of the 50th anniversary of the William Alanson White Institute in 1993, I wrote an article about teaching a course with Erich and titled it "The Constant North," from that famous speech in Sheakespeare's *Julius Caesar* (III,1): "I am constant as the northern star, / Of whose true-fix'd and resting quality / There is no fellow in the firmament." Although Erich passed away more than a quarter-century ago, a day rarely passes that I do not think of him. Until my retirement last year, his teachings informed my psychoanalytic work and personal life, and raised questions I still reflect upon.

To write about personal, everyday exchanges with Erich, however, with their biographical and self-referential implications, has its hazards. It feels like balancing on a tightrope between idealization and gossip. Erich disliked idolatry and mere chatter in any form and he was intensely private. Yet it is the purpose of this book to delve into the personal to present Erich Fromm the man, not solely the teacher, analyst, supervisor or, for some, even the prophet. In that spirit, I balance on the tightrope and offer certain memories in no particular order, but as a series of resonant encounters. Shortly after meeting Fromm, I reread *The Art of Loving* (1956a). I told him how discouraged it left me, because I could never meet the standards for loving he described. Erich smiled. "I am describing the mountaintop," he said gently, "It's the direction you take that matters. What's important is to be on the right path." His encouraging manner let a weight fall from my shoulders.

Years later, I drove Erich to a train that would take us to Boston, to the Massachusetts Institute of Technology (MIT), where he was to talk of his current work on human destructiveness and necrophilia. Erich seemed unhappy, however, when I picked him up at his New York Riverside Drive apartment. I asked how he felt. He'd had a bad night, he said, because of chest pain. It was the first time I had heard he had a heart condition, and it depressed me, because I had preferred to think he was invincible. But it's what followed that I prefer to relate here.

In the MIT seminar Erich spoke of the roots of different types of human destructiveness. The 15 or so professors, drawn into a circle, listened closely—except for one physiologist, who kept criticizing Erich's work in an overtly hostile manner. Erich responded courteously, but the physiologist was relentless. I wondered how Erich would handle this. Rather than waste more words and listen to more sour hostility, Erich shifted his chair, offered the critic his back, and continued his talk. That moment revealed another human side to Erich; he was no saint, but a man who could express his anger effectively, when needed.

And yet two hours earlier I had watched Erich warmly engaged with a man that most people would have ignored: the taxi driver who took us from the Boston station to MIT. Ten minutes after the taxi pulled up on campus, Erich and the driver remained deep in conversation. Whereas I would have stayed quiet during the ride, preparing to give my talk, Erich was enjoying himself and interested in what the taxi driver was like, and in his beliefs. That led me to see him as far more than a wise intellectual, but as a man who relished life.

I saw this again in Locarno, Switzerland, when Erich was living there. I visited for a month—with 22 American students—and together, Erich and I taught a daily seminar. One morning, we walked along the lake to the market, where he stopped to buy a bouquet of flowers and fell into a long conversation with the saleswoman. At first I just waited this out. Then I began to notice that he was clearly fond of her, and that they spoke comfortably together. As Erich turned a routine errand into a moment of real appreciation for another person, I wondered what part of humanity the rest of us might be blind to each time we payed for our purchases and turned to leave.

Erich's daily walks to the market were also times when he meditated on early experiences and their effects on him, as well as on present-day affairs. "Even if, as a child, one has limited choices, one must take responsibility retroactively," he said on one of those walks, "because even a child might possibly have acted differently. Without accepting this possibility, present day change is not likely to occur."

Erich was not one to be fooled, and he spoke his mind to those he knew well. Toward the end of the Locarno seminar in 1974, my students threw a party for Erich at a local inn. Three cases of wine went quickly, and a fourth was called for. Erich, in a happy mood, wanted to pay for the fourth case. I knew it would have been his pleasure to do so. But I stubbornly insisted the party was for him. Warmly, he continued to try to pay. I argued that he should not. The next day as we talked, in a direct but not unfriendly way, he said, "You are a controlling person." It shocked me, for it was not at all how I saw myself but after reflection I realized that Erich was right, and it was helpful that he minced no words.

In New York, after one of Erich's Sunday morning seminars, I asked if he was an atheist. "No, I am not a theist or an atheist, but a non-theist," he said. Erich explained that he did not believe in a personal God. The term "non-theist" was new and significant to me. We also spoke of politics around that time. It was during the period of international debate on the formation of the state of Israel. Erich said it wasn't a good idea. I asked him why. "Because," he said, "nations can't maintain principles. All governments lie. Nations get inescapably enmeshed in political pressures."

Erich and Annis invited me and my wife, Erica, to their apartment for dinner, along with a guest lecturer and his wife, who showed up with a beautiful plant. Though Erich discouraged gifts, I felt badly that I'd come empty-handed. To make matters worse, the other professor spoke with gracious fluency. On every issue, he agreed with Erich. He radiated charm to the point I thought—of sycophancy. Was I envious?

The next day, I told Erich how badly I felt about coming to dinner with no gift. He brushed it off. "That man," he said, "I saw to be an opportunist. He's just an ambitious, ingratiating person." Although invariably courteous with others, Erich had grown to be quite candid with me, and I was glad to share in his confidence. Parenthetically, when we showed up that evening, Erich was in the kitchen mixing the salad dressing. Men in this era did not lean toward housework or help with dinner. Yet here was Erich the visionary, a major figure in psychoanalysis, in the kitchen with a whisk, absorbed in an ordinary chore—with visible pleasure on his face.

He was an extraordinary observer; he caught small, uncomfortable moments and held them up to the light. This happened to me once, rather painfully. In one of our Locarno seminars, Erich analyzed a dream told to him by the Nazi architect Albert Speer, whom he had met several times. I slipped Erich a note, offering a markedly different interpretation.

He confronted me afterward. "Why didn't you say this in front of the class? Were you fearful of embarrassing me? If you were protecting me, that's a kind of bribery, acting nice to blunt any criticism." I had, in fact, been protecting him, but not to blunt criticism: I'd thought that a challenge to his authority before 22 young students might cause him discomfort. I know now that he would have welcomed it.

An incident with even greater impact occurred after an evening analytic session. I was so struck by what we'd discussed that I walked for hours in the dark. At the next morning's session, I told him what I'd learned the night before. Instead of nodding his approval, he looked at me and demanded, "Well, what have you done about it?"

"When could I have done anything?" I asked. After the reflective walk I'd gone to bed; in the morning, our session began early. Erich just gazed at me and repeated, "What have you done about it?" I finally grasped the point. Insight without action was useless. Action was an imperative. Change, in fact, could be telegraphed promptly in one's voice, posture, and other non-verbal ways; one had to show an awareness of the new reality. Fromm wanted to facilitate change and autonomy. He believed that psychoanalysis was too often an exchange of words and thoughts alone, not leading to change. "When we hear the word," he told me, "the reality is already lost."

For Erich's 70th birthday, I asked to prepare a festschrift in his honor. Dr. Edward S. Tauber collaborated. Erich consented, and mentioned some people whose work he'd like included. One man, a close friend of Erich's, submitted a manuscript that I found shallow. Erich, informed of this, asked that we give this man, whom he regarded highly, a second chance. The second effort was worse than the first. To our surprise, Erich thought that a respected colleague deserved a third chance at inclusion. It was a generous stance, and we agreed. Alas, what arrived was a reprint of a rather poor article that had run in an obscure journal. The festschrift accepted no reprints and Erich, though disappointed, said no more about it. He was delighted with the finished book and we learned how forbearing he could be regarding an esteemed friend.

One final, and deeply personal experience: In the late 1960s, when I was developing my practice, Erich invited me to move to Mexico and work with him. He offered a good salary, and to supplement it, he would establish a private practice for me. We would work together on three books, he proposed, over a two- to three-year period.

My wife agreed, and I, just starting out on my career, felt honored. I told Erich the deal was on. Over the next two weeks, however, I began to see this venture in a different light. I came to realize there would undoubtedly be times when we would disagree, and that Erich, as senior author, might always have final say. I concluded it was time to go my own way.

When I told this to Erich, he nodded with understanding. We both realized my decision was right.

Fromm Didn't Want to Be a Frommian

Michael Maccoby

In 1959 while I was finishing my doctorate at Harvard, David Riesman, the sociologist, introduced me to Erich Fromm who was looking for a psychologist with knowledge of statistics and projective testing to work with him on his study of a Mexican village. In exchange for working with him, Fromm offered me training in psychoanalysis at the Mexican Institute he had founded and analysis with him.

The year before leaving for Mexico in 1960 with my wife Sandylee, I participated with Fromm, Riesman and others in two political meetings. One focused on the dangers of nuclear war with the Soviet Union which led to establishing a group called *Committees of Correspondence*. Riesman published a newsletter, *The Correspondent*, to which both Fromm and I contributed in the years that followed.

The other was a meeting to discuss revitalizing the Socialist Party in the United States. Fromm had written a manifesto which was the topic of discussion [cf. 1960b]. Although I agreed with much of what Fromm had written, I wasn't convinced that a Socialist Party had any chance in America, a country where class differences are denied. Riesman, who was also at the meeting, and I decided our best hopes were to work within the Democratic Party, and subsequently, we presented a paper to a group of progressive Democratic Congressmen which was published in a collection of essays called *The Liberal Papers* (1961).

From 1960 to 1970, I was Fromm's student, analysand, apprentice, and colleague, co-author of a debate *On Thermonuclear War* with Herman Kahn (H. Kahn, 1960; E. Fromm and M. Maccoby, 1962b) and finally the book *Social Character in a Mexican Village* (E. Fromm and M. Maccoby, 1970b).

It is difficult to summarize a decade of profound learning and experiences with Fromm. The analysis was a deep exploration of Self, rich in dreams and insights that woke up sleeping parts of the Self and forced me to take full ownership of my life in making critical decisions. At one point, I had a dream of being in a Harvard examination hall with others. In front of us was a map of the world. I started to work on my map but I noticed the others just sitting there, not working. "That's a good dream," said Fromm, "We are all given the world as a test, but most people don't know it's a test they have to take until it's too late and they can no longer decide what they are here for."

Fromm's view of the Self was like a mansion of many rooms in which most people lived in one or two with the others closed off. Like Freud, he agreed with Terentius that "nothing human is alien to me." One's ability to experience and contain all the irrational as well as transcendent emotions, from the murderous to the loving and sublime, from deep despair to encompassing joy, determined how deep the analysis could go. To contain this awareness required a philosophical frame of meaning which Fromm had found first in Judaism but later in different forms of Buddhism and religious mysticism. Together with my analysis, Fromm had me read Aristotle's and Spinoza's *Ethics*, Herbert Marcuse's study of Hegel (H. Marcuse, 1941), Sören Kierkegaard's *Purity of Heart Is To Will One Thing* (S. Kierkegaard, 1938), Meister Eckhardt's stages of spiritual development and writings in Zen and Indian Buddhism.

During the time I knew him, including periodic meetings in the 1970s, Fromm significantly changed some of his views. In the early 1960s, his outlook combined a messianic belief in humanistic socialism with a practice of Zen Buddhism, learned from D. Suzuki. He was in contact with the Yugoslavian *Praxis* Marxists and encouraged me to lecture in Belgrade and Zagreb in 1964 and later to attend the meetings of *Praxis* in Korčula.

His analytic style at this time was very influenced by Zen and he had me practice Zen meditation every day. Like a Zen master he could be punishing when he thought I was holding back or being inauthentic. When I complained that he was not being helpful, he said "I am not here to be helpful but to analyze." He repeated the Zen story of the master who smacks his disciple with a stick. "But I haven't even said anything," says the student. "Why should I wait?" says the master.

After his heart attack [December 1966], Fromm became gentler, more sympathetic. He said that one could believe all illness was psychosomatic until reaching one's 60s. Then one had to accept the fact that the body wears out. In 1968, we were both very active in the anti Viet Nam war movement and Eugene McCarthy's campaign for president. After the election was over, Fromm expected McCarthy to join him in leading a humanistic movement based on his book *The Revolution of Hope* (1968a), but McCarthy let him down, even failing to show up for an agreed-upon meeting. Fromm became more pessimistic. The Messiah was not going to come any time soon. The Socialist movement was being buried in the rebellious acting out of the late 1960s, more in tune with what Fromm considered Herbert Marcuse's distortion of both Freud and Marx than with Fromm's humanism. He became more interested in individual spiritual development, more in tune with the Buddhist vision of transcendence, of becoming one with nature. In his New York apartment, he lay on the floor and showed me how he was practicing dying. His book *To Have Or to Be?*

(1976a) expressed his conviction about purpose, the aspiration to fully love life and to not be held back by greed and enslaving attachments.

Working with Fromm could be difficult but also extremely enjoyable. Even when difficult, it was stimulating. Never before had any professor ripped my drafts apart and forced me to clarify my thoughts, fully express the logic of my arguments. Fromm had no patience for unfounded disagreements, but when we wrote together, he was open to my ideas and criticisms.

One of the most memorable days of my life was when he asked me to critique his manuscript of *The Anatomy of Human Destructiveness* (1973a) and we met in his New York apartment, dialoguing and arguing from 11:00 am to 11:00 pm, getting up only to go to the bathroom. Food and drink was brought in by Annis, his wife. What intensity and concentration! Yet, at 11:00 pm, neither of us was at all tired. We were fully awake, full of enthusiasm from the intellectual journey we had shared.

Fromm's tough criticism was, I believe, a compliment, for he was equally tough on himself and extremely self-critical of what he considered his narcissism. Like Freud, he saw himself as a narcissistic personality. However, in retrospect, I think he overemphasized the negative aspects of this personality type and underestimated the positive side, the lack of internalization of the father, replacing the Super-Ego with an Ego ideal, giving one the freedom to create, for good or evil, one's own sense of meaning without being tied to cultural norms.

Fromm and I loved telling each other jokes. He had a wonderful sense of humor and a joyful laugh. He believed that a sense of humor was the emotional equivalent of a cognitive sense of reality. He especially enjoyed humor that punctured self-importance.

Fromm became an idolized figure in Mexico, based on appreciation of his wisdom but also strengthened by transferential idealization. His disciples lacked his knowledge and vision and few questioned anything he pronounced. I once asked him how it felt to be idealized and he answered that it was frustrating in the sense that his followers, with few exceptions, only repeated what he gave them, that there was a lack of creativity in their followership. This is a problem for many extremely creative thinkers who never finish learning and revising their ideas; it is the reason why the Freuds, Marxes and Fromms don't want to be Freudians, Marxists or Frommians.

His Way to Clarity and Humaneness

Jorge Silva García

From the moment I first heard Dr. Fromm present his critical views on the Oedipus complex, which he contrasted to the child's strong emotional needs and his deep dependency on his mother (pregenital fixation), a thick blindfold fell from my eyes: no more juggling data, all became quite clear about myself and my patients. When I came to realize my deep longing for mother's love, as well as that of my patients, the essential problem was to make the unconscious conscious—which is, as we all know, easier said than done.

I had found my Teacher at last; what he said made so much sense, I realized this was only the beginning of what I would and must learn from him. The Oedipus complex, the castration complex etc. had been my stumbling blocks, they had confused what I could see, feel and begin to understand about human behavior, including my own. Where would Sigmund Freud be if Erich Fromm had not increased the meaning, significance and scope of his findings and the theories he derived from them?

Fromm was right when he stated: "Man in each society, seems to absolutize the way of life and the way of thought produced by his culture, and to be willing to die rather than to change, since change to him, is equated with death." (1961a, p. 5.) I began to understand the clinical significance of pre-genital fixation on the mother, the psychological intensity of the dependency on her, so far removed from an incestuous sexual desire.

After a year-and-a-half of Freudian psychoanalysis on the couch in Chicago in 1947 and 1948, my psychoanalysis with Dr. Fromm from 1950 on was a very intense experience, rather trying at times, disquieting and even painful because of what I was learning about myself and others. There were days when I had to stop at a nearby ice cream parlor to console myself over a hot fudge sundae, before starting my afternoon practice. His use of face-to-face dialogue was a totally different experience from previous analyses: meaningful, intense, direct. The dialogue happened in the *here and now*. Whereas in the silence of the couch I would ponder what I was saying or what I had said, tomorrow was always another day, unless something moving had occurred to me.

During my first sessions, sitting face-to-face, as should be the case in any meaningful dialogue, he could see me and I could see him. *I saw him but I did not see him*; I could feel his piercing blue eyes peering into my soul. Little by little I began to see him and to notice how his eyes would flicker when I said something that helped him tie up loose ends, which sometimes he would share with me to stimulate my reactions, asking me what it brought to my mind.

At times I was so scared at what he was saying that I was paralyzed, I could not say a word. At other times his insistent but kind and patient prodding would help me express the horrors and/or pain in my mind. With infinite patience he listened to my stammering, halting speech or to my gibberish. Slowly I learned that he was my friend and teacher. Above all, I learned to remain silent, to listen carefully to what was being said to me, ultimately to be able to enquire, clarify, question that which was not clear. Thus I came to understand the intimate, inner logic of the unconscious process of myself and others.

Our training was formally initiated in 1950, according to the by-laws of the Universidad Nacional Autónoma de México (UNAM). It included two hours a week of individual analysis, three two-hour seminars a week in theory (studying Freud, Jung, etc., as well as Fromm). We were frequently visited by analysts from New York City who taught theoretical and clinical seminars, as well as providing individual clinical supervision: Drs Edward Tauber, Rose Spiegel, Nathan Ackerman, Walter Thompson and others. Though our training was formally terminated in June of 1956, I continued to be a frequent and constant visitor at my Teacher's door, knowing I would always learn from him, because of his experience and his creative, rational capacity. A phrase from "Pirke Avot" ("Sayings of the Fathers") remained in my mind: "Wear down the steps of your Teacher's home, learning from him."

Fromm taught me the experiential analysis of dreams that increased my understanding of my patients and of others, and gave me a high degree of insight into their unconscious conflicts, ideas or feelings, even *prior* to any association to the dream. Their associations, stimulated by my ideas suggested by their manifest dream, further broadened and deepened my understanding of the dreamer and his or her unconscious.

Once graduated, Dr. Fromm told us during a clinical meeting that no psychoanalytic Institute, as far as he knew, owned the building they occupied. This piece of knowledge stuck with me. In 1960 I was elected President of the Sociedad Mexicana de Psicoanálisis A.C. During my acceptance speech, I stated that I would build our institute, which statement raised a loud derisive laugh, for the funding I received amounted to only seven thousand pesos. Some months later, we bought the land where the Instituto Mexicano de Psicoanálisis A.C. now stands. I was able to raise the funds from parties interested in such a worthwhile idea.

The Institute was built, and inaugurated by Dr. Fromm on March 8, 1963, on which occasion he gave the keynote address *Humanism and Psychoanalysis* (1963f). In the speech, he set down the humanist basis of our discipline, in his usual very concise, clear manner—a perspective of psychoanalysis quite opposed to Freud. Included in the seven-story small white building, there was an apartment that Dr. and Mrs. Fromm could use while in Mexico City, equipped with all that was necessary to make their stay comfortable. They furnished it to their liking. I must say I was very proud and happy of the achievement.

My professional development was greatly enhanced by being bilingual in English and Spanish, which resulted naturally in my frequently presenting clinical material in English. Of course I reaped abundant criticisms, some reasonable, some not, others rude and merciless, but Dr. Fromm always tempered these normal and natural outbursts of collegial rivalry, and his critical observations were quite to the point, some rather painful, but always stimulating. Slowly I began to learn aspects of my patients' unconscious, despite all the criticisms—or maybe because of them.

During supervision, whether individual or in a group, he was always most attentive, letting nothing escape him. He would inquire why there had been a change in tone of voice, or a change in the way an idea was being expressed would suggest to him something different than it did to us. If we remained silent, he would express his own associations, which not infrequently were very much to the point, for he kept in mind all the pertinent information that the patient had expressed. He did not mind being wrong, for, as he said, we were not in a "vanity show," where one must always be right. Gradually, as we lost our fear of being wrong, we grew in spontaneity, which was very much his point. He would say that the only time when being right and being wrong was of any significance, was in an automobile accident.

I have always been slow in processing a lecture; I need time to ponder. Whenever he read one of his papers, I usually had no immediate comment. After a time, while alone or with the group, I could tell him what I thought about his paper, or what I associated with it—hoping secretly, he would value my comment. Whatever his response, it always enriched my perspective.

Dr. Fromm, time and again would tell me to count ten times ten before opening my mouth, and having done so, to remain silent. I have never stopped thanking him for this piece of advice, for it has enabled me to appreciate the value of learning to listen to others—and to myself. After 6 years of training, in June of 1956, we all graduated from the Post-Graduate Course in Psychoanalysis, presided by Dr. Jesús Zozaya, who gave each of us our Diploma.

In the early autumn of 1971, at 8:30 a.m. in the morning, Dr. Fromm arrived at the Buenavista Railroad Station in Mexico City, from the United States. Dr. José F. Díaz, Dr. Aramoni and I awaited him on the platform. As always, it was a felicitous event and a great joy to watch him descend from his Pullman coach, warm, affable, his blue eyes shining with gladness at the sight of us. He had an appetite, so we all went to the Aristos Hotel and had a nice breakfast followed by a wonderful conversation. He told us of a book he had recently read: *The Wolf Man* (M. Gardner (Ed.), 1971).

The volume compiled the impressions that Freud and others had drawn from the Wolf Man dream. Dr. Fromm began to laugh—laughter that was so contagious until we were all laughing at the humor in Dr. Fromm's voice. He laughed until he cried. He related to us Freud's inference, reinforced by the others, so lacking in any solid basis. In the dream of the Wolf Man (S. Freud, 1918b), six or seven white wolves were sitting on their haunches in the branches of a large pine tree, staring at the dreamer. Freud concluded, and the others concurred, that this was evidence that the dreamer had been witness to his parents' *coitus a tergo* (like dogs or wolves?). The tale was so gracefully told and with such glee, that we all had to laugh. Freud was right when he stated that dreams were "The Royal Road" to the unconscious, but his theoretical understanding was wrong (cf. 1979a, pp. 16-19).

I believe I was one "who wore down the steps of his home" everywhere from his stay at the Hotel Río, his apartment on Gutenberg Street (where his former wife Henny died), to the apartment on Anatole France Street. The same was true for his home with Annis at Neptuno 9 in Cuernavaca, Morelos, and finally at his apartment in Casa La Monda, his last home on Via Franscini 4, Locarno-Muralto, Switzerland.

When he was in Mexico City, my wife Inés would prepare fresh tomato juice, duly strained for him, which he enjoyed very much. It was always fun for Inés and me to plan our Saturday drives to Cuernavaca to see him and Annis; they were a delightful couple. Our trip would begin with a phonecall to ask them if there was something special we could bring: rough country bread, sour pickles with tarragon, at times, anchovy paste. When we arrived, Alicia, the house keeper, would open the door. We felt the peace and quiet of their garden as we made our way to the brook below. We would sit in the cool shade, listening to the murmur of the brook, eating and chatting at our ease. My appointment was always at 4 pm, during which time Inés sat chatting with Annis Fromm. After half an hour, kind and gentle Alicia would serve us coffee.

Dr. Fromm first met Inés in 1968 on his return from New York City by boat to Acapulco. Because of his heart, he had to climb to Cuernavaca in easy stages, and so we met with them at Alfonso Millán's home in Jiutepec. Dr. Fromm was waiting for us on the driveway, in a blue shirt—the color of his eyes. He already knew Inés from photographs. He, Annis and Inés took to each other at first glance.

One Saturday, Annis fell and hurt her knee, which immediately became inflamed causing her intense pain. Since the skin was not broken, I asked to apply a Folk Remedy I knew that would allow her to walk again in three days; I had used this remedy several times with success, including on myself. We carried Annis upstairs and Alicia and I proceeded to the kitchen to prepare the poultice; in the process I taught Alicia how to make it. When the knee could tolerate the heat of the poultice, I applied it. A layer of cotton and an elastic bandage followed. She felt immediate relief. Later I heard that she had slept soundly. The next morning they removed the poultice, upon which she could bathe carefully before applying a new one. By the third day she could walk, though I requested that a new poultice be applied to assure the effectiveness of the cure.

Annis was a tall, graceful woman with a fine sense of humor, a natural joyfulness. Both she and Dr. Fromm were loving and affectionate towards each other and every evening before going to bed, they would stand facing each other, place their hands on their shoulders and repeat a Mantra that they should not go to bed with anger in their hearts, only love.

Dr. Fromm was always orderly and highly valued his time. He studied or wrote in the mornings, his afternoons were devoted to us, his students, patients, friends or those who wished to interview him. We all had an allotted time, which was kept rigorously. Thanks to this discipline, he was able to meditate every evening, relaxing his breathing while sitting and letting his head hang, thinking of the events of his day. His meditation in turn allowed him to change profoundly in his bearing and in his life perspectives, from the arrogant man in his fifties with a cigar in his mouth, to the unpretentious, humble, gentle, warm, kind teacher of his sixties and seventies.

Excepting a short time in his youth, Dr. Fromm was never fond of Zionism. All of his teachers and professors were renowned humanists. In 1967, when the Port of Aqabah was closed to Israeli navigation and the Suez Canal to all ships, Israel, together with France and England, declared the "Six Day War" on Egypt. Dr. Fromm made public his disagreement with this alleged *casus belli*, and quite clearly stated that the situation warranted at the utmost a legal demand before the International Court at The Hague. For this reason, the Jewish community of the United States (itself comprised of many Zionists), banned all his lectures in the US. This did not stop his charges, nor his demand that justice be done. The United Nations held the same viewpoint. Finally, Sir Anthony Eden was deposed as Foreign Minister of Great Britain, and the attack on Egypt was stopped.

On another occasion, in 1962, he traveled to Moscow, fully aware that this was a dangerous decision and that he was putting his freedom in jeopardy. He went nonetheless, determined to intercede on behalf of his cousin Heinz Brandt who had been unlawfully kidnapped from West Berlin by the KBG. Thanks to the brave intervention of Erich and others, his cousin was eventually released.

One Saturday, I proudly brought Dr. Fromm a clinical paper on a case of agoraphobia. I very much needed his opinion, which he kindly agreed to give and I left my paper with him. Little did I dream he or Trixie (his personal secretary Beatrice Mayer) would misplace it. Weeks and months passed by and he said nothing. I finally got up the courage to ask for his opinion on my paper. "What paper?" he asked. I was aghast, but persisted. With his usual candor, calm and patient demeanor, seemingly innocent of any misdeed, he said he must have misplaced it. He then asked for a copy to make a point of reading it after I left. I was very annoyed, and, doing my best to keep calm, I answered that I had given him my only copy. He looked at me with his big blue eyes and told me I should never hand in a paper without keeping a copy of it—damn it, of course he was right! It took me three years to write again on the theme, get his input and publish it.

He often told me that I must always write as if I were writing a very important paper that I could present to my peers: well-documented and well-written. A propos, I saw him several times tearing apart a thick, typewritten manuscript of a book; he would then rewrite it and tell Trixie to please type it again.

In 1964 he read my paper "Man's Fear of Women" (of course, this time, I had a copy) and he made a very significant suggestion by differentiating three stages of male development (cf. J. Silva García, 1966):

- the *chronological* stage: the social group determines when one is considered a man, for example the Bar Mitzvah of the Jewish people (at thirteen), the coming to military age at eighteen;
- the *anatomic-physiological* stage: when the male is able to reach a strong, efficient erection that permits him and his sexual partner to reach an orgasm;
- the *characterological* stage or the age of manliness: when he as an adult is capable of thinking as well as being, loving himself and others, having transcended the neonate's Ego-centricity; knowing that he is the one who must change and can no longer demand that others change.

He encouraged me to present this paper at the Second International Forum of Psychoanalysis that was held in Zürich in June of 1965. Since we were one of the three founding members of the "International Federation of Psychoanalytic Societies" (IFPS), a large group of Mexicans attended the Forum (more than 20), and Dr. Fromm kindly and generously invited us all to a splendid dinner at the Red Fox. It was a happy gathering, presided by our Teacher, with good food and excellent wines. He beamed and was very pleased that so many of the second generation of students had made the special effort to come. Dr. Jorge Derbez and I were the only two of the original group.

On August 17-22, 1969, the Third International Forum of Psycho-analysis took place at the Hotel Aristos in Mexico City. We were unable to host it in 1968 because the Olympic Games of that year were being held in Mexico, making hotel space scarce. Postponing the forum turned out for the best because of the tragic event of that year: the culmination of a peaceful student movement that insisted on the need for a more democratic regime with an army ambush and a bloody massacre. Dr. Fromm was to preside over the Forum and I was in charge of the scientific and social organization. He telephoned from Europe to tell me that he was unable to come because of his health, and that I had to preside. I told him I could not do this for I held all the strings of the scientific and social organization he had entrusted to me. By telephone we decided to invite Dr. Ramón de la Fuente to preside; he accepted, but unfortunately, was not very committed. The Forum was nonetheless a success and all participants enjoyed the scientific and social events.

Inés and I went to Locarno after the Third Forum to inform Dr. Fromm in person of all that had transpired. He already lived at Via Franscini 4 and we, as usual, were most happy to be able to see Dr. Fromm and his wife on their balcony waving at us as we waved from our train window. We had telephoned ahead to inform them when we would switch trains at Bellinzona so he would know when we should arrive. Since childhood, he had been a railroad fan and would buy the Almanac each year to have the train schedules on hand.

We always stayed at the Muralto Hotel in Locarno and had reserved a very nice room on the 5th floor with a wonderful view of the Lago Maggiore; the hotel administration also had our precise instructions to bill only ourselves, so that we could feel free to stay as long as we wished and visit the Fromms as much as their time allowed them. On our arrival, a letter from Dr. Aniceto Aramoni awaited us in which he informed us of Dr. Arturo Higareda's death, asking that I inform Dr. Fromm of this sad event. He was one of our generation of psychoanalysts and thus, still young—in his late fifties, not quite sixty. He had died of a sudden heart attack. I did not know how best to tell Dr. Fromm, for in Mexico we dally somewhat in coming to the point. He showed me the direct and correct procedure with his usual patience and love—and again, I learned.

In Locarno, while I worked with Dr. Fromm, our wives would either go shopping for our supper or prepare what was already at the house. When he and I finished, we would set the table and prepare drinks; at times he prepared a punch, which he seemed to favor. We would converse as we dined and often (in the most interesting conversations), he would tell us of world-famous people he knew well. This led us, once, to visit Albert Schweitzer's home in Günsbach (Alsace) after he had extolled on his humility and wisdom, his humaneness. The same visit stimulated us into reading about Schweitzer and some of the books he had written, which again showed Fromm to be right.

Sometimes he would invite us to concerts in some beautiful old church in Ascona or Locarno. He always had the tickets. He also informed us that in Switzerland, people did not applaud in a church; they simple stood up to show approval.

Dr. Fromm had always enjoyed classical music and played the piano. On my 58th birthday, he performed a favorite of his: Bizet's Suite *L'Arlesiènne*, as a personal gift. I was very moved and still treasure the recording.

There is much left unsaid as is to be expected after a rich relationship of almost thirty years (1950-1978); we were unable to visit in 1979 because he had been ill. We talked over the telephone in January of 1980, and I told him this year we would most certainly meet even if for only five minutes; he answered that he was sure it would be more. I never saw him nor heard him again. I miss him greatly.

His Deeply Inspirational Presence and Thoughtfulness

Salvador Millán and Sonia Gojman de Millán

We were Erich Fromm's students at the end of his tenure in Mexico, in his last two classes of psychoanalytic training (1970 and 1972), for which he conducted seminars and supervised clinical cases.

Rainer Funk proposed that we try to write down our memories of Fromm, so we have attempted to recover some of those experiences. We present them here together because most of them were shared experiences. Certainly, his presence and thoughtfulness deeply inspired much of the work that we have developed over the years, and affected our lives in a profound and meaningful way.

Salvador collaborated with Fromm on the study of the Social Character of Mexican peasants (begun in 1957, cf. E. Fromm and M. Maccoby, 1970b). Later, Salvador conducted a research project about biophilia and necrophilia in contrasting groups of orphans that was supervised by Fromm for social connotations and by Michael Maccoby for methodology. Fromm had been close to Alfonso Millán, Salvador's uncle, since the early fifties. Alfonso was a crucial figure in Fromm's participation at that time in the National University of México (UNAM).

We will first describe Sonia's impressions of Fromm, both public and private. We also share Salvador's memories of his personal or direct experiences with Fromm, as well as indirect accounts from Salvador's family members and from members of the Mexican family that worked and lived in Fromm's house in Cuernavaca, México.

IN SONIA'S VOICE

I had read a number of Fromm's texts, e.g. *The Sane Society* (1955a), *The Heart of Man* (1964a), *Man for Himself* (1947a) and *Escape from Freedom* (1941a), when I was studying psychology at the University in Mexico (1963-1966). I was impressed to meet him in person during the conferences he gave at the Medical Center of the Mexican Institute for Social Security (1963f; 1966p).

In 1972 I had the opportunity to know Erich Fromm as a teacher, when Salvador encouraged me to undergo training as a psychoanalyst with a social orientation. Fromm was conducting an introductory seminar on psychoanalysis in the first semester of the training program, and interacting with him in the classroom was a very important event for me. To some extent, I had already been familiar with the experience of travelling every weekend to Cuernavaca to attend Fromm's clinical seminars (S. Millán and S. Gojman, 1997), in accompanying Salvador and his classmates. During those two years, I would stay at the hotel with the children.

For my training class of candidates in 1972, the introductory seminar sessions were focused on "Psychoanalysis as a science," i.e. on what we thought was or was not scientific for the social sciences. Fromm insisted on the notion that statistics and the leading nature of apparently quantifiable data, with no human content and no profound dynamic significance, were not appropriate ways to understand Man, not least because of their underlying positivistic approach.

This was the last generation of psychoanalytic trainees whom Fromm mentored in Mexico, as he would later leave for Switzerland. For this reason, my class sat at the table with him without having to share his attention or expertise, as previous classes had to do, with other alumni "observers." Since we had no regular visitors, my class could interact with Fromm more closely and directly.

Word has it that my grandfather Shimen Jezior (cf. M. Finkelman de Sommer, 2007) , who was one of the leaders of the *Bund*—a Jewish socialist organization that did not accept the need for Jews to have a separate, independent State—had attended a meeting with Fromm years before in México to share their concerns. My grandmother Tzila Jezior lived in Cuernavaca in the 1970s and when she heard that I was taking classes from Fromm, she insisted that I tell him that she wanted to invite him to a Jewish meal of her specialties. I never did it. I ended up thinking that Fromm's position on the matter of Judaism turned out to be more universal than the one the *Bund* held (see I. Deutscher, 1971).

Sometimes when we went out with our children in Cuernavaca, Morelos, we met Fromm, strolling about the Zapata roundabout on his way downtown, perspiring through his jacket. We didn't know at the time that he went out precisely to exercise, so I remember the first time we saw him, we offered him a ride in our car. I saw there that Fromm was fiercely determined: without much explanation, he refused the ride and continued his walk.

We visited Fromm in his apartment in Locarno after attending the International Federation of Psychoanalytic Societies Forum in Zurich in 1974, accompanied by Michael Maccoby. Just after we arrived in Locarno, we met Fromm's wife Annis in the street: she had gone out to get something to eat and to buy a cake for the afternoon's get-together. Fromm's apartment had a beautiful view of the lake, which reminded us of the view from his house in Cuernavaca. There, Fromm fed us a honey cake, and more than once offered us another piece. He asked us about the Zurich conference, and commented with some sarcasm and irony on his impressions of John N. Rosen (English 1965) and his treatment of psychotic patients. It was obvious that Fromm did not regard Rosen or his treatment very highly.

Fromm then asked us about our plans after the visit to Locarno. His attitude was one of intense, deep concentration in spite of this being an informal social gathering.

IN SALVADOR'S VOICE

Family portrait with Fromm

Members of my family, specifically Román Millán, my father, who was a lawyer, and my uncle Ignacio Millán, an oncologist, were both interested in social issues, in particular the possibility of alleviating the suffering of those most in need. I frequently witnessed and participated in discussions with Alfonso Millán on the idea of starting a project that would help people in disadvantaged social classes and those who used public health services, in venues like Mexico City's General Hospital. The presence of Professor Fromm in Mexico led us to discuss and delve deeper into the University's concerns and its obligation to social projects. I am convinced that for Fromm, the fact that there were intellectuals, the Milláns among others, who were interested in social issues, fuelled his interest in Mexico and his search for psychosocial understanding of its people (S. Millán, 1995; S. Millán and S. Gojman, 2000).

When in 1954 I began my medical training, I had already learned about Fromm's life in a direct and familiar manner: the way he travelled, the meticulous way he arranged prolonged journeys; his arrival on precisely the day he had announced; his habit of travelling with more than 10 suitcases, most of them filled with books; and above all, his determination to keep busy throughout the journey, reading and revising manuscripts.

He usually travelled from Mexico by land. When headed for Europe, he would take a train to New York, stay for a short time in his apartment there, then take a boat to Le Havre and another train to Locarno. One of the trips was quite special, when he came to Mexico while recovering from a heart condition in 1968. He arrived by boat in Acapulco from New York, passing through the Panama Canal; from there he went to the state of Morelos, to the town of Jiutepec, where the Millán family had a country home, and where we welcomed him. His phobia of airplanes explained the long journeys. When the family learned of his arrival dates, I used to go to welcome him and his wife, Annis.

Alfonso Millán was the head of the Department of Mental Health of the Medical Faculty of UNAM, which he had established with the support of the Director of the Faculty, Dr. Raul Fournier. He established a mental health and humanization program for the entire UNAM Medical faculty (S. Millán, 1990). Millan's position and influence at UNAM certainly favored a wider awareness of Fromm's work at the University, and allowed Fromm's psychoanalytic training to be recognized for decades. Under Millan's leadership, Fromm became a Professor Emeritus of the University's Medical Faculty.

Fromm analyzed Alfonso Millán and, more than 15 years later, his son Ignacio as well. Through my family ties, I learned that Ignacio had graduated as an engineer and that he was interested in psychoanalysis and its social projection; I assume that in this pursuit, Ignacio was accepted and stimulated by Fromm. This perhaps attests to Fromm's flexible understanding of the requirements for becoming an analytic candidate and his advice to not conform to academic bureaucratic processes that can dissolve and lose significance. Ignacio had joined the School of Superior Studies for Social Sciences at the Sorbonne in Paris, which at that time allowed graduates from programs in the hard sciences to have their qualifications re-evaluated in order to be recommended for a masters program in sociology. Thus, Ignacio was able to formally enter a course taught by Fromm at the University of Mexico.

The administrative formalities were overseen by Fromm's first students, who dictated that the candidates for training in these courses were required to be medical doctors or PhDs in psychology, forgetting that Fromm did not hold either of these professional degrees.

In 1971, keeping in mind the need to systematize his clinical ideas on first interviews, Fromm authorized Ignacio to tape the classes during the training. It was a task with a specific purpose, but it was considered a "privilege," a selective gesture. At least this is how it was perceived by colleagues who were in charge of the course's administrative aspects and were also dutiful followers of the "master's" teachings. Actually, it was not such a dramatic "preference." Rather, the assignment illustrated how Fromm was willing to pursue a practical purpose that would both help facilitate his own interest in systematizing clinical ideas and also further Ignacio's interests and development as a student. In this way, Fromm was both a gifted teacher and a great mentor.

The relationship between Fromm and Ignacio was the source of some family conflict, particularly with Alfonso, Ignacio's father, who was apparently trying to get closer to Fromm again, insisting on renewing ties with him. Fromm respectfully kept Alfonso's requests and demands at a distance, undoubtedly in the interest of protecting the ongoing therapeutic process with Ignacio.

Participative action research

In 1958 I sought out Michael Maccoby, who at that time was working on methodological results for the final draft of the book *Social Character in a Mexican Village* (E. Fromm and M. Maccoby, 1970b), in which he sought to elucidate the impact of modernity on traditional *campesinos* in the state of Morelos. I wanted to find ways for non-academics to study and become aware of Fromm's conceptualizations of biophilia and necrophilia (S. Millán, 1980a). The interpretative questionnaire, used as a guide for a personal interview, allowed for sensitization to the interview subject and stimulated acquisition of new personal and social insights.

So, I wondered how one might develop a method that would allow for the same objectives when administering to a group. In the United States, Michael Maccoby had created and used a questionnaire with specific answers to select through the questions regarding biophilia and necrophilia. This encouraged me to start a project using some of the same questions with the children in the organization *Nuestros Pequeños Hermanos* (NPH) (Campbell, 1975; E. Fromm and M. Maccoby, 1970b, pp. 213-217). This organization offered a secure space and development opportunities for children who had lost their mothers and were faced with the serious disadvantages arising from a lack of any defined social support or protection.

Fromm closely collaborated with Father William Wasson, the head of *Nuestros Pequeños Hermanos*, in developing the project's structure, which included legally adopting the children, thereby becoming like a large family. This approach stands in stark contrast to the typical scenario that one might find in an official correctional institution, where youngsters from similar precarious social situations were housed in an institution focused primarily on legal considerations and an attempt toward "readaptation" (S. Millán, 1980b).

Fromm celebrated my proposal. He wanted to know how the responses of these groups could reflect the impact of the different organizations. He agreed to work directly with me in the development and interpretation of results. Going over some of the results while humming the melody of Beethoven's Ninth Symphony, his state of inward contemplation, concentrating on the development of his own understanding, suddenly changed to a stare of disbelief when he was struck by the fact that some orphans talked about their mothers as if they were still alive. Moreover, the children frequently named their mothers when responding to the question of whom they most admired.

Fromm was visibly upset by these responses and asked me directly whether I was aware of the final aim of the project. The *Nuestros*

Pequeños Hermanos project was intended to accept only motherless children without exception; otherwise, the institution would be breaking the children's most elementary links. Evidently concerned, he made an impulsive phone call. He was alarmed and doubtful about what the facts showed. Some children said they had seen their mother, or that she had visited.

I now realize that these responses could have been understood in two different ways: a) that the mothers were alive and that they had been admitted by error or outright deceit of their families, or b) that these responses could reflect that the mourning process had not been resolved. It could thus be showing the children's inability to fully accept the loss, a process that has been known to take many years (eight, ten, or even more), such as those that have been described in attachment research studies through the responses to the Adult Attachment Interviews, and has been thought to be linked to severe pathology (M. Main and E. Hesse, 1990; E. Hesse, 1999a and 1999b; S. Gojman and Millán, 2003). Otherwise, the families might have been hiding the truth, possibly driven by a desire to secure the social advantages offered by the *Nuestros Pequeños Hermanos* project.

In my psychiatric orientation to the conflicted and problematic behaviors of the children and adolescents of *Nuestros Pequeños Hermanos*, I later witnessed the conditions of a young child who was sent away to the orphanage by his own "aunt-mother"—"aunt" to the organization, but real biological mother to him. He was chronically depressed, conflicted, and suffered from severe states of confusion. I now ask myself if Fromm had an insight to the dimension of this social reality that compelled these mothers to select the material advantages that the NPH institution would offer their children without regard for their emotional condition, mental health and development. Fromm's anger was indeed justified in this case, as it was directed at the mothers for their short-sighted opportunism at the expense of their children's long-term health.

These revelations serve as a reminder that researchers should take into account the potential for subjects of social intervention projects to make inaccurate and unrealistic statements out of self-interest and desperation. As such, social character questionnaires and periodic evaluations are both important and necessary as a basis for regular review of these processes. This has been confirmed in several of our projects conducted at the Seminario de Sociopsicoanálisis A.C. (SEMSOAC) (cf. S. Gojman, 1990, 1992, 1993; S. Gojman and S. Millán, 2000, 2003, 2004).

Erich Fromm in private

Fromm liked to throw parties, even though he would only spend a short while chatting with the guests in the garden of his home. He preferred to speak privately with people in his library. Fromm once remarked to Dr. R. Fournier, "Let's leave the people with the [joyous and noisy mariachi] music outside, and let's go listen to opera." The story illustrates Fromm's passion for classical music. He particularly loved Mozart's opera "The Magic Flute." I don't think it's a coincidence that the opera's plot revolves around the conflict between a young woman and her mother, in which values of courage, virtue and wisdom help her free herself of a dependent relationship, and help her develop possibilities for personal growth. The hubbub outside attested to Fromm's generosity and hospitality, with ample food and drink for his guests.

I particularly remember the time I attended, with many other guests, a party at Fromm's residence at Cerritos no. 14 in Cuernavaca. The reason for that party was either the end of classes for the second class, or the imminent opening of his own house on Neptuno no. 9, next door to the old house he rented. In building this new home, Fromm showed tremendous persistence and dedication. He was clearly interested in every detail, as can be seen in the photograph discovered by Carmen Delachica in that house. He was interested not only in its design but also in the garden and the special place where vegetables could be grown for his meals.

In 2001, we interviewed Sabina Camacho Garcia, along with her husband and her nephew Fernando Ibarra (cf. S. Millán and S. Gojman, 2001). She was hired exclusively to cook for Daisetz T. Suzuki in the cabin Fromm had built for Suzuki's visit in 1957, in the garden of his home. Fernando was the son of Fromm's housekeeper, Alicia Camacho Garcia, who lived for many years in the house, together with her family, in the servants' quarters. They considered Fromm to be part of their own family.

As described by Alicia Camacho García's family members, Fromm also had the help of Oguri, a Japanese gardener, who took charge of growing all the vegetables prepared in his home, particularly when Suzuki visited. With them both, he redesigned the garden to include the Japanese lamp that Suzuki—years later—sent as a gift. (Fromm later donated the lamp to the Bradley museum of Cuernavaca).

Some details about Fromm's private life in the home came out in our interview with Sabina, and with Alicia's son, Fernando. The family was witness to and shared in Fromm's daily life. When they first began working for Fromm, they were struck by the solidarity he showed with his wife Annis. The couple had returned to Mexico after Annis underwent a serious surgery and she was following a strict diet. It consisted of a wide variety of vegetables, boiled and blended together with veal liver, which they drank 3 or 4 times a day. The diet prescribed for Annis was in fact the only food they both ate for six months. Fromm asked those working in the home not to bring salt into the house, and to prepare their own food on a different schedule from theirs, to avoid cravings.

According to them, Fromm seemed to work incessantly. They did not know at what time he would wake, but they would see him on the balcony together with his wife watching the sun rise. They also did not know at what time he would go to bed, but knew that when they finished their household chores and retired for the evening, Fromm continued working in his office or writing in his room. Sometimes he would concentrate so intensely on his writing that when they brought his tray of food in the morning or afternoon, they would find the previous tray there untouched.

When Fromm worked with his secretary, Beatrice Mayer (who periodically lived in the house), he stayed beside her dictating letters or editing the pages that came out of the typewriter. All the books Fromm wrote were in fact originally produced by his own hand, before Beatrice Mayer did the typewriting. A more rushed and tense atmosphere pervaded the house when a project had to be completed by a certain deadline. At those times, Annis would eat alone and everyone remained on the alert.

His relationship with Alicia was fatherly: he followed the health and education of her children and he urged her not to work when they were sick; on those occasions, he told her she should go home (before they began living in the house) and take care of them, because that "was most important." When Alicia told Fromm that one of her children was having trouble in school, Fromm advised her: "Look, I don't have children, but if one of them didn't want to study, I would have told him it was alright. I would really say to him, 'If you want to be a carpenter, go ahead, become one, but do it well.'" Alicia's son Fernando once said that it was not fair to say that Fromm had no children, because, he stated proudly, he and his siblings had felt as if they were.

The family that worked with him on a daily basis harbors pleasant memories, a mixture of surprise and gratitude; they always "felt incredibly respected and protected."

A Crucial Encounter

Gérard D. Khoury

Some human beings affect you so deeply that your life is forever changed. For me, Erich Fromm is among them. When I was about twenty—he gave me the means to cope with some difficulties emerging in my youth out of my family history and nationality. My family has its roots in the Middle East, another universe, as it were. It took me more than thirty years to understand this universe, since it follows different cultural and anthropological codes.

UNDERSTANDING CULTURE

I had been brought up in a bourgeois world, where trade and money were the only valued standards, as they could provide, besides security and status, identity and freedom. It was quite hard to affirm myself, and to disentangle myself from such a world. I had also been exposed to a family world which did not value culture and art, which I really had to challenge to dare to believe in the strength of ideas—ideas which could change the unjust world that I had before my eyes. I was not aware, at the time, that these bourgeois values were going to be so relevant for the West as well, under the influence of other legitimizing factors connected with the Protestant work ethic, or for contemporary liberal America in which the market was the supreme arbiter.

I do not need to go into the details of the crucial meeting with Erich Fromm. It had been preceded by my reading of his works throughout the years 1959-1960. At that time, I was still struggling with parental authority, which was no simple affair at all. It was only much later that I realized that in the Middle East every aspect of life was still led by family, clan and community.

I was up against a wall of determinism, and no choices were available to me except those offered by my father. It was unthinkable for me to oppose him; daring to defy him caused his anger and my feeling of guilt. I felt I had no way out; each time I managed to escape from paternal wrath, I had to face my mother's emotional insistence, a different means to achieving the same goal. She tried to convince me to take up the career path which had been prepared for me by my father, and to transform the family business into a more modern and finance-oriented one (in my father's hands it had remained quite archaic).

No personal choice seemed possible: a boy was supposed to fall into his father's steps, marry his first cousin, live under the same roof with his parents, *pour le reste de son âge*, to quote Joachim du Bellay. It was only later that I understood the meaning of endogamy.

On the political, social and economic level, I found it hard to analyze Lebanese reality. In those days, many were talking about the "Lebanese miracle," "the strength of a weak state," Beirut as "the Paris of the Middle East," "a young country that was 6000 years old," "the Switzerland of the Near East" and so many other *clichés*. This small country, recently independent, was glittering with all the lights of liberalism and material success, and it looked as though it was untouched by the history of the region, except in taking advantage of the various coups and troubles affecting the bourgeois of neighboring states, who came to seek refuge, with their financial capital, in the haven of Lebanon. Social inequalities did not seem to trouble anyone within the *milieu* of the powerful. When I was young—at a rebellious age, and one where I cried for justice—everything was a source of anguish. I was deeply confused about the history of Lebanon, the history of the Middle East, the existence of Israel, the presence of Palestinian refugees in Lebanon, and so on.

THE FIRST MEETING

When I was a third-year student in Economics, I received an invitation from the American State Department, to visit the United States with a group of Arab students. One of my reasons for accepting the invitation, was the secret hope to meet Erich Fromm, after reading all his writings available in English. I wrote to him "care of Routledge and Kegan," not knowing what his reaction would be. It was to my great surprise that I received an answer from Erich Fromm, and an invitation to meet him in New York.

I immediately informed him of the time period I was to stay in New York, and he proposed that I call him on my arrival to agree when to meet. Was it the fact that I was from the Middle East, from an Arab country, that had elicited Fromm's curiosity? Was he curious to meet me since he was a German Jew, and a former militant of the Zionist youth organization, who had in time opposed the creation of a Jewish state and then embraced an anti-Zionist position? The surprise left me speechless, and I felt as though I could fly!

By chance, aside from the invitation to the United States, I got another invitation to present the Lebanese situation in a sociology conference in Mexico. When I called Fromm in July 1960, before leaving for Mexico, to arrange a meeting in New York, he proposed that we meet in Mexico instead, where we would have more time to see each other. I promised to call him there as soon as the conference was over.

Later on, Fromm himself told me how surprised he had been on our first meeting. He expected a professor in his forties and found himself face to face with a 22-year-old student. First of all, he tried to understand the reasons that brought me to see him from so far away. Then, without delay, he proposed that I take a room in a *hacienda* in Cuernavaca owned by a Frenchman he knew (which was actually temporarily closed, but Fromm nevertheless assured me he could get me a room there). This way, we would be able to meet intensively, which we then did. Two or three times a week, he allotted me four or five hours in the afternoons. I will not talk about these meetings in Cuernavaca, as they are of a very personal nature, but I would like to recall Erich Fromm as I knew him back then.

First of all, I was impressed by his clear glance, sweet and intense, penetrating but respectful. This very glance immediately expressed his openness, and transmitted the unspoken feeling of trust, reassuring and questioning at the same time. This glance expressed the great humanity of Erich Fromm, showing both vulnerability and strength; it expressed his openness to the other and a silent invitation to open up in response. I rediscovered this subject-to-subject-relationship, that Fromm called a "central relationship" (1992g [1959], p. 177), when I was editing *Revoir Freud* (2000e), the work published in France for the 100th anniversary of his birth.

I was also deeply impressed by the harmony between Fromm the author and Fromm the man. He thoroughly lived up to his ideas. Born as a German Jew from an orthodox family, he had disentangled himself from the bounds of religion without losing Jewish spirituality. A man of the Enlightenment, he was still capable of thinking paradoxically; a stern defender of reason, he explored the world of religion and mysticism, both western and oriental. He kept his interest in mystical experience alive throughout his whole life, studying Saint John of the Cross, Master Eckhart, Mansur al-Hallaj, and especially Zen Buddhism. His meetings with Suzuki and the work they completed together, with the help of de Martino (cf. 1960a), bridged mystical experience and psychoanalysis.

As to me, coming from Lebanon, where religion is spelled out on identity papers and where everything is shaped by religion, Erich Fromm helped me start on a long and complicated journey through my own cultural framework, particularly through such works as *The Dogma of Christ* (1930a) and *You Shall Be as Gods* (1966a). This helped me distance myself from all that is referred to as collective enterprises (family, clan, community), and consequently enhanced my aspirations as an individual. I still had to separate individual aspirations and narcissism, which was a completely different work. Gradually, I renounced an almighty Ego, and learned what sharing is all about—which has helped me to defend politically relevant values. In the Middle East, individuals exist only as members of a group (clan, community, etc). Such a society finds it ontologically impossible to develop a political project which may affirm individual freedom, in any domain. Yet the political project reflects the relationship its members have as individuals with society itself.

My inward situation was reflected by Erich Fromm in a letter he wrote in March 1964:

> "The real problem seems to be a certain lack of determination and aim in your life, a certain passivity, perhaps some amount of narcissism. I also cannot help thinking how much all this has to do with your father and your family. Whether you are not avoiding the solution of the conflict between independence and temptations of what I assume to be the protective and powerful family."

Again, in August 1964, he repeated:

> "When I read your last letter my main impression was that you are in the situation in which so many people are, especially if they are the sons of wealthy fathers, that they cannot really put themselves on their own feet because their wish for independence is so weakened by the seduction of the comforts of luxury which they can have if they do not break with their fathers. You apparently live with this conflict all the time [...] I do not know whether what I am saying here is correct, but I cannot help thinking it because that is what I sense between the lines. As I wrote in my previous letter, I think the main problem is this decision, and to overcome the fear of standing on your own, and the longing for the 'flesh-pots of Egypt'. You must also consider that in your past you were probably so afraid of life that your wish for security has an undue weight in your decision."

POLITICAL COMMITMENT

In the political field Erich Fromm, a dedicated socialist, knew that nothing could be built without the knowledge of the past. He was aware that revolutions could no longer happen the same way as in the 18th century, nor as the Russian Revolution of 1917, because Western societies had become societies of techno-structures. He presented these ideas in his *The Revolution of Hope*, written in 1968 to be the program for Eugene McCarthy's presidential campaign against Richard Nixon, which I have translated with the title *Espoir et Révolution* (cf. 1968a).

As to me, I have become familiar with Marxism through a deepened study of both Karl Marx's writings (including the 1844 *Economic-Philosophical Manuscripts*) and Erich Fromm's writings on Marx—such as *Marx's Concept of Man* (1961b) or *Beyond the Chains of Illusion* (1962a)—which have prevented me from falling prey to communism as framed by the ideological dogmatism typical of Marx's exegetes.

In welcoming me so warmly, Fromm gave me a "gift of trust" when he helped me to interpret the hidden language, not only of psychological reality, but also of political, social and economic reality. He has truly changed my life, and gave me the courage to open up to all inquiries and all struggles. He even advised me to follow a very large reading program spanning writers from pre-Socratic philosophers to George Orwell. In other terms: Fromm pushed me towards the wide world of ideas, well beyond the field of psychoanalysis, to which he introduced me. In so doing, he communicated to me his conviction that ideas are strong enough to move mountains, even though they may seem helplessly far from daily life concerns. By introducing me to the prophetic tradition, he also made me receptive of that stream of thought that nurtures Western modernity together with Greek thought—and, as I would learn later—with the Arab philosophical tradition. It is so easy today, while all of us are going through such a global crisis of civilization, to doubt that ideas might be strong enough to change the world!

The ideas of Erich Fromm have doubtlessly changed my life. Fromm taught me to mistrust the dichotomy between sensitivity and thinking, to mistrust the opposition between using thought to strengthen power and domination, and using thought to enhance liberation and freedom. I lacked self-confidence and the ability to think for myself. Fromm taught me to mistrust conventional and merely descriptive thinking; he always encouraged me to look for the hidden face of reality. He taught me to try new ways to understand social and political problems from within, and grasp their profound implications, instead of being satisfied with cataloguing and describing them. He thus helped me very much in my work as a historian: I knew him as an heir of Spinoza and Marx; today I discover him as an heir of Giambattista Vico as well. When I re-read my correspondence with Fromm between the 60s and the 80s, I can still feel his presence, his penetrating spirit, his openness and availability to others, his lucidity and his attention to words. He never accepted words to be just empty shells, they had to be symbols of flesh and life, where emotions and concepts were joined. Words such as love, freedom, justice, respect, courage, were at the same time his plan and his song for life.

In regard to what I owe Erich Fromm, I would like to stress that Fromm's openness is a gift in itself. His writings are clear and reader-friendly; since they are not meant to be accessed only by specialists, they are not protected by codes of any kind. Erich Fromm offers himself, and can be read without protection. Sometimes, he has been criticized for a supposedly weak theoretical framework, but his main concern was *lively* and *living* thinking. When I was reading him in 1959 and in the following years, I found his theoretical approach perfectly suitable to my own story, a true matching of reality and ideas. Born in Lebanon, I was suspended between two cultures, two sensibilities, two worlds. Fromm's emphasis of the schizoid character of contemporary societies, as opposed to the hysterical character of 19th century societies, was the perfect answer for me. I would also like to cite his critique of the world of appearances and of the value of money, which supported me in my own critique of Lebanese society. The last book published when Fromm was still alive was *To Have Or to Be?* (1976a), about which we had long discussions on my visits in 1978 and 1979 to Locarno.

CRITIQUE OF TERRORISM

Last but not least, I keep a memory of our last meetings in Locarno, of the evenings spent discussing so many topics, in particular the Israeli-Palestinian question and terrorism—already quite vocal at the time! His critique of both Israeli and Palestinian terrorism went hand in hand with his defense of the Palestinian cause; in 1948, he was among the first, with Hannah Arendt, to advocate the right of the refugees to return.

At the time when I was translating *The Revolution of Hope*, he asked me about Palestinian organizations, and in a letter dated March 7, 1970 I gave him a short summary of the most important ones, among them Al Fatah, pointing out their leaders and the principles of each of them. On April 4th, he wrote in response:

> "It was enlightening to me and I have now for the first time an idea of the various currents and groupings in the Arab resistance movement. This is really very helpful to me, and I appreciate very much the trouble you have taken to send me such a detailed memo.
>
> "I am against terror tactics. I was against them when the Israelis applied them against the British, and I am against them when the Arabs apply them against the Israelis. I do not believe in hate as a constructive sentiment for the liberation of any nation, and of course I am not a friend of nationalism, be it Arab or Israeli. This is something different from understanding deeply the motivation for Arab nationalism and from my severe criticism of Israeli policy, not only since the foundation of the State, but altogether, of a completely Jewish State as such. I think the only solution would have been that suggested

by Rabbi Magnus, of a bi-national Jewish-Arab state, similar to the Swiss canton system."

I answered him on May 31, 1970:

"The bi-national Jewish-Arab state would be a rational solution if only the two parts were sincerely willing to accept each other and live in peace. Resistance and war are logical consequences of occupation and violence. We can speak of terrorism only when some Palestinian extremist group deliberately attacks ... civilians, as Israeli extremists (such as the 'Stern') did in the past, e.g. when they blasted off King David Hotel. In this meaning, I am also against terror, but resistance has another content when it is the only possibility left for the Palestinians to assert their rights."

To conclude my testimony, I shall quote from Fromm's response concerning terrorism, which seems to be still relevant today, when the only effect of US policy has been to strengthen Arab terrorism, despite declaring a war against it using the language of a crusade against evil:

"Thank you for your letter of May 31st just arrived. I have read with great interest your remarks on the Arab-Jewish situation. I realize what you mean by differentiating between resistance and terror, but I think that while the distinction can be made theoretically, it is very difficult to uphold it practically. As long as the guerrilla fighters can attack an opposing army, the distinction is pretty clear and realistic. But when the liberation fighters do not attack an army, and for practical reasons this is often impossible, and instead attack peaceful settlers or other civilians, then the resistance necessarily employs terroristic methods.

"With attacks against individual settlements, buses, etc. the liberation fighters have actually, it seems to me, used terroristic methods just as the Zionist extremist groups like the Stern gang used the same method of terror in their fight against the British. I do not for a moment forget that the air attacks of the Israeli army against so-called military targets near Cairo are also for all practical purposes terroristic and that it is no excuse if it is explained that killing children was due to an error or whatever excuse is.

"It seems to me one should introduce another element and that is, the question whether military moves of the resistance have any realistic chance to change the political and military picture or whether they just vent indignation and hate of those who have been deprived of their land against those who sit on it. It is quite clear and has proved for many years, that the resistance of the NLF in Vietnam has a real and indubitable military function. It is not clear to me whether at this moment the Arab resistance has any such function.

"I should like to comment on the fact that until and including the First World War, the use of force had been voluntarily restricted by certain compassionate considerations mainly in two directions. One did not kill civilian populations, and by and large did not use torture, even if its use would produce important military information. Since and during the Second World War these restrictions have been abandoned first by all great powers, and are now in a situation where force is used on all sides without restrictions.

"Of course all this has nothing to do with the full condemnation of Israeli aggressiveness, its refusal to evacuate the conquered territories, etc. etc. The refusal of the Israeli government even to permit Nahum Goldman, the most intelligent, realistic and humanist of Zionist leaders, to meet with Nasser is only a glaring example of the intransigence of Israeli government."

Thirty-five years later, Fromm's analysis remains prophetic, and is joined by the analysis of Edward W. Said. Seeing the failure of violence in all its forms, and the challenges posed by demography in the coming years, is there any possible solution other than a bi-national state and giving up terrorism? Or will Israel continue to practice a policy of exclusion, and to be protected by a wall which turns the whole state into an enormous ghetto with the blessing of the US? In the meantime, Islamism and international terrorism, which the American war in Iraq cannot but enhance, will become more and more radical. We have reasons to fear that the Middle East will remain an earthquake area for a long time, untouched by any solution inspired by fairness and respect, in spite of the prophetic vision of just men such as Fromm and Said.

Fromm's Genius
Was in His Actual Presence

Leonard C. Feldstein

George Seferis stated that the soul inscribes itself upon a man's face. In the subtlety of its movements, in the immediacy with which it registered every nuance of feeling, and in its sheer aliveness, Erich Fromm's face was the most marvelous face I have ever known. It was the kind of face which draws itself deep into one's memory, and whose image lasts forever. By the reverberations which it sets up within someone, it transmits itself to another, thence to another, until, in the end, it has echoed among countless strangers who, by those reverberations, have, for a brief moment, become intimates.

Surely, Fromm's face must have etched itself upon hundreds who, like myself, were privileged to have known him as teacher, personal psychoanalyst, supervisor, and guide. How much the more for those who, unlike myself, were privileged to have known him as friend. And, if Seferis is right that the soul inscribes itself upon a man's face, then the more profoundly a face reveals the soul, the more, when one looks upon that face—especially when, like Fromm's, it is so mobile, so fine, its lineaments so varied and vibrant—one peers into one's own soul. To have known Erich Fromm in any capacity is somehow also to have known him as a friend. It is at the same time to have delved deep into the very labyrinth of one's Self. With utmost precision, his face registered the entire range of human emotions.

Unlike the legendary psychoanalyst, so impassive and removed, Fromm was an astoundingly vital presence. His every gesture lived and resonated with his spirit. Before you, his face was luminous with soul, its contours shaped directly, spontaneously, and in perfect synchronicity. Unalloyed and pure, Fromm's countenance, once experienced, endures, and never ceases to sink into one's inmost depths. It had the power to penetrate. Fromm's eyes sang, his facial lines danced, his voice pulsed with conviction, integrity, and openness. Above all, he was humane ... and so very human. So human that there was a certain childlike joy which, clearly, he felt in his own powers—a certain audacious self-centeredness, some might say. But to touch that self-centeredness was for me, and I imagine for so many others, to invite me to touch my own center. Never obtrusive, it was a Self so centered upon itself that it inspired one fully to encounter one's entire being, and to join one's very center to his center.

As psychotherapist, Fromm abhorred mere technique. For him, it implied trickery, hence deceit. He always spoke from his center. As both teacher and psychoanalyst, I could not forget his example. I learned, often painfully, to trust myself: at least, to entrust myself to myself. Let flow forth what will—the flaws, the absurdities, the contradictions, the downright blunders—at least, in the end, I will have possessed myself. Such, for me, was Erich Fromm's message.

More than anything else, I learned this precept: be who I am; never be other than myself; allow my own words to flow. Not randomly, hardly uncritically, but truly; now haltingly, now gushingly, but always spoken, with feelings which are my feelings. And feel my feelings fully, to the last draught. Not to wallow in them, nor to indulge a false self-romanticism; but to speak my feelings deliberately, circumspectly, reverentially—and always, in the end, spontaneously and, insofar as possible, easily. Respond to the other as he or she moves me to respond: tenderly, kindly, and with profound respect, but authentically, and without duplicity. This ideal, which Erich Fromm's entire being stood for, became my ideal. And, though I often deviated from it, I could still hold it before me as the ideal which alone is worthy of either teacher or psychoanalyst.

To experience Fromm, even in his eccentricities, was invariably to liberate the creative surge within oneself. Compassion, warmth, strength, and firmness radiated from him. They flowed toward you, and caught you up in their embrace. They so intermingled that, in his presence, one felt totally accepted, wholly without need for pretense, sham, or cant. If only momentarily, one was transformed by that presence, even quite radically metamorphosed. One felt oneself to be larger than one had been, to pulsate with new life. For a face so to affect one, and, through one, others as well, is to immortalize the soul which illumines that face. Fromm's vitality was so enormous that it had the power to spread, and by its impact, even upon a single person, to grow.

Erich Fromm's writings were powerful, lucid, and deceptively simple. They have stirred a whole generation into reflection upon the meaning of love, authority, human wholeness. When he was at his best, his face, and his voice, shone through his words. For, in the end, Fromm's genius was in his actual presence, and in the surgings of that presence, through each who was affected, to another. Others will judge, in times to come, the ultimate stature of Fromm's written words, but no person who has ever encountered Erich Fromm, face-to-face, can doubt the ultimate stature of the man. His face, his voice, and his spirit-illumined physical presence are inviolable. They will not perish.

References

Bacciagaluppi, M. (1989). Erich Fromm's Views on Psychoanalytic Technique. *Contemporary Psychoanalysis*, 25, 226-243.

Burston, D. (1991). *The Legacy of Erich Fromm.* Cambridge, Mass.: Harvard University Press.

Campbell (1975). Tu Eres Mi Hermano. *Our Sunday Visitor*, Noll Plaza Huntington.

Deutscher, I. (1971). *El Judío no Sionista* (The Non-Zionist Jew) Madrid: Editorial Ayuso.

Ehrenberg, D. B. (1990). Playfulness and the psychoanalytic relationship. *Contemporary Psychoanalysis*, 26, 74-95.

English, O. S., et al. (1965). *Análisis Directo y Esquizofrenia*, Buenos Aires: Editorial Paidós.

Evans, R. I. (1966). *Dialogue with Erich Fromm*, New York: Harper & Row.

Feiner, A. H. (1975). Reminiscences of Supervision with Erich Fromm. *Contemporary Psychoanalysis*, 11, 463-4.

- (1990). Playfulness and the interpersonal ideology. *Contemporary Psychonalaysis*, 26, 95-107.

- (1991). The analyst's participation in the patient's transference). *Contemporary Psychoanalysis*, 27, 208-241.

Finkelman de Sommer, M. (2007). Shimon Jezior. Un Hombre Pilofacetico. *Expresiones. Comunidad Ashkenazi de Mexico*, No. 14 (8. 1. 2007), 23-4.

Frie, R. (2003). Erich Fromm and contemporary psychoanalysis: From modernism to postmodernism. *The Psychoanalytic Review*, 90, 855-68.

Freud, S. *The Standard Edition of the Complete Psychological Works of Sigmund Freud* (S. E.), 1-24, London. The Hogarth Press, 1953-1974:

- (1900a). *Dream Interpretation*, S. E. 4 and 5.

- (1918b). From the History of an Infantile Neurosis, S. E. 17, 1-122.

- (1919a). Advances in Psycho-Analytic Therapy, S. E. 17, 157-168.

- (1937c). Analysis Terminable and Interminable, S. E. 23, 209-253.

Fromm, E. 1930a). The Dogma of Christ. *The Dogma of Christ and Other Essays on Religion, Psychology and Culture*, New York: Holt, Rinehart and Winston, 1963, 3-91.

- (1941a). *Escape from Freedom*, New York: Farrar and Rinehart.

- (1947a). *Man for Himself. An Inquiry into the Psychology of Ethics*, New York: Rinehart and Co.

- (1955a). *The Sane Society*, New York: Rinehart and Winston, Inc.

- (1955d). Remarks on the Problem of Free Association. *Psychiatric Research Report*, Washington: American Psychiatric Association, II, 1-6.

- (1956a). *The Art of Loving. An Inquiry into the Nature of Love* (World Perspectives 9, planned and edited by Ruth Nanda Anshen), New York: Harper and Row.
- (1960a). Psychoanalysis and Zen Buddhism. *Zen Buddhism and Psychoanalysis*, D.T. Suzuki, E. Fromm and R. de Martino, New York: Harper and Row, 77-141.
- (1960b). *Let Man Prevail—A Socialist Manifesto And Program*, New York: The Call Association.
- (1961a). *May Man Prevail? An Inquiry into the Facts and Fictions of Foreign Policy*, New York: Doubleday.
- (1961b). *Marx's Concept of Man.* With a Translation from Marx's Economic and Philosophical Manuscripts by T.B. Bottomore, New York: F. Ungar Publisher Co.
- (1962a). *Beyond the Chains of Illusion. My Encounter with Marx and Freud* (Credo Perspectives, planned and edited by Ruth Nanda Anshen), New York: Simon and Schuster.
- (1962b (together with Michael Maccoby). A Debate on the Question of Civil Defence. *Commentary. A Jewish Review*, New York, 33, 11-23.
- (1963f). Humanismo y psicoanálisis. *Revista de Psicoanálisis, Psiquiatría y Psicología*, México (No. 2, 1966), 5-12; engl.: Humanism and Psychoanalysis. *Contemporary Psychoanalysis*, New York: The Academic Press, Inc., 1 (1964), 69-79.
- (1964a). *The Heart of Man. Its Genius for Good and Evil* (Religious Perspectives, 12, planned and edited by Ruth Nanda Anshen), New York: Harper and Row.
- (1966a). *You Shall Be as Gods. A Radical Interpretation of the Old Testament and Its Tradition*, New York: Holt, Rinehart and Winston.
- (1966p). Conciencia y sociedad industrial. *Ciencas Politicas y Sociales*, México, No. 43/44 (Jan-Jun 1966), 17-28; engl.: Scientific Research in Psychoanalysis. *Contemporary Psychoanalysis*, New York, 2 (1966), 168-170.
- (1968a). *The Revolution of Hope. Toward a Humanized Technology* (World Perspectives, 38, planned and edited by Ruth Nanda Anshen), New York: Harper and Row. French: *Espoir et Révolution*, translation by Gérard D. Khoury, Paris: Stock 1970.
- (1970b) together with Michael Maccoby. *Social Character in a Mexican Village. A Sociopsychoanalytic Study*, Englewood Cliffs: Prentice Hall.
- (1973a). *The Anatomy of Human Destructiveness*, New York: Holt, Rinehart and Winston.
- (1974b). In the Name of Life. A Portrait Through Dialogue. *For the Love of Life*, Hans Jürgen Schultz (Ed.), New York: The Free Press, 1986, 88-116.
- (1976a). *To Have Or to Be?* (World Perspectives 50, planned and edited by Ruth Nanda Anshen), New York: Harper and Row.

- (1977i). Das Zusichkommen des Menschen. Interview with Micaela Laemmle und Juergen Lodemann. *Basler Magazin*, Basel (No. 47, 24. 12. 1977), 3; reprint under the title. Die Kranken sind die Gesündesten. *Die Zeit*, Hamburg (21. 3. 1980.
- (1979a). *Greatness and Limitations of Freud's Thought*, New York: Harper and Row 1980.
- (1989a [1974-75]). *The Art of Being*, R. Funk (Ed.), New York: Continuum 1993.
- (1991c [1964]). Factors Leading to Patient's Change in Analytic Treatment. *The Art of Listening*. R. Funk (Ed.), New York: The Continuum Publishing Corporation 1994, 15-41.
- (1991d [1974]). Therapeutic Aspects of Psychoanalysis. *The Art of Listening*. R. Funk (Ed.), New York: The Continuum Publishing Corporation 1994, 45-193.
- 1992g [1959]). Dealing with the Unconscious in Psychotherapeutic Practice (3 Lectures 1959). *International Forum of Psychoanalysis*, 9 (No. 3-4, October 2000) 167-186.
- (1992h [1975]). Die Bedeutung der Psychoanalyse für die Zukunft. *Erich-Fromm-Gesamt-ausgabe in 12 Bänden*, R. Funk (Ed.), Munich: Deutsche Verlags-Anstalt and Deutscher Taschenbuch-Verlag 1999, XII, 369-390.
- (2000e). *Revoir Freud. Pour une autre approche en psychoanalyse*, Gérard D. Khoury (Ed.), Paris: Armond Colin.
Funk, R. (1982). *Erich Fromm. The Courage to Be Human*, New York: Crossroad/Continuum; first published in German under the title *Mut zum Menschen*, Stuttgart: Deutsche Verlags-Anstalt 1978.
- (2000). *Erich Fromm—His Life and Ideas*. An Illustrated Biography, New York: Continuum International; Softcover Edition 2003.
Gardiner, M. (Ed.) 1971). *The Wolf-Man*, with a supplement by Ruth Mack Brunswick, New York: Basic Books.
Glover, E. (1955). *The Technique of Psychoanalysis*, London: Bailliere, Tindall.
Gojman, S. (1990). Experiencias de Clase en los Sueños de los Niños. *Erich Fromm al Siglo XXI, Cuadernos*, Enep Zaragoza 1, Serie Psicología UNAM. México.
- (1992). A Socio-psychoanalytic Intervention Process in a Mexican Mining Village. *Science of Man. Yearbook of the International Erich Fromm Society*, 3, Muenster: Lit-Verlag, 47-56.
- (1993). An Overview of the Mexican Project of Sociopsychoanalytic Participative Research in a Mining Community. *Cuadernos IV. Social Character, its study. An experiential Interchange*, Seminario de Sociopsicoanalisis (Ed.), Mexico, 59-84.
Gojman, S., and Millán, S. (2000). Attachment patterns and social character in a Nahuatl village. Socialization processes through social character interviews and videotaped attachment current methodology. *Fromm Fo-*

rum, International Erich Fromm Society (Ed.) English version No. 5 (2001), Tuebingen: Selbstverlag, 38-42.

- (2003). Integrating Attachment and Social Character Approaches to Clinical Training. Case Studies from a Mexican Nahuatl Village. *Attachment Theory and the Psychoanalytic Process*, Cortina & Marrone (Eds.), London: Whurr Publishers.

- (2004). Identity in the Asphalt Jungle. *International Forum of Psychoanalysis*, 13, No. 4.

Gourevitch, A. (1981). Tribute to Erich Fromm. *Contemporary Psychoanalysis*, 17, 435-6.

Hesse, E. (1999a). The Adult Attachment Interview. Historical and current perspectives. *Handbook of Attachment. Theory, Research, and Clinical Applications*, J. Cassidy and P. Shaver (Eds.), London: The Guilford Press, 395-433.

- (1999b). *Unclassifiable and Disorganized Responses in the Adult Attachment Interview and in the Infant Strange Situation Procedure. Theoretical proposal and Empirical Findings*, Doctoral Dissertation, Leiden University 1999.

Horney, K. (1937). *The Neurotic Personality of Our Time*, New York: W. W. Norton & Co.

Kahn, H. (1960). *On Thermonuclear War*, Princeton: Princeton Univ. Press.

Kierkegaard, S. (1938). *Purity of Heart Is to Will One Thing*, New York: Harper.

Koestler, A. (1941). *Darkness at Noon*, New York: The Macmillan Company.

Kohut, H. (1971). *The Analysis of the Self.* New York: International Universities Press.

Kretschmer, E. (1921). *Körperbau und Charakter*, Berlin: Springer Verlag.

Landis, B. (1981). Fromm's approach to psychoanalytic technique. *Contemporary Psychoanalysis*, 17, 337-351.

Landis, B. and E. Tauber (Eds.) (1971). *In the Name of Life. Essays in Honor of Erich Fromm.* New York: Holt, Rinehart & Winston.

Landis, B., und Tauber, E. S. (1971). On Erich Fromm. *In the Name of Life. Essays in Honor of Erich Fromm*, B. Landis and E. S. Tauber (Eds.), New York: Holt, Rinehart, Winston, 1-11.

Levenson, E. A. (1982). Follow the fox. *Contemporary Psychoanalysis*, 24, 1-15.

Main, M., and Hesse, E. (1990). Parents unresolved traumatic experiences are related to infant disorganized attachment status. Is Frightened and/or Frightening Parental Behavior the Linking Mechanism? *Attachment in the Preschool Years. Theory, Research and Intervention*, M.T. Greenberg, D Cicchetti and M.G. Commings (Eds.), Chicago: University of Chicago Press, 161-182.

Marcuse, H. (1941). *Reason and Revolution*, Cambridge Mass.: Harvard Univ. Press.

Marx, K. (MEGA). *Karl Marx und Friedrich Engels, Historisch-kritische Ge-samtausgabe* (= MEGA). Werke - Schriften - Briefe, im Auftrag des Marx-Engels-Lenin-Instituts Moskau,. Adoratskij (Ed.), 1. Abteilung. Sämtliche Werke und Schriften mit Ausnahme des Kapital, quoted I, 1-6, Berlin 1932.
- MEGA I, 3. *Ökonomisch-philosophische Manuskripte aus dem Jahre 1844*
- MEGA I, 5. *Die deutsche Ideologie*
Millán, S. (1995). Mexican Time. Erich Fromm in Mexico. A Point of View. *Gesellschaft und Charakter (Society and Character). Jahrbuch der Internationalen Erich-Fromm-Gesellschaft,* Münster: LIT Verlag 6, 69-75.
- (1980a). Preponderancia Materna. Estudio Sociopsicoanalítico. *Memorias,* Mexico: Sociedad Psicoanalítica Mexicana, 411-424.
- (1980b). Un Modelo de Sistema Autoritario. Estudio Sociopsicoanalítico. *Memorias.* México: Sociedad Psicoanalítica Mexicana A.C., 609-620.
- (2000). El Psicoanálisis de las Costumbres y los Mitos Acerca de la Muerte Reflexiones sobre el Encuentro Internacional Octubre-Noviembre 1999. Cuernavaca Morelos. *La Jornada de Morelos,* Enero 5, 2000. México.
Millán, S., and Gojman, S. (1997). The weekly Clinical Group Supervision Chaired by Erich Fromm. Paper presented at the International Conference on Erich Fromm- Psychoanalyst and Supervisor, Ascona, April 4-5, 1997, Typescript, 15 p.
- (2000). The Legacy of Fromm in México. *International Forum of Psychoanalysis,* 9, 207-215.
- (2001). *Entrevista a la Sra. Sabina Camacho García,* Cuernavaca Morelos Febrero 10. Documento mecanografiado. Seminario de Sociopsicoanálisis A.C. México, Typescript, 23 p.
Ortmeyer, D. H. (1997). Self-Analysis, Learning and Literature. *Connecticut Society of Psychoanalytic Psychologists Newsletter,* 10 (No. 1, Winter 1997), 8-9.
- (2002). Clinical Relevance of Social Character and Social Unconscious. *International Forum of Psychoanalysis,* 11, 4-9.
Rothenberg, A. (1988). *The Creative Process of Psychotherapy.* New York: W. W. Norton and Company.
Sheldon, W. H. (1942). *The Varieties of Temperament,* New York/London: Harper and Brothers.
Silva García, J. (1966). El temor del hombre a la mujer. Una contribución al estudio del complejo de castración. *Revista de Psicoanálisis, Psiquiatría y Psicología,* México, 2 (1966), 13-24.
- (1989). Erich Fromm in Mexico. *Contemporary Psychoanalysis,* 25, 244-257.
Spiegel, R. (1981). Tribute to Erich Fromm. *Contemporary Psychoanalysis,* 17, 436-441.
Taylor, C. (1988). Forward. In *Social Action and Human Nature,* A. Honneth and H. Jonas, vii-ix. Cambridge: Cambridge University Press.

Tauber, E. S. (1954). Exploring the Therapeutic Use of Countertransference Data. *Psychiatry*, 17, 331-336.

- (1959). The Sense of Immediacy in Fromm's Conceptions. *American Handbook of Psychiatry, II*, S. Arieti (Ed.). New York: Basic Books.

- (1981). Tribute to Erich Fromm. *Contemporary Psychoanalysis*, 17, 448-9.

Winnicott, D. W. (1947). Hate in the Countertransference. *Through Paediatrics to Psychoanalysis*. New York: Basic Books, 1958.

About the Contributors

Akeret, Robert U.
Ph.D., born 1928.—Dr. Akeret received his doctorate in psychology from Columbia University and his certificate in psychoanalysis from the William Alanson White Institute, where he trained with Rollo May and Erich Fromm. He is the author of *Photoanalysis* (1973), *Family Tales, Family Wisdom* (1992), *Photolanguage* (2002) *Tales from a Traveling Couch* (1996).

Crowley, Ralph Manning
M.D., 1905-1984.—As Psychiatrist, Dr. Crowley practiced at Sheppard and Enoch Pratt Hospital in Baltimore, after completing training supervised by Frieda Fromm-Reichmann at Chestnut Lodge. In 1946, he became a faculty member and training and supervisory psychoanalyst at the young William Alanson White Institute, and was elected fellow two years later, in 1948. During his lifetime, Crowley also served as president of the American Academy of Psychoanalysis, consultant at Roosevelt Hospital-St. Luke's Medical Center, and lecturer at Albert Einstein College of Medicine.

Davis, Harold B.
Ph.D., ABPP, born 1930.—Dr. Davis is currently supervisor at the New York University Postdoctoral Program in Psychotherapy and Psychoanalysis, faculty and supervisor at the Institute for Contemporary Psychotherapy, and in private practice in New York City. He is a former president of the International Federation for Psychoanalytic Education.

Eckardt, Marianne Horney
M.D., born 1913.—Dr. Eckardt completed her training at the American Institute of Psychoanalysis, and went on to become an assistant professor of psychiatry, though most of her career has been spent in private practice as psychoanalyst. She has taught at the Psychoanalytic Institute of the New York Medical College and Post Graduate Center for Mental Health and been an active member of the American Academy of Psychoanalysis. Eckardt was Fromm's analysand from 1938 to 1941, and his friend from 1950 on.

Feiner, Arthur H.
Ph.D., 1922-2005.—Dr. Feiner spent most of his career at the William Alanson White Institute, as fellow, training and supervising analyst. In 1970, he became editor of the Institute's journal, *Contemporary Psychoanalysis*, a position he held until 1995.

Feldstein, Leonard Charles
Ph.D. 1922-1984.—Aside from being a practicing psychoanalyst in New York City, Dr. Feldstein worked as professor of philosophy at Columbia University, the Albert Einstein College of Medicine, the Mannes College of Music and other institutions over the course of his life. He is the author of *Homo Quaerens* (1978), *The Dance of Being* (1979) and Choros (1984).

Funk, Rainer
Ph.D., born 1943.—Dr. Funk is a psychoanalyst, the current proprietor of the Fromm Archives in Tuebingen and Fromm's sole literary executor. His doctoral dissertation was about Fromm's ethics and social psychology, and in 1974, he became Fromm's last assistant and editor. He co-founded the International Erich Fromm Society.

Gojman de Millán, Sonia
Ph.D., born 1945.—Dr. Gojman de Millán is a training and supervising analyst, social researcher, and the current secretary general of the International Federation of Psychoanalytic Societies (IFPS), a post she has held since 2000. She is also a certified trainer of the Adult Attachment Interview. Her contact with Fromm dates from 1963 to 1974.

Goldman, George D.
Ph.D., born 1923.—Dr. Goldman studied under Erich Fromm at the William Alanson White Institute in New York in 1958. He is a clinical professor of Psychology, director of the Postdoctoral Psychotherapy Center and supervisor of Psychotherapy at Adelphi University in GardenCity, New York.

Gourevitch, Anna
1898-1981.—Anna Gourevitch was faculty member, training and supervising analyst at the William Alanson White Institute. In 1970, she became a consultant at the Department of Psychiatry at the Albert Einstein College of Medicine.

Khoury Gérard D.
Ph.D., born 1938.—Born in Lebanon, Dr. Khoury studied economics and is now living in Aix-en-Provence, France, working as a writer and histo-

rian. He visited Fromm in 1960 in Mexico to study psychoanalysis, and since then, has done a significant amount of translating, editing and promoting Fromm's writings in France. Most of his books reflect his particular interest in the dialogue between the Arabic and the Western culture.

Kwawer, Jay S.
Ph.D., born 1945.—Dr. Kwawer is the current director of the William Alanson White Institute. He is working as training and supervising analyst and supervisor of psychotherapy at the William Alanson White Institute. He is also a clinical professor of psychology at the Postdoctoral Program in Psychotherapy and Psychoanalysis at the New York University and at the Institute of Advanced Psychological Studies at Adelphi University.

Landis, Bernard
Ph.D., born 1926.—Dr. Landis has worked as a clinical associate professor of psychology at the Cornell University Medical College and the New York Hospital, a visiting Professor at the Department of Psychiatry at Cedars-Sinai Medical Center, Los Angeles and as psychoanalyst. His contact with Fromm dates from 1961 until Fromm's death.

Lesser, Ruth M.
Ph.D., 1923-2004.—Dr. Lesser was a training and supervising analyst at the New York University Postdoctoral Program, and the Westchester Center for the Study of Psychoanalysis and Psychotherapy. She was also clinical professor of psychology at the Graduate School of Arts and Science at New York University and a faculty member at the William Alanson White Institute.

Maccoby, Michael
Ph.D., born 1933.—Dr. Maccoby studied and worked with Fromm from 1960-1970 in a training analysis and as a research and writing collaborator. Over the course of his career, he has worked as training analyst and lecturer at the Washington School of Psychiatry and as guest professor at universities in the US and Europe. From 1978-1990, he was director of the Program on Technology, Public Policy and Human Development at Harvard. Since 1977, he has worked as consultant to leaders in business, unions, government and universities.

Millán, Salvador
M.D., born 1936.—Dr. Millán is a trained psychiatrist, and has worked as training and supervising analyst at the Instituto Mexicano de Psicoanálisis. He has worked as professor, social researcher, and is the co-director of the

Seminario de Socio-psicoanálisis. His contact with Fromm dates from 1954 to 1975.

Ortmeyer, Dale H.
Ph.D., born 1926.—Over the course of his career, Dr. Ortmeyer has held positions as director of the Continuing Professional Education Divison, training and supervising analyst at the William Alanson White Institute. He has also worked as professor at the Westchester Center for the Study of Psychoanalysis and Psychotherapy at Adelphi University and as instructor in psychiatry at Columbia University.

Schecter, David E.
M.D. 1926-1981.—In 1957, Dr. Schecter became a faculty member at the Albert Einstein College of Medicine, where he later became an associate clinical professor in 1967. He joined the William Alanson White Institute in 1962, first as fellow and training analyst, then as supervising analyst five years later. From 1964 to 1971, Dr. Schecter participated in a research project on early Ego development in natural family settings.

Silva García, Jorge
M.D., FAAP and DP, born 1919.—Dr. García underwent training in psychoanalysis with Erich Fromm from 1950 to1956. He served as training and practicing analyst and lecturer at the Mexican Psychoanalytic Institute until 1979. From 1965 to 1980, Dr. García was a member of the Scientific Committee of the International Federation of Psychoanalytic Societies (IFPS). In 1973, he was named honorary consultant at the Instituto Nacional de Ciencias Médicas y Nutrición Dr Salvador Zubirán.

Tauber, Edward S.
M.D., 1908-1988.—Over the course of his career, Dr. Tauber was fellow, training and supervising analyst at the William Alanson White Institute, as well as charter fellow at the American Academy of Psychoanalysis. He also worked as adjunct professor of psychology at the New York University Graduate School of Arts and Sciences and at Yeshiva University. He began analysis with Erich Fromm in 1946 and collaborated with him for many years. Besides being an expert in psychoanalytic theory and practice, and the neurophysiology of sleep, Dr. Tauber did pioneering work in the field of dreams in animals.

Acknowledgements

Akeret, Robert U.: "What Have You Learned about Yourself from Your Patient?" is a partial reprint of R.U. Akeret, *Tales from a Traveling Couch. A Psychotherapist Revisits His Most Memorable Patients*, New York and London (W. W. Norton) 1995, pp. 112-120.—Permission to reprint generously granted by W.W. Norton and Company, New York.

Crowley, Ralph M.: "Psychoanalysis: An Adventure in Learning to Think Critically" was first published under the title "Tribute on Erich Fromm," in: *Contemporary Psychoanalysis*, New York, Vol. 17, No. 4 (1981), pp. 441-445.—Permission to reprint generously granted by *Contemporary Psychoanalysis*, New York.

Feiner, Arthur H.: "Now, Look here..." is taken from A. H. Feiner, "Reminiscences of Supervision with Erich Fromm," in: *Contemporary Psychoanalysis*, New York, Vol. 11 (Oct. 1975), pp. 463-464., as well as from his paper "The Thrill of Error: Image and Appearance, Articulation, Union," in: *Contemporary Psychoanalysis*, New York (William Alanson White Psychoanalytic Society), Vol. 27 (1991), pp. 624-653.—Permission to reprint generously granted by *Contemporary Psychoanalysis*, New York.

Feldstein, Leonard C.: "Fromm's Genius Was in His Actual Presence" was first presented at "An Evening in Memory of Erich Fromm" on June 18, 1980, at the William Alanson White Institute in New York and then published under the title "The Face of Erich Fromm," in: *WAW Newsletter*, New York, Vol. XV, No. 1 (Winter 1981), p. 5.

Goldman, George D.: "What Is this Patient Really After?" was first published under the title "Some remembrances of supervisory sessions with Erich Fromm," in: Robert C. Lane, Ed., *Psychoanalytic approaches to supervision. Current issues in psychoanalytic practice*, No. 2, New York (Brunner/Mazel, Inc.), 1990, pp. 71-83.—Permission to reprint generously granted by the *Society for Psychoanalytic Training*.

Gourevitch, Anna: "Elation and Fortification" was first published under the title "Tribute on Erich Fromm," in: *Contemporary Psychoanalysis*, New York, Vol. 17, No. 4 (1981), pp. 435-436.—Permission to reprint generously granted by *Contemporary Psychoanalysis*, New York.

Kwawer, Jay S.: "His Main Interest: The Human Passions" was first published under the title "A Case Seminar with Erich Fromm," in: *Contemporary Psychoanalysis*, New York (The Academic Press, Inc.),

Vol. 11 (1975), pp. 453-5.—Permission to reprint generously granted by *Contemporary Psychoanalysis*, New York.

Lesser, Ruth M.: "There Is Nothing Polite in Anybody's Unconscious" is a reshaped and enlarged paper that was presented at a Workshop on Frommian Therapeutic Practice, August 30 - September 1, 1991, in Verbania-Pallanza. It was published under the title "Frommian Therapeutic Practice: 'A Few Rich Hours,'" in: *Contemporary Psychoanalysis*, New York (William Alanson White Psychoanalytic Society), Vol. 28 (1992), pp. 483-494.—Permission to reprint generously granted by *Contemporary Psychoanalysis*, New York.

Schecter, David E., "Awakening the Patient" is a compilation of two papers David Schecter has written. The first ("He was above all a truth-seeker") originally entitled "On Fromm" was written in 1980 after Erich Fromm's death and shortly before David Schecter's own death. The second paper is taken from a presentation to the Association of Psychoanalytic Psychologists on February 13, 1958. With minor editing, it was published for the first time through the generosity of Mrs. David Schecter under the title "Contributions of Erich Fromm," in: *Contemporary Psychoanalysis*, New York Vol. 17, No. 4 (1981), pp. 468-480.—Permission to reprint generously granted by *Contemporary Psychoanalysis*, New York, and by Estelle Schecter.

Erich Fromm's Writings
on Psychoanalytic "Technique"

1955d: Remarks on the Problem of Free Association. In: *Psychiatric Research Reports* 2 (December 1955).

1960a: The Nature of Consciousness, Repression and De-Repression. Chapter 4 of: D. T. Suzuki, E. Fromm and R. de Martino, *Zen Buddhism and Psychoanalysis*, New York (Harper and Brothers) 1960, pp. 95-113.

1966f: Interviews with Richard I. Evans. Unpublished ad verbum transcript of the two Interviews with Richard I. Evans according to the two 16-mm films taken in December 1963 in Cuernavaca/México. Evans' publication as a book entitled *Dialogue With Erich Fromm* was never authorized by Fromm. Fromm tried to prevent further publication of the book.

1966k: The Oedipus Complex: Comments on the "Case of Little Hans". In: E. Fromm, *The Crisis of Psychoanalysis*, New York: Holt, Rinehart and Winston, 1970, pp. 69-78.

1989a [1974-5]: Self-Analysis. In: E. Fromm, *The Art of Being*, New York (Continuum) 1993, pp. 69-86.

1990f [1969]: The Revision of Psychoanalytic Therapy. In: E. Fromm, *The Revision of Psychoanalysis,* Boulder (Westview Press) 1992, pp. 70-81.

1991c [1964]: Factors Leading to Patient's Change in Analytic Treatment. In: E. Fromm, *The Art of Listening*, New York (The Continuum Publishing Corporation) 1994, pp. 15-41. Reprint in Part One of this volume.

1991d [1974]: About the Therapeutic Relationship (including: Christiane. A case history with remarks on therapeutic method and on understanding dreams). In: E. Fromm, *The Art of Listening*, New York (The Continuum Publishing Corporation) 1994, pp. 96-162 and pp. 192-193.

1992g [1959]: Dealing with the Unconscious in Psychotherapeutic Practice. In: *International Forum of Psychoanalysis*, Vol. 9 (No. 3-4, October 2000) pp. 167-186. Reprint under the title "Being *Centrally* Related to the Patient" in Part One of this volume.

1992h [1975]: Die Bedeutung der Psychoanalyse für die Zukunft. In: *Erich Fromm Gesamtausgabe in zwölf Bänden* (GA), München (DVA and dtv) 1999, GA XI, pp. 271-284.